WHO WOULD JESUS KILL?

AUTHOR ACKNOWLEDGMENTS

There are many I would like to thank for making this book possible. First my wife, Emily, whose support has made all of my professional endeavors possible. Your sacrifices have made my successes achievable. I am forever grateful.

I would also like to thank Tobias Winright (Saint Louis University) for his detailed reading of the drafts and thoughtful and constructive comments—I am honored to be your colleague and your friend; Brian Orend (University of Waterloo) and Kathryn Kueny (Fordham University) for reading drafts and providing excellent commentaries; Jerry Ruff and Leslie Ortiz from Saint Mary's Press for their confidence, encouragement, advice, and patience; and Eleanor Beach (Saint Ambrose University), whose copyediting and other editorial contributions significantly improved the final product.

Finally I dedicate this book to my children, Ezekiel (Zeke) and Agnes. May you never know a world at war and may you always be instruments of God's peace.

PUBLISHER ACKNOWLEDGMENTS

Our thanks to the following individuals who advised the publishing team or reviewed this work in progress:

Tobias Winright, PhD, Saint Louis University, Missouri

Brian Orend, PhD, University of Waterloo, Ontario

Kathryn Kueny, PhD, Fordham University, New York

WHO WOULD JESUS KILL?

WAR, PEACE, AND THE CHRISTIAN TRADITION

MARK J. ALLMAN

Saint Mary's Press®

The publishing team included Leslie M. Ortiz, general editor; John B. McHugh, director of college publishing; and Jerry Ruff, editorial director; iStock, cover image (RF); prepress and manufacturing coordinated by the production departments of Saint Mary's Press.

Printed in the United States of America

7010

ISBN 978-0-88489-984-6

Library of Congress Cataloging-in-Publication Data

Allman, Mark J.
    Who would Jesus kill? : war, peace, and the Christian tradition / Mark J. Allman.
    p. cm.
    Includes bibliographical references and index.
    ISBN 978-0-88489-984-6 (pbk)
    1. War—Religious aspects—Christianity. 2. Peace—Religious aspects—Christianity. I. Title.
BT736.2.A45 2008
241'.6242—dc22
                                                          2008038976

CONTENTS

FOREWORD

One of the highlights of the Christian liturgical year for me has always been gathering with friends, family, and others at a late Christmas Eve service to glorify God and celebrate the birth of Jesus Christ. With the passing of time, however, this experience has become rather bittersweet. On the one hand, echoing the heavenly host that appeared to the shepherds some two thousand years ago, we proclaim, "peace on earth, good will toward all" (Luke 2:14). Yet a quick glance at the news, with its graphic images of suffering, displaced, and dying men, women, and children due to war and conflict in places such as Kenya, Afghanistan, Iraq, and the Darfur region of Sudan — not to mention the terrorist attacks and loss of innocent lives on September 11, 2001, events tattooed onto our minds since that now infamous date — obviously reveals an excruciating absence of peace in the world for all too many people.

Nevertheless Catholics and other Christians continue to worship each week in sanctuaries where we experience in the here and now a foretaste of the peace of Christ. In the liturgy, people from all nations and backgrounds gather and unite in prayer for God's peaceable kingdom to come and God's will to be done on earth as it is in heaven, and for God to forgive us our trespasses as we forgive those who trespass against us. At the Catholic Mass, after everyone recites the Lord's Prayer, the priest adds, "Deliver us, Lord, from every evil, and grant us peace in our day." At this point, he says, "The peace of the Lord be with you always," and the congregation responds, "And also with you." This is followed by everyone's exchanging with one another a sign of peace. Not simply a hello or a greeting, this gesture is a visible symbol of our reconciliation with God and one another. There is peace among us. Indeed the United States Catholic bishops "encourage every Catholic to make the sign of peace at Mass an authentic sign of our reconciliation with God and with one another. This sign of peace is also a visible expression of our commitment to work for peace as a Christian community."[1] After this gesture of peace and before receiving the Eucharist, the assembly sings the *Agnus Dei*, praying that the Lamb of God, who takes away the sins of the world, will "grant us peace." That word keeps coming up.

Moreover when receiving the Body of Christ in Communion, Catholics profess that we, in turn, become his body. To paraphrase Augustine, we are what we eat. In his *Confessions*, Augustine writes that he heard God's voice, saying, "Grow and you shall feed on me. But you shall not change me into your own substance, as you do with the food of your body. Instead you shall be changed into me."[2] Christ is our peace, and we are called to embody and practice that peace. Indeed the peace we experience during worship is not supposed to be left behind the stained glass windows of the church building. At the conclusion of the Mass, during the dismissal, the priest blesses us and usually says, "The Mass is ended, go in peace to love and serve the Lord," to which we enthusiastically respond, "Thanks be to God." We now get to share that peace through love and service to others outside the church doors. This, though, is easier said than done. The chasm between what we experience during the liturgy and what we encounter in the world is stark and deep.

More specifically, when we go forth from worship and attempt to pass Christ's peace on to a planet where peace is often absent, the question of *how* to do so comes to the forefront. When conflict erupts, how should Christians respond in a way that is congruent with Christ's call for love, mercy, and reconciliation?

May Christians ever resort to the use of force, including killing, to restore or establish a just peace? If, for example, an enemy, whom we are called to love, threatens an innocent neighbor, whom we are also commanded to love, what should we Christians do? We know that we ought to do something, but what? What would Jesus have us do? Can we imagine that Jesus would use lethal force to protect someone from an attacker? Or as the title of this important book asks, "Who would Jesus kill?"

That is not merely a theoretical or provocative question. I myself struggled with it when I worked for several years in law enforcement (in corrections while I was a young person in college and in policing some years later) and participated in Army ROTC (during my undergraduate days when I considered a possible career in the military). As a Christian who had attended parochial school and youth group Bible studies while growing up and who regularly attended Mass, I found that I struggled with the question of whether I could use lethal force in the performance of my duties. I hoped to serve others and protect them from harm, but the conflicts and violence that I encountered in the line of duty—and the use of force that might be required to prevent or stop such violence—seemed in tension with the peace of Christ I experienced at church and was called to pass along to the world. Too bad this book was not available back then! It would have helped me sort through these difficult questions.

Now, many years later, I teach my own course on war and peace in the Christian tradition each semester, and I often find myself unsatisfied with the textbooks that are available. I keep trying out new texts (and some old ones) for this class, but I think with *Who Would Jesus Kill?* we finally have one that I will use and keep on using. The fruit of careful research and instructional experience in the college classroom, this text provides a comprehensive yet accessible treatment of the various Christian ethical approaches to peace and war: pacifism, holy war, and just war. A fine appendix also discusses that ethical approaches to peace and war are not the sole domain of Christians but are important considerations in the Jewish and Islamic faith traditions as well.

Easily discernible throughout the book is the author's passion for teaching undergraduates and providing them with the tools and information they need for thinking critically about this timely yet perennial moral issue. I am grateful for this opportunity to introduce the reader to this wonderful book written by my good friend and fellow ethicist Mark Allman.

Tobias Winright, PhD
Assistant Professor of Christian Ethics
Saint Louis University

ENDNOTES

1 National Conference of Catholic Bishops, *The Challenge of Peace: God's Promise and Our Response* (Washington, DC: United States Catholic Conference, 1983), no. 295.

2 Augustine, *Confessions*, trans. R. S. Pine-Coffin (New York: Penguin, 1961), book VII, no. 10.

INTRODUCTION

War is about killing. One of my greatest frustrations as a professor of war and peace studies is that we often lose sight of this fact. The conversation quickly moves to heady academic discussions. We casually throw around terms and phrases like "casualties," "collateral damage," "target," "troop deployment," and "engaging the enemy," which mask the bloody reality of war. When wars are waged, ordinary citizens are turned into killers. In war, men, women, and children are violently killed. I think part of the reason we have trouble keeping the brutality of war fresh in our minds is that violence has become ordinary in our lives. We watch television programs and movies in which violence is a normal theme; we play video games in which decapitations and shooting not only are part of the game but are actually celebrated and rewarded; and for decades our nightly news has been filled with images of war. War and violence have become not only a normal part of our lives, they are actually a form of entertainment.

Christians should be uncomfortable with violence in general and especially with war. The title of this book, *Who Would Jesus Kill?*, is intentionally provocative. When faced with this question, as a Catholic Christian I want to immediately cry out, "No one! Jesus would have nothing to do with violence and killing." But then why are most of the men and women in our armed services Christian? Why do we have chaplains serving in the military?

How is it that a predominantly Christian nation is also the world's superpower and the only nation ever to resort to nuclear warfare? If it is so obvious that Jesus wouldn't kill anyone, then why are Christians responsible for so much killing?

This book explores the three traditional Christian approaches to war and peace: pacifism, holy war, and the just war theory. But first, we must define *war*.

WHAT IS WAR?

Language is powerful; it is not morally neutral. This is especially true when it comes to describing and evaluating war. One person's "freedom fighter" is another person's "terrorist," and one nation's "victory over the insurgents" is another nation's "bloodbath." Defining war proves to be especially difficult. We have such terms as "civil war," "cold war," and the "war on terrorism." The word *war* is used with different senses. Sometimes it means armed conflict (for example, armies shooting at each other), and sometimes it is used metaphorically to mean a prolonged and concerted effort to overcome or put an end to something, such as in "the war on drugs" or "the war on crime." I once saw a sign outside a middle school proclaim, "We Declare War on Mathematical Illiteracy!" The popular phrase "the war on terrorism" is still more confusing because it involves military action but is not really a war. Terrorism is not an enemy in the formal sense. It is a way, a technique, a method of fighting. It is not a nation-state or a unified political entity; one cannot really fight a war on terrorism.

Clearly war involves conflict, but not all conflicts are wars. I can have a conflict with my neighbor over her loud music or barking dog, but it's not a war. Typically we reserve the word *war* for conflicts between political groups (for example, states, nations, or organizations with a political agenda). Carl von Clausewitz (1780–1831) opens his classic work *On War* by stating:

> I shall not begin by expounding a pedantic, literary definition of war, but go straight to the heart of the matter, to the duel. War is nothing but a duel on a larger scale. . . . Each tries through

physical force to compel the other to do his will. . . . *War is thus an act of force to compel our enemy to do our will.*[1]

Clausewitz goes on to connect war to politics:

> The reason [people go to war] always lies in some political situation, and the occasion is always due to some political object. War, therefore, is an act of [political] policy. . . . We see, therefore, that war is not merely an act of [political] policy but a true political instrument, a continuation of political intercourse, carried on with other means. What remains peculiar to war is simply the peculiar nature of its means. . . . The political [objective] is the goal, war is the means of reaching it.[2]

Clausewitz is no naïve idealist; he reduces both politics and war to a single motivation — power.

In a similar manner, Brian Orend, a contemporary expert on the ethics of war and peace, also defines war in terms of politics and force:

> War should be understood as an *actual, intentional* and *widespread* armed conflict between political communities. Thus, fisticuffs between individual persons do not count as war, nor does a gang fight, nor does a feud on the order of the Hatfields versus the McCoys. War is a phenomenon which occurs *only* between political communities, defined as those entities which either are states or intend to become states (in order to allow for civil war). Classical war is international war, a war between different states, like the two World Wars. But just as present — and apparently growing in incidence — is war within a state between rival groups or communities, like the American Civil War. I suppose that certain political pressure groups, like terrorist organizations, might also be considered "political communities," in that they are associations of people with a political purpose and, indeed, many of them aspire to statehood. . . . Indeed I would argue that *all warfare is precisely, and ultimately, about governance.* War is a violent way for determining who gets to say what goes on in a given territory regarding, for example, who gets power, who

gets wealth and resources, whose ideals prevail, who is a member and who is not, what laws get made, what gets taught in schools, where the border rests, how much tax is levied, and so on. War is the ultimate means for deciding these issues if a peaceful process or resolution can't be found.[3]

Although some argue that the idea of war should not be limited to physical combat and should include the threat of violence, Orend dismisses this idea:

> The mere *threat* of war and the presence of mutual disdain between political communities do not suffice as indicators of war. The conflict of arms must be actual, and not merely latent, for it to count as war. Further the actual armed conflict must be both intentional and widespread: isolated clashes between rogue officers, or border patrols, do not count as acts of war. The onset of war requires a conscious commitment and a significant mobilization on the part of the belligerent in question. There's no real war, so to speak, until the fighters *intend* to go to war and until they do so with a heavy *quantum* of force.[4]

There is a substantive difference between threatening to use force and actually resorting to violence. Thus we see some key elements to war: political or ideological motivation, use of physical force, and the desire for power.

Michael Walzer, a preeminent scholar on the ethics of war and peace and author of the widely popular *Just and Unjust Wars*, calls war "a form of tyranny."[5] He stresses that wars are the result of human choice. War is an action that humans choose based on their perception of reality and of the options they have before them. As such, war is a social and historical creation. War is not natural or inevitable:

> War is not usefully described as an act of force without some specification of the context in which the act takes place and from which it derives its meaning. . . . [T]he social and historical conditions that "modify" war are not to be considered as accidental or external to war itself for war is a social creation. . . . What is war and what is not war is in fact something that people decide.[6]

Nor is war accidental, says Walzer. Wars are not like hurricanes or earthquakes, acts of destruction that occur in nature; wars are acts of violence perpetrated by individuals acting in the name of states.

> The tyranny of war is often described as if war itself were the tyrant, a natural force like a flood or a famine or, personified, a brutal giant stalking its human prey. . . . Wars are not self-starting. They may "break out," like an accidental fire, under conditions difficult to analyze and where the attribution of responsibility seems impossible. But usually they are more like arson than accident: war has human agents as well as human victims.[7]

The human agency (free choice) involved in warfare leads Walzer to conclude that war is best described as a crime, what the prosecutors at Nuremburg called "crimes against peace" and what international law terms "the crime of aggression." Wars break out because individuals choose to pursue political goals through force.

For our purposes here, we draw on Clausewitz, Orend, and Walzer and define war as *the freely chosen use of physical and usually deadly force by one political community against another political community to compel the latter to submit to a social, political, economic, or ideological objective.* Of course, there are further distinctions within the category of war itself, such as justified or unjustified war, defensive or offensive war, preventative or preemptive war, and so on. We will address these in due time.

HOW TO USE THIS BOOK

This book explores the three major approaches to war and peace within the Christian tradition: pacifism, holy war, and the just war theory. It is helpful to have preliminary definitions of these terms, which we will expand upon later. *Pacifism* can be understood negatively as simply advocating for the absence of war or the threat of war. Framed in more positive terms, it is a commitment to peace grounded in justice and a refusal to resort to violence as a means of settling disputes. *Holy war* refers to war waged either because God commands it (or at least because people believe that God has commanded it) or for other religious reasons (for example, to defend or spread one's faith). *Just war* refers to a religious or philosophical theory that contends that war, although regrettable, is sometimes warranted, but only if certain criteria are met, such as last resort, just cause, right intention, and if the actual fighting is carried out in an ethical manner (for example, civilian causalities are limited, prisoners of war are treated humanely, and so on). The just war theory is fairly complex and will be explored in depth in chapters 4 and 5.

These three approaches to war and peace are well established within the Christian tradition, and, ironically, they contradict one another. I see these three theologies of war and peace as a continuum, with pacifism occupying the far left, holy war the far right, and just war standing in the middle. As we set out to explore these three positions, I encourage you to think about your own attitude toward war and peace. If you are a Christian, how do you answer the question, "Who would Jesus kill?" Can one rightly claim to be a follower or disciple of Jesus Christ while simultaneously holding that war and violence can sometimes be justified or even commanded by God? If you are not a Christian, how do these Christian theologies of war and peace affect your own personal stance toward war and peace? By way of comparison, an appendix in this book briefly outlines Jewish and Muslim perspectives on war and peace.

A chart follows this introduction on page 18. The chart graphically represents a range of positions on a continuum of approaches to war and peace. Periodically you will be asked to refer back to this chart to consider where you find yourself on this continuum. I encourage you to consider and reconsider your attitudes, beliefs, commitments, and apprehensions about war and peace as you read. How does encountering the arguments for and against pacifism, holy war, and just war affect your own beliefs, and why? Realize that these are not three distinct "camps." That is why we have placed these approaches on a continuum; a person can occupy the positions in between.

Start this reflection now. Based on what you know now, are you a pacifist, a holy warrior, or a just war theorist? Either actually or mentally place an X on the continuum to mark where you fall today, then track your shifting attitudes toward war and peace as you read. In chapter 1, we will begin with an overview of ethics in general and Christian ethics in particular, to establish the theoretical foundations upon which the more complex arguments about war and peace rest.

ENDNOTES

1 Carl von Clausewitz, *Vom Kriege*, book 1, chapter 1, section 2. English translation, Michael Howard and Peter Paret, *On War* (Princeton, NJ: Princeton University Press, 1976), 75–76, quoted in Gregory Reichberg, Henrik Syse, and Endre Begby, *The Ethics of War: Classical and Contemporary Readings* (Malden, MA: Blackwell, 2006), 554.

2 Clausewitz, book 1, chapter 1, sections 23–24. English translation, Howard and Paret, *On War*, 101–106, quoted in Reichberg, Syse, and Begby, *The Ethics of War*, 555–56.

3 Brian Orend, *The Morality of War* (Peterborough, Ontario, Canada: Broadview, 2006), 2–3.

4 Ibid., 3

5 Michael Walzer, *Just and Unjust Wars: A Moral Argument with Historical Illustrations* (New York: Basic, 1977, 2000), 31.

6 Ibid., 24.

7 Ibid., 30–31.

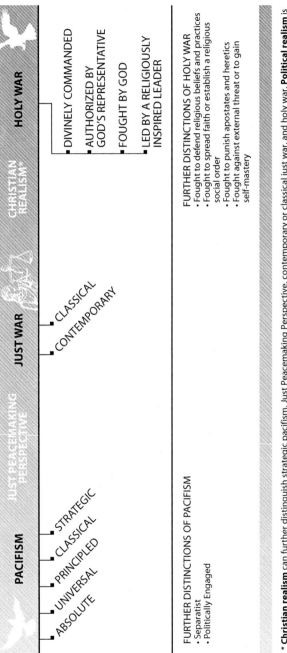

CONTINUUM OF APPROACHES TO WAR AND PEACE

PACIFISM
- STRATEGIC
- CLASSICAL
- PRINCIPLED
- UNIVERSAL
- ABSOLUTE

JUST PEACEMAKING PERSPECTIVE

JUST WAR
- CLASSICAL
- CONTEMPORARY

CHRISTIAN REALISM*

HOLY WAR
- DIVINELY COMMANDED
- AUTHORIZED BY GOD'S REPRESENTATIVE
- FOUGHT BY GOD
- LED BY A RELIGIOUSLY INSPIRED LEADER

FURTHER DISTINCTIONS OF PACIFISM
- Separatist
- Politically Engaged

FURTHER DISTINCTIONS OF HOLY WAR
- Fought to defend religious beliefs and practices
- Fought to spread faith or establish a religious social order
- Fought to punish apostates and heretics
- Fought against external threat or to gain self-mastery

* **Christian realism** can further distinguish strategic pacifism, Just Peacemaking Perspective, contemporary or classical just war, and holy war. **Political realism** is not religious theory per se, but influential on the Christian tradition. It includes descriptive and prescriptive realism.

CHAPTER 1

A Crash Course in Christian Ethics

This is a book on the ethics of war and peace, which is a sub-category of the larger field of ethics. Throughout the book, you will be asked to consider moral questions about issues related to war and peace. For example, is it ever acceptable to use weapons of mass destruction (for example, chemical, biological, or nuclear weapons)? Can armed forces ever intentionally target civilians in the name of the overall good of winning a war? Is there any such thing as military ethics, or is the only objective in war to win "by any means necessary"? Which is worse, to invade a country to protect a persecuted minority group or to stand back and do nothing? Can one claim to be a Christian while at the same time supporting war? Before we can begin to answer these and other such questions, we must first establish *how* one makes a moral decision.

The process is extremely important because the way one goes about making a moral judgment (what you consider relevant or irrelevant and why, whom you consult, what you ignore, the principles you uphold, and so on) strongly influences the decision. In an ethical decision, as with all decisions, the *why* determines the *what*. In other words, when faced with making a decision (What should I do?), one must first ask *why* do A instead of B, C, or D? What reasons justify one decision or course of action over other options? This chapter takes our moral reflection even deeper and asks, "*How* did you arrive at the *why* that determines the *what*?" The *how* focuses on what ethicists call the *moral* or *ethical method*. A moral or ethical method is the process one goes through to make a moral or ethical decision.

Let's consider an example. Think of a tough decision you have had to make (for example, where to go to college, whether to break up with a sweetheart, whether to quit or accept a job). Working backward, start with the *what*. What did you decide to do? Now look at *why*. Why did you choose to do what you did? What reasons can you give to justify or defend your action (or inaction)? Finally, consider *how*. How did you make this decision? What process did you engage in, whom did you consult, did any basic principles, commitments, or other factors influence your decision? The *how* is your moral or ethical method, and the *how* precedes the *why* that determines the *what*.

When I present this to my students they often say, "I don't know why or how I chose to do what I did, I just followed my gut." But gut feelings or instincts are not automatic; we simply process *why* and *how* very quickly. In this chapter, we slow down the process of moral reflection so we can explore a variety of moral methods (a number of *hows*). Without this foundation in ethics, our debate about the issues surrounding war and peace won't move beyond the level of emotional reaction.

It is normal to have an emotional reaction when faced with a moral decision, but ethics involves more than just strong feelings. It includes critical thinking and rational argument. For example, do you think the U.S. invasion of Iraq in 2003 was justified? Why? How did you arrive at that conclusion? Do you think the United States' dropping of nuclear bombs on Hiroshima and Nagasaki at the end of World War II was justified? Why? How did you arrive at that decision? War and the conduct of war are always moral and ethical issues. As we discussed in the introduction, wars are not like hurricanes, earthquakes, or other acts of nature. Wars arise out of human choices, and thus we are able to make judgments about their rightness or wrongness. Before addressing the particulars of war and peace ethics, let's establish a foundation in ethics.

Ethics and morality are about making judgments concerning the rightness or wrongness of actions and the standards used in making those judgments. For most, "ethics" and "morals" mean the same thing: right and wrong behavior. This is understandable, considering that the term *moral* comes from the Latin *moralis*, the same root word from which we get the term *mores* (customs). *Ethics* comes from the Latin *ethica* and the Greek *ēthos,* meaning custom or habit. But there is a subtle difference between these terms. Jozef Zalot and Benedict Guevin provide a fairly standard explanation of the difference between the two:

> Morality refers to the standards or norms that an individual or group holds concerning good and evil as well as what constitutes right and wrong behavior. It concerns the basic moral principles that are considered beneficial to society. Ethics is the inquiry into, or the investigation of, the subject of morality, or the study of how we are to act in morally good ways.[1]

My own interpretation focuses more on the difference between personal choice and social implications.[2] Morals (and morality) are about right and wrong personal choices and actions. Morality tends to focus on issues of conscience, motive, and interpersonal relationships. Ethics has to do with right and wrong choices and actions within a larger community and systemic patterns of behavior. Hence we often talk about *personal* morality and *social* ethics (for example, sexual morality and business ethics). Obviously ethics and morals are related. The personal choices and actions of an individual affect the larger society, and society has an influence on personal choices, attitudes, and behavior.

Many people are reluctant to judge the ethical behavior or personal morality of others. They don't want to be judgmental or they fear being hypocritical ("Who am I to say what she did was wrong? I've done bad things too!"). But there's a difference between making a judgment and being judgmental. A judgment is a decision or a conclusion. A good or valid judgment is one based on sound reason. We make judgments all the time: what to wear in the morning, what to eat for lunch, what to do when faced with a tough decision, and so on. We could never get through the day without making judgments. Being judgmental, however, refers to entirely condemning or dismissing a person or a group of people for no valid reason. The error of being judgmental is twofold: it fails to distinguish between what a person does in a particular situation and who that individual is as a person, and it renders its conclusion based on invalid reasons.

CHRISTIAN ETHICS

There is a wide variety of ethical approaches, methods, and theories, each with its own set of principles and strengths and weaknesses. Christian ethics is one approach. Christian ethics looks to the life, teaching, and example of Jesus Christ in forming ethical standards, but that's not all. Christian ethics also looks to other sources. Most Christian denominations (although not all) draw on the same four primary sources when addressing moral and ethical questions:[3]

- **Scripture:** The Bible is the primary source for Christian doctrine and ethics. For many Protestant Christians, the Bible is the sole source of truth (*sola Scriptura*). The three other sources are understood as means through which one comes to a richer understanding of the core biblical truths. For Catholics, by contrast, Scripture and tradition enjoy a complementary relationship.

- **Tradition:** The Bible does not explicitly address every possible moral or ethical issue. How Christians in the past have wrestled with the moral problems of their day is often illuminating to

SCRIPTURE AND TRADITION

"Sacred Tradition and Sacred Scripture, then, are bound closely together and communicate one with the other. For both of them, flowing out from the same divine well-spring, come together in some fashion to form one thing and move towards the same goal. . . . Tradition transmits in its entirety the Word of God which has been entrusted to the apostles by Christ the Lord and the Holy Spirit. It transmits it to the successors of the apostles [that is, the bishops] so that, enlightened by the Spirit of truth, they may faithfully preserve, expound, and spread it abroad by their preaching." (*Divine Revelation*, no. 9, as quoted in *Catechism of the Catholic Church*, nos. 80–81)

contemporary moral problems. Tradition refers to the history of how Christians through the centuries have interpreted and adapted the faith to their own particular context. We might call it the wisdom of the ancients.

- **Reason:** As mentioned previously, ethics is more than strong feelings. Ethical reflection involves critical thinking and making defendable judgments (that is, drawing logical conclusions) based on objective facts and on a commitment to sound principles. Christian ethics draws heavily from other ethical methods, especially philosophical ethics.

- **Experience:** Christianity affirms a God that is personally involved in our lives. Personal experiences of God through prayer, contemplation, or examination of one's conscience are a source for Christian ethics. But Christian ethics is not developed in a vacuum; we consult others, particularly other members of the Christian community. Descriptive accounts of what it means to be human (for example, from psychology, sociology, biology, economics, political science, anthropology, and so on) are essential in forming both personal and communal understandings of what it means to live a Christian life in the contemporary world.

Although Scripture is typically held as the primary source for Christian ethics, it is not the exclusive source. A holistic approach to Christian ethics engages all four of these sources in tandem and uses them in dialogue with one another. In the following chapters, as we explore the ethics of war and peace in detail, we will draw on all four. We will look at biblical passages that defend and condemn war; we will examine how Christians through the centuries have wrestled with issues of war and peace; and we will engage the reasoning and experience of philosophers, theologians, and social scientists on the topic. Let's look more closely at the four primary sources for Christian ethics.

SCRIPTURE

Scripture is the foundation of Christian ethics. An ethic that does not draw explicitly or implicitly from Scripture can hardly be considered a Christian ethic. Scripture is important for Christian ethics for at least two primary reasons:

1. For Christians, the Bible is a source of revelation, that is, it brings to light the will of God. But it is not the only source of God's revelation. Creation (God's handiwork) is also a source of revelation, as is Jesus Christ, the Word of God made flesh.

2. Stories are the principal medium through which the Bible communicates ethics. Jesus was a storyteller. He did not present his ethic in the form of an erudite treatise; instead he told stories like the parable of the good Samaritan (Luke 10:25–37) or the rich man and Lazarus (Luke 16:19–31). After his death, *Jesus the storyteller became Jesus the story told.* In other words, in his lifetime Jesus used stories (parables) in his preaching, and, after his death, his disciples began to tell stories about Jesus (not just the stories Jesus told). Finally, Jesus is the model of the Christian life. Our knowledge of his

beliefs, morals, actions, and attitudes comes almost exclusively through the Gospels. We know Jesus through the Scriptures.

Although it is impossible to review comprehensively the entire biblical ethical tradition in a single chapter, we can address how to use Scripture in ethics and some of the common themes found in both the Hebrew Scriptures and the New Testament.

HOW TO USE THE BIBLE IN ETHICS
Richard Gula observes:

Scripture is a normative criterion of judgment in Christian morality and ethics, [including the morality and ethics of war] because Christians believe that in the events recounted in Scripture, pre-eminently in the life of Jesus, God's intentions for human living are revealed. Hence the authority of the Bible for ethics and morality is that it is the word of God—the privileged, though not exclusive, source of our knowledge of God and of God's intention for us. That Scripture ought to inform and shape the Christian moral life, then, follows from its authority. But just how it does so is a difficult and complex matter.[4]

Scripture as a source of revelation is not self-interpreting. Interpreting Scripture requires paying attention to when and where it was written; the context in which it was written (that is, the social, political, economic situation); the author; the author's intention; the original audience; and the genre of the literature (for example, history, poetry, hyperbole, analogy, metaphor, philosophical treatise, code of law).

One must avoid three dangers when interpreting Scripture:

- *Fundamentalism:* A fundamentalist approach to reading Scripture views the Bible as a rule book that directly applies to all circumstances and times. Fundamentalism fails to consider the social, political, and economic contexts in which the Scriptures were written. The danger in the fundamentalist (or biblical literalist) approach is that it assumes passages written centuries ago, in a radically different context, apply to contemporary situations without adaptation and with little interpretation.

- *Proof Texting:* This involves making a decision about a moral or ethical issue first, and then going to the Scriptures to find passages that support the preformed opinion, which is then justified as biblically based. The danger is that one ignores the passages that contradict or challenge the preformed opinion.

- *Caricature:* This refers to reducing the image of God, Jesus, or the entire biblical ethic to a facile commandment, most usually of love. I've encountered many who believe the popular misconception that "Jesus preached a message of unconditional love." Nowhere does Jesus endorse unconditional love; in fact, Jesus attaches several conditions to discipleship, as the following so-called hard sayings illustrate:

> If you wish to be perfect, go, sell what you have and give to the poor, and you will have treasure in heaven. Then come, follow me. (Matt 19:21)

> It is easier for a camel to pass through the eye of a needle than for one who is rich to enter the kingdom of God. (Matt 19:24)

> Do you think that I have come to establish peace on the earth? No, I tell you, but rather division. (Luke 12:51)

> If anyone comes to me without hating his father and mother, wife and children, brothers and sisters, and even his own life, he cannot be my disciple. (Luke 14:26)

This belief in a "warm and fuzzy Jesus" represents a therapeutic Christianity, one that affirms without challenging and that tends to endorse the American, middle-class, suburban status quo. The danger in this image is that it is profoundly unbiblical and bears little semblance to the radical first-century Jewish prophet from Nazareth whose preaching ultimately cost him his life.

Avoiding these dangers of interpreting is not enough. To responsibly engage Scripture in ethical reflection, Kenneth R. Himes suggests attending to four tasks:[5]

THERAPEUTIC CHRISTIANITY

H. Richard Niebuhr, an American Protestant theologian, was a strong critic of reducing the biblical ethic to one of affirmation without challenge. He lamented that American theology and spirituality had become a cross-less Christianity, a diluted gospel intended to make us feel better about ourselves without making any demands. He concluded that most American Christians believed, "A God without wrath brought men without sin into a kingdom without judgment through the ministrations of a Christ without a cross."[6]

- *Exegetical Task:* This step tries to uncover what a text meant to its author and the original intended audience. This involves a variety of types of biblical criticism (academic study of the Bible) including the historical-critical method (what were the historical circumstances of the author, audience, and depicted period?), source criticism (what are the original sources from which a text was derived?), form criticism (what genre of literature is a text?), and redaction criticism (how has a text been changed or edited over the centuries?).

- *Hermeneutical Task:* This step is interpretive; it asks, "What does this passage mean to us today?" Operating under the belief that the Bible is eternally relevant, this task focuses on discovering how a centuries-old passage illuminates a contemporary situation. The task of interpretation can be highly subjective, thus there is need for a method of interpretation, which is the third task.

- *Methodological Task:* This step is how one accomplishes the hermeneutical task. James Gustafson identifies a host of ethical sources in Scripture including laws, ideals, and analogies. He encourages taking a "great variety" approach, wherein one supports an ethical norm by citing passages from multiple books and authors.[7] Another similar method, the great themes approach, looks for common themes that run throughout the Scriptures. We will explore this approach in the following section.

- *Theological Task:* This step moves moral reflection beyond the confines of personal conscience into a conversation with the wider church community. Recognizing that no one person could simultaneously master the exegetical, hermeneutical, and methodological tasks, the theological task grounds the interpretation and application of Scripture in ethical reflection in the larger church. It involves consulting teachings of popes and bishops; the work of theologians, ethicists, and Scripture scholars; experts in other fields (for example, history, sociology, medicine, economics, psychology, and politics); and prayer, reflection, discussion, and debate.

BIBLICAL ETHICAL THEMES

A number of common themes runs throughout the Bible. Although not present in every book of the Bible, themes do repeat with regularity, leading many scholars to compose lists of themes.[8] The problem with such an approach centers on the question, "Who decides what counts as a central theme?" Nevertheless, many of these lists are remarkably similar. The following list focuses on ethical themes that run throughout the Bible.[9]

- *Creation:* The book of Genesis provides two creation stories (Gen 1:1–2:4a and 2:4b–3:24). Despite significant differences, these two accounts affirm that human beings hold a special place in God's ordering of the universe. In the first account, humans are made in *imago Dei* (the image and likeness of God). In the second, humans receive *ruah* (the breath or spirit of God). In both accounts, humans enjoy a special relationship with God. Also the goodness of creation is established. In both accounts, creation is given to humans for their use and enjoyment, and they are to exercise dominion (care or stewardship) over creation.

- **Sin:** In the second creation story, we learn how Adam and Eve exercise their free will and disobey God, which results in a disordering of the relationships between God and humanity, between humans, and between humanity and creation. The theme of sin runs throughout Scripture, often indicating a human tendency to act selfishly or in ways contrary to God's will. According to the Christian tradition, God responds to human sinfulness with the Incarnation and redemption (see below).

- **Covenant and Torah:** The covenant is the special relationship between God and the Israelites, best captured in the promise made by God, "I will be your God, and you will be my people" (Lev 26:12). The Scriptures often use the image of a marriage to describe the covenant. The Torah (meaning "instruction" in Hebrew and referring to the first five books of the Bible, or to God's instruction as a whole) is seen as a means to safeguard this relationship.

- **Justice:** The Hebrew word for justice is *tsedaqah*, which means justice, righteousness. The great Hebrew Bible scholar Gerhard von Rad said, "There is absolutely no concept in the Old Testament with so central a significance for all the relationships of human life" as that of *tsedaqah*.[10] John Donahue summarizes the biblical concept of justice as "fidelity to the demands of relationship."[11] This points to the covenant. Being righteous means being in right relationship not only with God but with others as well, which is why the Decalogue (Ten Commandments in Exodus 20 and Deuteronomy 5) opens with commandments concerning how humans relate to God, followed by how they relate to one another. In a similar fashion Jesus answered the question, "What is the greatest commandment?" with a two-part response: "You shall love the Lord your God with all your heart, with all your soul, with all your mind, and with all your strength. . . . The second commandment is this: You shall love your neighbor as yourself" (Mark 12:28–31; see also Matt 22:34–40 and Luke 10:25–28).

- *Incarnation:* The New Testament proclaims that Jesus was God taking on human form or, as the Gospel of John declares, "The Word became flesh and made his dwelling among us" (John 1:14). In taking on human form, Jesus the Christ is not only the perfect revelation of God's will, but he is also a model and example for how Christians ought to live. Theologically for Christians, the Incarnation is a necessary first step toward redemption.

- *Redemption:* Christians believe Jesus' death on the cross and resurrection from the dead have reconciled a sinful humanity with God and have freed us from the grip of sin and death.

- *Discipleship:* One of the unique features of Jesus' life and ministry was that he personally invited people to follow him. Discipleship refers to the practice of devoting oneself to spreading the good news of Jesus Christ with the expectation that such a commitment will involve sacrifice and persecution.

- *Love:* In English we have only one word to express the concept of love, but Greek (the language of the New Testament Scriptures) has multiple words for love, among them: *storgē* (natural affection); *philadelphia* (love between brothers or friends); *eros* (sexual love); and *agapē* (sacrificial love). *Agape* is the term used most often in the New Testament to describe God's love for humanity; it is a freely given, unearned love or, as the Gospel of John declares, "For God so loved the world that he gave his only Son" (John 3:16).

- *Preferential Option for the Poor:* A major biblical theme is the idea that God exercises a predilection or partiality toward the weak, poor, and vulnerable. This does not suggest that God does not love the strong and wealthy, only that the biblical story from the Exodus to the life and example of Jesus teaches that God possesses a strong sympathy for the weak, the poor, and the outcast. In other words, it is part of God's nature to defend the vulnerable. Anyone who wishes to be like God must also exercise an option for the poor.

- **Kingdom of God (or Reign of God):** This New Testament phrase presents a key theme in the teaching of Jesus, as well as of many of the Hebrew prophets. It refers to the expectation that sometime in the future God's definitive Reign will be established on earth. Part of the Jewish messianic hope, this expectation is of a time when humans will live in perfect harmony with one another and with nature, and they will know God personally and intimately.

TRADITION

Tradition is the "wisdom of the ancients." How Christians in the past wrestled with the moral problems of their day often illuminates how we today ought to think about our own quandaries. For example, the Bible says nothing about nuclear weapons. The Catholic Church's position on the use of nuclear weapons has been informed by medieval teachings on war. In the Middle Ages, the introduction of the longbow and crossbow changed the nature of warfare dramatically. The Church condemned these weapons on the grounds that they were *indiscriminate* (the longbow could not distinguish between soldiers and civilians) and *disproportionate* (their use greatly increased casualties).[12] The Church cited these same two principles as the main reasons why nuclear weapons ought to be condemned. Every new moral problem need not be addressed in isolation. The way Christians through the centuries have thought about and debated moral and ethical problems can serve as a means of achieving insight into how we address contemporary moral issues.

As noted above, tradition plays a key role in ethics, especially within the Catholic tradition, where there is a body of literature by popes and bishops on social, political, and economic issues called Catholic social teaching (or Catholic social doctrine). An even larger collection, Catholic social thought, includes these magisterial teachings as well as the writings of theologians, economists, philosophers, political theorists, and others.

THE MAGISTERIUM AND LEVELS OF TEACHING

Many Catholics don't realize that not all Church teachings carry the same level of authority. For example, while the Church teaches that popes can teach infallibly (that is, free from all error), the Church has never held that everything the pope teaches is infallible. The magisterial teaching authority of the Church is comprised of bishops and the pope (who, as the bishop of Rome, exercises authority over all of the bishops). The Extraordinary Magisterium (Sacred Magisterium) refers to the infallible teaching of the Catholic faith. This is the belief that God, through the Holy Spirit, protects the Church from error. Infallible teachings are extremely rare. They must either be declared *ex cathedra* (by the pope "from the chair" of Saint Peter; that is, papal infallibility) or produced in a General Council (sometimes called an Ecumenical Council, such as Vatican II, the Council of Trent, the Council of Nicaea), in which the bishops teach in unison with the pope. But not every teaching from a General Council is infallible, only those teachings that are declared as such. Papal infallibility is a relatively new addition to the Catholic faith. It was first claimed by Pope Pius IX in 1854 and was later recognized by the First Vatican Council in 1870 and reaffirmed at Vatican II (1964). This teaching holds that the pope is preserved from error when teaching on matters of faith and morals and only when teaching *ex cathedra*. Only two dogmas have been declared infallible: the Immaculate Conception of Mary (1854) and the Bodily Assumption of Mary (1950). The idea of papal infallibility has been and continues to be strongly debated.

The Ordinary Magisterium refers to teachings by popes, bishops, and councils of bishops that are not considered infallible; that is, they are open to change over time. Most magisterial teachings fall under this category and include statements such as decrees, constitutions, encyclicals, and pastoral letters.

A third source of authority within the Church is the *sensus fidelium* (the sense of the faithful), which Austin Flannery describes as

The Magisterium *(continued)*

"the instinctive sensitivity and discrimination which the members of the Church possess in matters of faith."[13] This belief affirms the common sense of the faithful (that is, the laity and the clergy) and is based on the belief that just as the Holy Spirit protects the Magisterium from grave error, so too the Holy Spirit is poured out on the entire Church (see *Dogmatic Constitution on the Church*, no. 12).

Although the Church has responded to social, political, and economic ethical issues for centuries, ever since Pope Leo XIII's 1891 encyclical *Capital and Labor* (*Rerum novarum*), nearly every pope has issued a social encyclical addressing "the social problem," that is, a pressing contemporary social, political, or economic issue. This has raised matters of social justice to the forefront of the Church's public life. When one looks at the larger body of Catholic social thought, one finds that popes, bishops, and a host of other experts on matters of social justice have written on nearly every social issue: capitalism, communism, poverty, economic and social development, globalization, capital punishment, the role of women in society, racism, war, human rights, nuclear weapons, labor issues, and more. While there is no official list of documents or principles of Catholic social thought, many ethicists have identified common ethical themes or principles to which these teachings and writings often appeal, which serves as a companion roster to the ethical themes found in the Scriptures. Lists of ethical principles of Catholic social thought typically include:

- *Dignity of the Human Person and Human Rights:* Based on the biblical creation stories in which human beings are declared to be made in the image and likeness of God, blessed with rationality and free will, and called into a special relationship with God, Catholic social thought teaches that all human beings, regardless of race, sex, religion, mental capacity, sexual orientation, or nationality, possess an inherent and inviolable dignity. Human beings must always be treated as an end in themselves, never simply as a means to an end. Because all human beings possess an inherent dignity, they can claim (have a right) to be treated in a manner appropriate for a human being. This includes not only basic human rights (such as life, food, clothing, shelter), but, within the Catholic tradition, a number of other rights including social, political, and economic rights (for example, a right to employment, freedom of association, freedom to have a family, freedom of conscience, freedom of speech, freedom to pursue art). All rights also come with concomitant duties; in other words, in claiming a right one also accepts the corresponding obligations that come with that right. (See *Peace on Earth*, nos. 8–38 and *The Church in the Modern World*, nos. 24–30.)

- *Solidarity:* According to Pope John Paul II, solidarity "is not a feeling of vague compassion or shallow distress at the misfortune of so many people, both near and far. On the contrary, it is a firm and persevering determination to commit oneself to the common good [see below]; that is to say to the good of all and of each individual, because we are all really responsible for all" (*Social Concerns*, no. 38). In other words, solidarity is more than a feeling of being connected to one another. It is a virtue that motivates one to act, a care that expresses itself in a willingness to work and sacrifice in order to alleviate the suffering of others. It is an expression of neighbor-love.

- *The Common Good:* The bishops at the Second Vatican Council (1962–1965) described the common good as "the sum total of social conditions which allow people, either as groups or as individuals, to reach their fulfillment more easily" (*Catechism*, no. 1906, quoting *The Church in the Modern World*, no. 26). In other words, the common good is nurtured by social, political, and economic structures, systems, and institutions that allow people to flourish. Securing the common good is typically seen as the primary responsibility of the state, but each citizen is also responsible for contributing to the good of all. The common good typically refers to the good of a nation, although there is also an emerging sense of a global common good (universal common good), which begs the question, "Who is responsible for the global common good?" (See *Peace on Earth*, nos. 98–108 and 130–41.)

- *Participation:* The right to participate (play a role) in the social, political, and economic spheres rests on the idea that all human beings possess an inherent dignity and human rights. It is a basic right because human beings are social animals, and we need to participate in social groups. As the U.S. bishops state, "Basic justice demands the establishment of minimum levels of participation in the life of the human community for all persons. The ultimate injustice is for a person or group to be treated actively or abandoned passively as if they were nonmembers of the human race. To treat people this way is effectively to say they simply do not count as human beings" (the 1986 U.S. bishops' pastoral letter, *Economic Justice for All*, no. 77; see also *The Church in the Modern World*, no. 31, and *Economic Justice for All*, nos. 68–78 and 296–97).

- *Family:* Catholic social thought sees the family as the basic building block of society, whose mission is to be "the first and vital cell of society" (*Apostolate of the Laity*, no. 11). It is the primary location in which the individual learns how to interact with others, how to share, forgive, compromise, and love; as such, the family has great social significance. (See *The Church in the Modern World*, nos. 47–52, and *On the Family*.)

- *Subsidiarity:* This principle concerns the level at which decisions ought to be made. As Pope Pius XI declared, "Just as it is gravely wrong to take from individuals what they can accomplish on their own initiative and industry and give it to the community, so also it is an injustice and at the same a time a grave evil and a disturbance of right order to assign to a greater or higher association what lesser and subordinate organizations can do" (*On Reconstruction of the Social Order*, no. 79). In other words, decisions ought to be made and actions carried out at the most appropriate level. For example, the federal government has its proper roles and responsibilities as do state and local governments. There are also in society other groups (unions, clubs, religious groups) that have their own proper roles to play.

- *Ecological Stewardship:* For centuries, the divine blessing in Genesis (1:28) that directs human beings to exercise "domin- ion" over nature was interpreted to mean domination (abso- lute control). In recent years, biblical scholarship has stressed that the term is closer to stewardship (that is, managed care of a limited resource). Creation is a gift from God entrusted to humankind. It has its own intrinsic worth and must be cared for accordingly.

- *Private Property:* The Church has long affirmed the right to private property as an effective means for meeting human needs, expressing human dignity, and securing the common good. The right to private property, however, is not absolute. It is always subordinate to the common good, especially the needs of the poor. (See *On Reconstruction of the Social Order*, nos. 44–48 and *On the Hundredth Anniversary of* Rerum novarum, nos. 30–32.)

- *Labor:* Catholic social thought has a long history of defend- ing the rights of workers, especially the rights to form unions, to bargain collectively, and to receive a living wage. This dates back to the first modern social encyclical, Pope Leo XIII's *Capital and Labor* (1891; see also *On Human Work*, 1981).

- *Preferential Option for the Poor:* As we saw previously, this biblical principle holds that the poor, weak, and vulnerable have the single most urgent claim on the conscience of the individual and on society as a whole. Social, political, and eco- nomic policies ought to be evaluated primarily by what they do to, with, and for the weakest and most vulnerable members of society. (See *Economic Justice for All*, nos. 86–95.)

- ***Development:*** Closely related to the preferential option for the poor, development refers to addressing the social, political, and economic conditions that contribute to or alleviate global poverty, sometimes called Third World poverty or underdevelopment. The commitment to development is not simply economic; it is a commitment to full or authentic human development. Poverty is not only an economic phenomenon. It has social and political ramifications. Full human development seeks to address the root causes of poverty (such as unfair trade agreements, lack of access to capital, poor education, lack of infrastructure, political or social instability) to foster an environment that allows human beings to live lives worthy of human beings. (See *On the Development of Peoples*, nos. 1–33 and *On Social Concerns*, nos. 27–33.)

- ***War and Peace:*** This principle is the primary subject of our study. Suffice it to say that Catholic social thought holds that "peace is not merely the absence of war"; it is "an enterprise of justice" (U.S. bishops' 1983 pastoral letter, *The Challenge of Peace*, no. 68, quoting *The Church in the Modern World*, no. 22).

These principles are not a new Ten Commandments, that is, new ethical laws. They are a set of ethical principles (commitments) that have emerged more or less organically over centuries of heartfelt reflection on how to confront contemporary ethical problems — including problems of war and peace — in a way that is faithful to Scripture and the life and example of Jesus Christ. They should not be appealed to as law; instead, they are ethical guidelines that frame our discussions about moral and ethical problems. In essence, Catholic social thought represents a summary of the Catholic ethical tradition.

REASON

Saint Anselm of Canterbury's description of theology as "faith seeking understanding" (*fides quaerens intellectum*) highlights the role of reason in the Christian life. Christianity does not espouse blind faith, that is, accepting teachings without questioning. Operating from a belief that God made humans curious and rational, the tenets of the Christian faith (including its morals and ethics) ought to be reasonable, intelligent, and convincing. As such, Christian ethics draws heavily upon many ethical theories. This is a question of moral method—*how* one arrives at the *why*, which determines the *what*. Christian ethics draws on a number of philosophically based moral methods. For our purposes, we will review four key moral methods: relativism, deontology, consequentialism, and teleology. These moral methods have been applied by various individuals, churches, and social and governmental bodies over the centuries to myriad questions surrounding the issues of war and peace.

RELATIVISM

Relativism refers to several methods sharing the premise that it is impossible to talk definitively about morality and ethics because every person, culture, and religion has a different concept of right and wrong. Thomas Carson identifies four types of relativism:[14]

- *Cultural Relativism:* This method observes that different cultures have different moral standards. For example, some cultures practice polygamy while others condemn it; some see homosexual behavior as wrong, others do not. On the descriptive level, cultural relativism is true. The mistake cultural relativists make, however, is that they jump from the observation "different cultures have different moral beliefs" to the conclusion "all morality is relative." The fact that cultures endorse different behaviors does not prove that morality is relative.

- *Normative Relativism:* This method claims that the rightness or wrongness of an action is based on personal or social standards. There are two types of normative relativism: individual

OTHER MORAL METHODS

It would be impossible to review every moral and ethical method. This chapter focuses on four: relativism, deontology, consequentialism, and teleology. Some other popular moral methods include the following:

- *Ethical Egoism:* This method is based on the premise that one should always act out of self-interest; one's primary duty is always to oneself.

- *Emotivism:* This method holds that moral judgments are nothing more than feelings. When we say, "This is right, good, or fair," what we really mean is, "Yeah! I really like this," and when we condemn something as wrong, sinful, or evil, all we are saying is, "Boo! I don't like this."

- *Ethical Intuitionism:* This method posits that we know right from wrong instinctively, by "following our gut."

- *Feminist Ethics:* Sometimes called the *ethic of care*, feminist ethics focuses on the primacy of human relationships. It tends to reject universal moral absolutes and other so-called objective approaches to ethics under the premise that human beings are social animals and our relationships are more than a "contract" or agreement.

normative relativism (an action is right or wrong depending on one's personal moral standards), and societal normative relativism (an action is right or wrong depending on a society's standards). The problem with individual normative relativism is that what one believes to be right or wrong could change, so what was right today could be wrong tomorrow (or even five minutes later). There are several problems with societal normative relativism as well. First, it follows the principle that "if everybody else is doing it, it must be okay." An extreme example of this would be to argue that the Holocaust was a good thing because it was in keeping with a societal belief (prejudice) in the inferiority and dangerous nature of Jews. Second, societal normative relativism never defines what constitutes a society. What about minority populations within a larger society: are they part of the larger society and its ethical norms, or do they operate with their own moral code? Finally, according to societal normative relativism, a society can never be wrong, even if it adopts contradicting standards over time.

- **Situational Relativism:** This method determines right and wrong through context. While a situation or context legitimately should be taken into account when making a moral judgment, taken to its extreme (called *situationalism*), this philosophy contends that universal moral rules or standards do not exist. Situation determines everything, so even actions like rape and genocide can't be condemned as "always wrong," since the context in which they occur and not the acts themselves determines their rightness or wrongness.

- **Ethical Relativism:** This method is best summed up in the phrase, "What's true for you is true for you, and what's true for me is true for me." This is utter nonsense, of course. Imagine you are in an algebra class and you conclude that $x = 10$. The teacher then corrects you, saying, "No, $x = 12$." Would you reply, "Well, for you $x = 12$, but for me $x = 10$"? Ethical relativists use the word true disingenuously. When we say information is true, we usually mean it is factual and that its accuracy is verifiable. To claim that "it's true for you that using torture is wrong, and it's true for me that using torture is permissible" is really saying, "You believe one thing, and I believe something else," but that is simply an observation about what we *believe*, not about what actually *is*. Ethical relativists, in claiming morality is subjective, are in essence the same as individual normative relativists.

We examined relativism first because it is a popular moral belief system, *not* because it is part of the Christian tradition.

Christian ethics belongs to a category called *moral realism*, which holds that moral standards are real. Moral realism stands opposed to *moral skepticism*, which holds that there are either no objective moral standards or, more moderately, that there might be objective moral standards, but there is no way we can verify them. According to Christianity, there are objective moral rules and some of them are known, for example, the Ten Commandments and the Golden Rule. The authority of these moral principles rests on the fact that they are based in Revelation.

Yet a word of caution is needed here. History is full of examples of moral realists, especially Christian moral realists, claiming to know the moral truth and then going out and doing horrible things to people who disagree with them. Believing there is an objective moral order does not imply one has automatic or infallible knowledge of it. A dose of humility on making moral claims goes a long way.

The remaining three moral methods are also realist theories. They are attempts (or methods) to discern what those objective moral standards are—in other words, to know right from wrong.

DEONTOLOGY

The Greek word *deon* means rule, law, duty, or obligation. Deontological ethics are rule-, law-, or duty-based ethics such as divine command theory, Kant's categorical imperative, and social contract theory.

According to divine command theory, right and wrong are based on what God commands. This theory typically looks to what are considered to be divinely revealed texts or teachings such as the Ten Commandments in the Bible or instructions in the Qur'an, the sacred text for Islam. There are many problems with divine command theory, among them:

- Can God command something immoral? As we will see, the Bible contains examples of God commanding what appear to be immoral actions (for example, killing innocent people). Do these usually immoral actions become moral simply because God commands them, or can God act in immoral ways?

- What if there isn't a rule? Most sacred texts are centuries old and do not address contemporary moral problems like nuclear war or embryonic stem cell research. What should we do if there is no divine command?
- What if the commandments contradict each other?

Divine command theory reduces ethics to power and authority. All one must do to be good is follow the rules, even if one follows them for the wrong reasons.

Immanuel Kant (1724–1804) proposed a deontological ethic based on pure reason. He saw his method, the categorical imperative, as applying to everyone, everywhere, all the time (thus categorical), and as identifying obligations that must be fulfilled (thus imperative). For Kant, morality was more than following the rules, though; you have to do the right thing for the right reason. He summarized his categorical imperative in two forms:

- *The Principle of Universalization:* An action is morally right if, and only if, one can logically wish (will) that everyone would act the same way in the same situation. In other words, when deciding what is the right thing to do, ask yourself, "What if everybody else did the same thing, if they were in the same situation?" For example, if everyone cheated on tests, then tests would become meaningless. You may be thinking, "Hey, that's a good thing!" But then what would happen? Professors would simply devise other ways of assessing students, or maybe colleges would simply become meaningless since there would be no way of measuring student learning. So when one cheats on a test, that person isn't simply being dishonest, he or she is eroding the very foundation upon which education is built. If a student doesn't care about that, then why attend school at all?

- *The Golden Rule:* Do unto others as you would have others do unto you. In other words, always treat others in a way that you want to be treated. For Kant, human beings could never be used as a means to an end only; rather each person must always treat others as an end in and of themselves. This follows from the principle of universalization; no one would logically wish to live in a world where people were treated like things.

The strength of the categorical imperative is its logic. It isn't based on any religion, and it is clear in its rationale. Its problems are that it can be rigid (under no circumstances are you allowed to break the rules), it doesn't look to consequences or outcomes, and it has trouble when one has conflicting duties.

The Social contract theory holds that morality is nothing more than an agreed upon set of social norms. Right and wrong, then, are nothing more than conventions. Thomas Hobbes (1588–1679) proposed that before there were societies and civilization, humans lived in the "state of nature." In the state of nature, life is "solitary, poor, nasty, brutish, and short."[15] It is a world in which might makes right, there are no rules, and talk of morality, right and wrong, fair and unfair, or just and unjust is meaningless. Everyone lives in a constant state of fear. Hobbes concluded that because of fear of one another, humans create government as an enforcer of rules and security. We surrender the absolute freedom that the state of nature provides in favor of security. The role of government is to enforce the rules of society, which brings us relative peace.

While Hobbes never claimed that the state of nature actually existed, he used this thought experiment to argue that morals, rules, and law are nothing more than socially agreed upon standards to which we surrender in the name of peace. We will encounter Hobbes again later, for he also argued that when the state fails to protect, we are thrust back into the state of nature, which is a state of war of all against all.

The war convention is a fitting illustration of social contract theory. While many decry the idea of battlefield ethics under the mantra, "all's fair in love and war," history has shown that customs, protocols, norms, and expectations have governed warfare for centuries. The rules of surrendering are the best example. A soldier who surrenders enters into an agreement with his captors. He promises not to fight, and his captors grant him benevolent quarantine. While the rules are not always followed, it is a widely accepted practice that often works. The practice preceded any formal treaty on surrendering. Michael Walzer characterizes these war conventions as common law, that is, widely accepted best practices, which only later become positive law (codified or black letter law) when they are ratified in treaties and agreements such as the Geneva Conventions (a collection of international laws formulated between 1864 and 1949 that addresses the treatment of battlefield casualties, maritime casualties, prisoners of war, and civilians during wartime).

Military ethics often tends toward deontology. Deontology, emphasizes protocols, honor codes, a clear chain of command, and duty. Deontological ethics works well in hierarchies (such as the military and the Catholic Church), but, as any military leader will tell you, the rules can't cover every possible situation, and sometimes what the rules require conflicts with the right thing to do. For example, I know a U.S. officer who served in Kosovo in the former Yugoslavia. This officer and his fellow soldiers had been commanded not to provide medical supplies to civilians because there was no way the military could meet all civilian needs, and their first responsibility was to their fellow soldiers. Besides, aid agencies were taking responsibility for medical aid to civilians. It happened that these soldiers came upon a community that had no medical supplies. Many in the community, which included an orphanage, were in need of basic medical attention (antibiotics, bandages, syringes, and so on). My friend and his soldiers gave everything they had to the community's doctor, which was a direct violation of an order, but in his opinion (and in the opinion of all his fellow soldiers), "It was the right thing to do." The strength of deontological ethics lies in its clarity — the rules are the rules. But it is a minimalist ethic. So long as I don't break the rules, I've done nothing wrong. Deontological ethics also tends to be rigid: it can't accommodate times when it's acceptable or even required to break the rules (such as speeding to get to the hospital); it fails to address what ought to be done in new or unimagined situations; and it often gets more and more complex as new situations arise, requiring new and more complex rules.

CONSEQUENTIALISM

Consequentialist ethical methods focus on outcomes, results, or (as the name implies) consequences. In consequentialist ethics, right and wrong are determined by what produces the best results; they are not based on any rules, obligations, character, or even motive. Utilitarianism is the most popular and famous consequentialist ethic. For utilitarians, right and wrong are based on what produces the greatest amount of happiness for the greatest number of people. Jeremy Bentham (1748–1832) proposed what is called act utilitarianism. According to this theory, when trying to decide what to do in a particular situation, one should assign a positive value (+) to whatever increases happiness and a negative value (–) to whatever produces unhappiness. One then adds up the plusses and minuses, and whatever scenario produces the greatest net happiness for the greatest number is the right thing to do. To illustrate, imagine a military commander in the field is faced with sniper fire from a local village. Using act utilitarianism, the officer would consider the options and weigh the advantages against the disadvantages by assigning values, as the chart below illustrates.

Option A: Do nothing.	Option B: Send in a strategic strike unit to eliminate the sniper.	Option C: Call in an air strike on the entire village.
Sniper continues to wreak havoc and slow troop movement in the area: –75	Sniper is eliminated, allowing better troop movement in the area: +100	Elimination of the sniper, allowing better troop movement in the area: +100
Civilian casualties: 0	Civilian casualties: –25	Civilian casualties: –350
Military casualties (short term): 0	Military casualties (short term): –25	Military casualties (short term): 0
Military casualties (long term): –100	Military casualties (long term): 0	Military casualties (long term): 0
Total: –175	Total: +50	Total: –250

According to act utilitarianism, option B is the right thing to do because it produces the greatest happiness (and least amount of unhappiness) for the greatest number. But this illustration points to one of act utilitarianism's greatest problems: assigning value to human happiness is terribly subjective. The point values are arbitrary, and determining what should and should not count is also subjective. For example, in the options from the chart, environmental destruction is not considered nor is the effect on the families and friends of civilian and military casualties.

John Stuart Mill (1806–1873) proposed rule utilitarianism as a way of improving Bentham's crass calculus. For Mill, it is nearly impossible to calculate the pleasure or pain of each particular action; instead, rules and laws in society are based on centuries of human experience and teach us generally what produces the greatest happiness for the greatest number. Instead of calculating consequences in this particular situation (act utilitarianism), simply look to long-established rules (for example, don't lie, don't cheat, don't steal). One important factor in rule utilitarianism is that one's own personal happiness does not count more than the happiness of others; it is a disinterested ethic.

Besides the difficulty of calculating pleasure or pain, other problems with consequentialist ethics include the following:

- It is based on speculation; one cannot predict the consequences of an action with certainty, and war in particular tends to generate unintended consequences.

- In these theories there are no intrinsically evil or wrong actions. Rightness or wrongness is determined by outcomes and nothing else, so intentional killing of civilians, rape, or genocide aren't wrong per se, but only because they might produce negative consequences.

TELEOLOGY

Teleological ethics gets its name from the Greek word *telos*, meaning "end" or "goal." As such, teleological ethics focuses on the end or goal of an action. This is different from consequences or outcomes because it includes intention. It considers not simply what happens but also the intended goal one is seeking when choosing one action over another. We will examine two types of teleological ethics: virtue ethics (Aristotle) and natural law (Aquinas).[16]

Virtue Ethics – Aristotle (384 – 322 BCE) proposed that everything has its natural end that it seeks. Acorns become oak trees, rivers flow toward the sea, sunflowers grow toward the sun. For Aristotle, happiness (*eudaimonia*) is the end that all humans seek, but happiness is not simply fleeting joy. *Eudaimonia* referred to happiness to the core, the kind of happiness that comes from a well-ordered life, a life lived with purpose, meaning, and direction. Aristotle concluded that happiness is our natural end because happiness is the only thing we pursue as an end in and of itself; everything else we want (money, fame, sex, power, popularity) is desired because it will bring us happiness. They are means to the end, but not an end in and of themselves.

Eudaimonia, for Aristotle, is achieved over the course of a lifetime and requires virtue. The virtues are traits, characteristics, skills, dispositions, and habits that are necessary for performing a task perfectly. For example, we can speak of the virtues necessary for military service: discipline, respect for authority, bravery, the ability to think quickly, and physical strength. For Aristotle, the virtues were both a means to an end and an end in and of themselves (instrumental to and constitutive of happiness). In other words, the virtuous person lived the virtues because they lead to happiness and because they are part of happiness. In deciding what's the right thing to do in a particular situation, Aristotle proposed the Doctrine of the Golden Mean. When facing a moral dilemma one should (1) identify which virtues seem to apply to the situation; (2) identify

Aristotle

ESSENTIAL VIRTUES

Aristotle taught that the virtues were both a means to happiness and an essential part of happiness. Over the centuries, many people have posited certain virtues as essential to human happiness.

- *Aristotle:* Temperance (self-control), Justice, Prudence, Fortitude, Courage, Generosity, Honesty, Wit, Friendliness
- *Thomas Aquinas:* Faith, Hope, and Love (1 Cor 13:13)
- *Benjamin Franklin:* Temperance (self-control), Silence, Order, Resolution, Frugality, Industriousness, Sincerity, Justice, Moderation, Cleanliness, Tranquility, Chastity, Humility

the two extremes (ask yourself, "What would a person lacking in this virtue do in this situation, and what would a person with too much of this virtue do in this situation?"); and (3) after identifying these two extremes, aim for the middle. For example, imagine a soldier pinned down in a foxhole on a battlefield. His comrade is severely wounded, and many enemy troops are quickly advancing. Clearly this is a situation that calls for bravery. A person lacking in bravery is a coward. A coward would run away leaving the other soldier behind. A person with too much bravery would foolishly jump out of the foxhole and attack the oncoming enemy. Aiming for the Golden Mean, in this situation, calls for retreating as quickly as possible with the wounded soldier.

Aristotle noted that often we don't have time for moral deliberation, which is why he extolled the importance of habit. Habit is like training the soul. By habitually forcing ourselves to act virtuously, we teach ourselves to desire naturally what is right and good. For Aristotle, ethics and morality are learned. We must surround ourselves with virtuous friends and examples of virtuous behavior (for example, in books or movies) so that we become accustomed to doing what is right. This way, when faced with a tough moral decision that needs to be made quickly, we can trust our instincts because we have habitually trained ourselves to choose what is good, right, and just. This pertains to military training especially, because in the heat of battle, soldiers need to trust their instincts; thus military education should stress those virtues that are seen as inherent in good military service.

Natural Law Theory. Natural law is another teleological method and enjoys a place of prominence in Catholic moral theology. The name, *natural law*, however, is misleading. It is not the same as a law of nature (for example, the boiling point of water or the law of gravity), nor is it law in the sense of a codified set of rules. There is no code of natural law in a law school library. Rather, it is best to think of the natural law as the rational order.

Thomas Aquinas (1225–1274), often cited as the foundational figure in Catholic natural law theology, adapted Aristotle's ethic to a Christian framework. According to Aquinas, because God is the Creator, everything in the universe functions as God wants it to. Aquinas called this the eternal law. Human beings can know God's will through the Scriptures (divine law) and through the natural law. For Aquinas, rational reflection on human experience yields knowledge of the natural law. Human beings are rational by nature. It is through the use of reason we discern God's will. According to natural law theory, human beings are able to know right from wrong through reason. The natural law is how rational creatures participate in the eternal law. The natural law (and therefore God's will) is knowable to all human beings regardless of their religious convictions or experience. In other words, by reflecting on how God structures nature (the universe), one can discern God's moral law. While at first the natural law seems esoteric, don't dismiss it too easily. The natural law serves as the foundation of many human rights theories (for example, the idea that people have rights should be immediately apparent to any rational human being), as the preamble to the Declaration of Independence illustrates when it states, "We hold these truths to be self-evident [in other words, truths about which any rational human being should agree], that all men [and women] are endowed by their Creator with certain inalienable rights, among these are life, liberty, and the pursuit of happiness."

Adapting Aristotle's ethic to fit a Christian worldview, Aquinas proposed that the natural end sought by all human beings is not *eudaimonia*, but heaven (that is, full and perfect communion with God). Aquinas then offered his "first principle" as a means to attaining heaven.

Thomas Aquinas

It's a simple moral rule, which he claimed as a universal moral absolute (that is, it applies to everyone, everywhere, all the time, no exceptions): "Do good and avoid evil." This immediately leads us to question, "But how do I know what is good and what is evil?" This brings us to Aquinas's second principle. According to Aquinas, four primary goods lead us (normally, but not always) to the ultimate good, namely God.

- Life: Act in ways that protect and promote life.
- Family: Act in ways that protect and promote marriage and family, including a strong emphasis on the good of procreation.
- Knowledge: Act in ways that support education and learning. Aquinas included knowledge of God (such as prayer, worship, and religious education) in this category.
- Community: Act in ways that build up community, because human beings are social animals by nature.

When faced with a moral dilemma, Aquinas counseled that choosing to act in ways that promote these goods will more often than not lead to choosing good over evil, which will ultimately

CHRISTIANITY AND THE NATURAL LAW

The natural law enjoys a long history within Christianity, especially Catholicism, as the following examples illustrate.

Saint Paul in the first century wrote, "For when the Gentiles [non-Jews] who do not have the law by nature observe the prescriptions of the law, they are a law for themselves even though they do not have the law. They show that the demands of the law are written in their hearts, while their conscience also bears witness." (Rom 2:14–15)

The early Church father Tertullian (around 200 CE) recognized that, "Alone among all animate beings, man can boast of having been counted worthy to receive a law [that is, the natural law] from God: as an animal endowed with reason, capable of understanding and discernment, he is to govern his conduct by using his freedom and reason, in obedience to the One who has entrusted everything to him." [17]

Pope Leo XIII declared in 1888, "The natural law is written and engraved in the soul of each and every man, because it is human reason ordaining him to do good and forbidding him to sin" (*Catechism*, no. 1954, quoting *Nature of Human Liberty*, no. 8).

The *Catechism of the Catholic Church*, published in the 1990s, states, "Man participates in the wisdom and goodness of the Creator who gives him mastery over his acts and the ability to govern himself with a view to the true and the good. The natural law expresses the original moral sense which enabled men to discern by reason the good and the evil, the truth and the lie" (no. 1954).

lead us to God. These four goods are not listed in any particular order (they are coequal in worth), and Aquinas admitted there were probably others. The natural law is a method of moral decision making; it doesn't tell you exactly what to do, but instead is a way of framing the way we think about what we ought to do when faced with a moral dilemma.

Virtue ethics and natural law move ethics beyond simply following the rules or seeking the best possible consequences; instead, they focus on the whole person and emphasize the importance of motive (the *why* behind the *what*). But one of the great weaknesses of teleological ethics is that it tends to be vague. It doesn't draw hard and fast conclusions. It simply proposes a way of thinking about what one ought to do or a way to frame the conversation about what ought to be done.

APPLICATION

We have reviewed four of the more prominent moral methodologies (relativism, deontology, consequentialism, and teleology), but many others could also have been included. In the interest of clarity, we conclude this section on the role of reason in Christian ethics using a centuries-old, five-step method for making moral decisions. When faced with a moral dilemma, simply address each of these five areas.

1. The Act: What are you thinking about doing? The first step in any moral or ethical reflection is descriptive. Accurately describe what you are considering. Is what you are considering intrinsically (that is, by its very definition) wrong?

2. The Person(s): Who is involved in this decision, and who will be affected by it? Who is affected immediately, and who will be affected in the long term? What is your state of mind? Are you free or are you being coerced? Is the stress of the situation clouding your judgment?

3. The Motive: What is the intention behind the action you are considering (the *why* behind the *what*)? What are you hoping to accomplish? What is the goal (*telos*)? What are the motivations of others involved?

4. The Circumstances: What is the context in which this decision is being made? Do you have all the facts? Are they facts or opinions? What other options are available? Have you considered them? If you dismiss any other options, why do you dismiss them?

5. The Consequences: Based on what you know, what will be the outcome of each of your options? How certain are your predictions?

For example, imagine you lost your college scholarship and you are facing the choice of either dropping out of school or enrolling in ROTC (Reserve Officers' Training Corps) in order to take advantage of the military's tuition assistance program. Running this decision through these five steps helps make the decision-making process more comprehensive.

- The Act: Enlisting in the military and staying in school
- The Person(s): You, your family, and friends
- The Intention: Is it only for money to stay in school, or is it also motivated out of a desire to serve your country through military service or for other reasons?
- The Circumstances: Is this really your only choice? Have you asked about other financial aid packages? Could you work full-time for a year and then return to school, or go to school part-time and work part-time?
- The Consequences: If all goes well you would graduate on time with little or no debt. Then you would owe the military several years of service, during which you could be shipped anywhere and might see active combat duty that could put your life at risk or even require you to take the life of another human being.

Although the above is used only as a brief illustration, it demonstrates the usefulness of this five-step methodology. The purpose of these five considerations is to help make intelligent decisions based on comprehensive reflection.

EXPERIENCE

Experience in Christian ethics refers to both personal experience and descriptive accounts of human experience, typically from the social sciences (psychology, sociology, anthropology, economics, and political science).

Ethics and morals always cut to the core of who we are. Think of a time when someone questioned your character, your honesty, or your faithfulness. There's no way not to take that personally. Or think of a time when you were faced with a tough moral decision, and you had to do some soul searching and ask yourself, "What kind of person am I really?" Christianity affirms belief in a personal, intimate, and loving God, a God who listens to and answers our prayers, a God who invites us into a personal relationship. As such, personal experience plays a foundational role in Christian ethics. Christian ethics requires prayer and contemplation.

Prayer is an act of surrender. For many Catholics, unfortunately, hearing the word *prayer* simply brings to mind words, memorized prayers from childhood like the Lord's Prayer and the Hail Mary. While this is one type of prayer (that can be very meaningful if done with full attention), the Catholic tradition is actually much richer than simply rattling off a script. Prayer involves not only talking to God but also listening. As the Scripture recommends, "Be still, and know that I am God" (Ps 46:10, NRSV), or as the example of Jesus in the garden of Gethsemane illustrates (Matt 26:36–46; Mark 14:32–42; Luke 22:40–42), prayer is often a dialogue—we speak, but we also listen. Hearing God speak rarely takes the form of "hearing voices"; rather it is more subtle: a sense of calm, a prompting, or a feeling of consolation. In my own life, I've never had a prayer answered in the way I answer a question from a student; rather, when I pray about a tough choice, I often get a sense of what God is asking me to do. Some prefer to use the words *contemplation* or *meditation* instead of *prayer*. Differences exist among the three, but all of them involve more than just thinking. They require one to abandon oneself and allow God to lead, a simple being in the presence of God.

Conscience is another source of experience (see *Catechism of the Catholic Church*, nos. 1776–1802). The bishops at Vatican II eloquently described conscience in a way that reflects the Catholic Church's commitment to natural law theory:

Deep within his conscience man discovers a law which he has not laid upon himself but which he must obey. Its voice, ever calling him to love and to do what is good and to avoid evil, tells him inwardly at the right moment; do this, shun that. For man has in his heart a law inscribed by God. His dignity lies in observing this law, and by it he will be judged. His conscience is man's most secret core, his sanctuary. There he is alone with God whose voice echoes in his depths. (The *Church in the Modern World*, no. 16)

Thus conscience is where we stand totally transparent before God, where the true intentions for our actions are laid bare. Nothing is hidden is this sanctuary.

In Catholic moral theology, conscience is not monolithic. In fact, there are three levels (or senses) of conscience.

Conscience 1 (*synderesis*): Synderesis is about perception, the capacity to know what is good and right. It is how one comes to know what is good and right and how one chooses to do it.

Conscience 2 (moral science): While synderesis is the way one knows what is the right thing to do and what motivates us to pursue it, moral science engages rational reflection. It searches for appropriate moral principles, rules, and virtues that apply to the particular situation. It is the process (method) by which one chooses the good, not abstractly, but concretely (in a real-life situation). Moral science is about critical thinking and rational reflection to make moral decisions.

Conscience 3 (judgment): This is the final judgment, when one finally concludes, "I must do this," and then acts upon that judgment. Judgment is about making a decision and acting upon it.[18]

In the Catholic tradition, conscience reigns supreme. While many Catholics assume that morality and ethics have to do with following what the Church teaches, this is not actually what the

Church teaches. Because conscience refers to how one knows good from bad, one is obligated to follow one's conscience, even if it runs contrary to Church teaching.

> It is through his conscience that man sees and recognizes the demand of the divine law. He is bound to follow this conscience faithfully in all his activity so that he may come to God, who is his last end. Therefore he must not be forced to act contrary to his conscience. Nor must he be prevented from acting according to his conscience, especially in religious matters. (*On Religious Freedom*, no. 3)

Thus while "a human being must always obey the certain judgment of his conscience," and, "if he were deliberately to act against it, he would condemn himself," nevertheless "it can happen that moral conscience remains in ignorance and makes erroneous judgments" (*Catechism*, no. 1790). Too often people hear about the supremacy of conscience and choose to interpret it as a license to do whatever one wants. But this is not what the Church teaches. Instead, the Church holds that the Church, and in particular the Magisterium, teaches moral truths that ought not to be violated lightly.

> In forming their conscience the Christian faithful must give careful attention to the sacred and certain teaching of the Church. For the Catholic Church is by the will of Christ the teacher of truth. Her charge is to announce and teach authentically that truth which is Christ and at the same time with her authority to declare and confirm the principles of the moral order which derive from human nature itself. (*On Religious Freedom*, no. 14)

Thus, the Church teaches that while one is obliged to follow one's conscience even if it is wrong or contrary to Church teaching, one also has the obligation to properly form one's conscience through study and to take what the Church teaches seriously. One is held morally responsible for wrong judgments based on a poorly formed conscience. This distinction is often described as the difference between *invincible ignorance* (not knowing due to no personal fault) and *vincible ignorance* (not knowing when one could have or should have known better). Before appealing to the supremacy of conscience, one must make sure that his or her conscience is properly formed (educated), which includes knowing what the Church teaches on various moral and ethical issues and why the Church holds certain positions. We will return to the importance of conscience in the following chapter when we discuss conscientious objection to war and selective conscientious objection.

Descriptive accounts of human experience are also a source for Christian ethics. These accounts normally come from the social sciences such as psychology, sociology, anthropology, economics, and political science. Their value lies in that they are empirically based, often using statistical evidence to support their claims about what is normative and what ought to be considered abnormal in human behavior. Each of these social sciences provides a unique window into human experience. Instead of positing how things ought to be, they tend to focus more on how things actually are, that is, they are descriptive accounts, not prescriptive (although sometimes they are both). If the first step in ethical reflection is descriptive, then empirical accounts of human behavior are essential to ethical reflection.

WAR IS AN ETHICAL ISSUE

Christian ethics does not function like mathematics or an exact science. There is no single formula, method, or rule that will tell you what's the right thing to do in a particular situation. Instead, Christian ethics functions inductively. Its moral rules and principles are derived from Scripture, tradition, reason, and experience. We place these sources in dialogue with one another to facilitate a public conversation about what we ought to do. While questions of morality often deal with personal conscience, questions about ethics must, by definition, be public.

War is primarily an ethical issue. The personal decision of whether to fight in a war is a moral matter; the judgment about whether a particular war is just or not just, or about whether in fact any war can be just, is a matter of ethics. With this foundation in Christian ethics established, we turn our attention to the specific topic of the ethics of war and peace. In chapter 2, we begin with pacifism.

DISCUSSION QUESTIONS

1. This chapter explores four primary sources of Christian ethics: Scripture, tradition, reason, and experience. What do you think of this approach to Christian ethics? Is it useful? What are its strengths? What problems might there be with this approach, especially when facing ethical questions?

2. The section on Scripture presents four tasks for using Scripture in ethical reflection, three dangers one ought to avoid when using Scripture, and a list of key ethical themes found in the Bible. Critique this approach to using the Bible in ethics by identifying its strengths and weaknesses.

3. What is your opinion about the relationship between Scripture and tradition? Do you agree or disagree with the Roman Catholic teaching on Scripture and tradition?

4. Catholic social thought is often called the best-kept secret in the Church, meaning that it is a rich source for ethics, but is largely unknown. Whether you are Christian or not, what is your critique of the principles of Catholic social thought?

5. Having explored a variety of moral methods (relativisms, consequentialist, deontological, teleological), how would you characterize your own approach to moral decision making? In other words, are you a relativist, utilitarian, egoist, Kantian, etc.?

6. The section on experience examines different types of conscience and the "supremacy of conscience." Critique the idea that conscience reigns supreme.

ENDNOTES

1 Jozef Zalot and Benedict Guevin, OSB, *Catholic Ethics in Today's World* (Winona, MN: Saint Mary's Press, 2008), 15–16.

2 It is worth noting that not everyone defines morals and ethics in the same way. According to James Gustafson, morals have to do with practical decision making (for example, "What should I do?") and concern questions of fundamental convictions, character, context, and norms. Ethics is the study of the theoretical foundations of morality and tends to be more abstract, focusing on concepts such as the good, justice, human free will and agency, and criteria for moral judgment. See James Gustafson, "Theology and Ethics," in *Christian Ethics and the Community* (Philadelphia: United Church Press, 1971), 85; and *Christ and the Moral Life* (New York: Harper & Row, 1968), 1–4. Richard Sparks makes a similar distinction: morality concerns values, choice, and actions, while ethics is the study of theories of morality. See Richard Sparks, *Contemporary Christian Morality* (New York: Crossroad, 1996).

3 Often these four sources are referred to as the Wesleyan Quadrilateral. John Wesley (1703–1791), founder of the Methodist Church, identified four sources that a Christian ought to and normally does consult when faced with an ethical decision, although in practice Christians have relied on these four sources for centuries.

4 Richard Gula, *Reason Informed by Faith: Foundations of Catholic Morality* (Mahwah, NJ: Paulist Press, 1989), 165.

5 Kenneth R. Himes, "Scripture and Ethics: A Review Essay," *Biblical Theology Bulletin* 15 (April 1985): 65–73. For an interpretation of Himes' four tasks, see Gula, *Reason Informed by Faith*, 165–72; and Russell B. Connors and Patrick T. McCormick, *Character, Choices, and Community: The Three faces of Christian Ethics* (Mahwah, NJ: Paulist Press, 1998), 102–106.

6 H. Richard Niebuhr, *The Kingdom of God in America* (New York: Harper & Row, 1959), 193.

7 James Gustafson, "The Place of Scripture in Christian Ethics: A Methodological Study," *Theology and Christian Ethics* (Philadelphia: United Church Press, 1974), 121–45. For interpretations of Gustafson, see Gula, *Reason Informed by Faith*, 169–71; and Connors and McCormick, *Character, Choices, and Community*, 102–104.

8 See Gustafson, "The Place of Scripture," 134; Timothy O'Connell, *Principles for a Catholic Morality* (San Francisco: Harper & Row, 1990), 36–48; Richard Crook, *An Introduction to Christian Ethics* (Upper Saddle River, NJ: Prentice Hall, 2002), 66–91; and Connors and McCormick, *Character, Choices, and Community*, 106–112.

9 For more on key biblical themes, see Connors and McCormick, *Character, Choices, and Community,* 106–112; and Richard Crook, *Basic Christian Ethics* (Upper Saddle River, NJ: Prentice Hall, 2002), 66–90.

10 Gerhard von Rad, *Old Testament Theology,* trans. D. M. G. Stalker (New York: Harper and Bros., 1962), I.370.

11 John Donahue, "Biblical Perspective on Justice" in *The Faith that Does Justice,* ed. John Haughey (New York: Paulist Press, 1977), 69.

12 The longbow and crossbow were also condemned because they were seen as cowardly. They allowed killing from a distance. They also contributed to the end of the age of chivalry because longbows and crossbows allowed peasants to gain an advantage in battle over knights. They could kill a knight in armor from a safe distance, rendering knights on horseback ineffectual in battle.

13 Austin Flannery, *Vatican Council II: The Conciliar and Post Conciliar Documents* (Boston: St. Paul Editions, 1975), translation note, 363.

14 Thomas Carson, "An Approach to Relativism," *Teaching Philosophy* 22.2 (June 1999): 161–84.

15 Thomas Hobbes, the Leviathan, part 1, chapter 12.

16 See Aristotle, *Nicomachean Ethics,* bk I, ch. 8–9 ; bk. II, ch. 1–9 and bk. III, ch. 1–12, trans. W. D. Ross (Oxford: Claredon Press, 1908), and Aquinas, *Summa Theologica* I–II, questions 49–67.

17 *Catechism of the Catholic Church,* no. 1951, quoting Tertullian, *Adv. Marc,* 2, 4, from J. P. Migne, ed., *Patrologia Latina* (Paris: 1841–1855), 2.288–89.

18 Gula, *Reason Informed by Faith,* 130–35; and Zalot and Guevin, *Catholic Ethics in Today's World,* 36–40. See also *Catechism of the Catholic Church,* no. 1780.

CHAPTER 2

Pacifism

This book's title comes from a peace rally I attended in Akron, Ohio, during the initial phase of the 2003 U.S. invasion of Iraq. At the rally, I saw a middle-aged woman holding a large yellow sign with black letters that read, "WWJK? Who Would Jesus Kill?" In its simplest form, her sign captured Christian pacifism at its core. Pacifism is a commitment to peacemaking and a rejection of violence. Through the centuries, many Christians have concluded that Jesus was a pacifist and that violence is antithetical to the gospel (that is, in direct and unequivocal opposition to the life, teaching, and example of Jesus). This chapter explores the "far left" in our continuum of approaches to war and peace (see page 18) by examining different types of pacifism, scriptural support of pacifism, the history of Christian pacifism (from Jesus to contemporary times), and challenges to Christian pacifism.

DEGREES OF PACIFISM

The word *pacifism* is often mistaken for its homonym, *passivism*. But typically, pacifists are not passive (inactive or submissive),

THE CYCLE OF VIOLENCE

The cycle of violence refers to the phenomenon that violence begets violence. Violence rarely erupts out of nowhere. It is usually precipitated by threats, fear, antagonism, or other forms of provocation. Individuals, groups, and even nations resort to the use of force because they feel threatened, humiliated, betrayed, or wronged. Their opponent likewise feels threatened, humiliated, and afraid, and in turn feels compelled to retaliate. Playground scuffles, barroom fights, gang warfare, and international wars often follow the same pattern. They begin with the perception, sometimes right and sometimes wrong, of being mistreated or humiliated ("She made fun of me," "He was hitting on my girl-friend," "They threatened us"), which the person or group then feels requires a response. But in receiving violence, the other side likewise feels wronged or humiliated and desires revenge, which only fuels the antagonism.

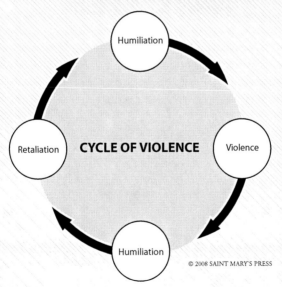

Humiliation

Retaliation   **CYCLE OF VIOLENCE**   Violence

Humiliation

© 2008 SAINT MARY'S PRESS

The Cycle of Violence *(continued)*

The best way to break the cycle of violence is for someone to choose not to retaliate, in essence to choose either (1) to take the hit, humiliation, or threat and not respond, or (2) if one finds "just taking it" to be a form of self-hatred or complicity in one's own abuse, then to leave, move on, or engage the help and protection of others, but in ways that do not demean the aggressor. The basic logic is by not repaying humiliation with violence, the "tit-for-tat" pattern ends. Groups (from families to nations) that have a strong sense of what is "honorable" may require education and training to reconceptualize nonretaliation as an honorable act for the common good and to develop alternative methods of conflict resolution.

which is why many pacifists prefer to call their commitment to peace *active nonviolence*. Pacifism comes from the Latin *pacificus* (*pac-* or *pax* meaning "peace" and *ficus* meaning "making"). Thus, pacifism means *peacemaking*. Pacifists actively pursue the creation of peace with justice.

One of the most common challenges levied against pacifists is the question of self-defense. When others learn that a person is a pacifist they often retort, "You mean if someone were to attack you, you wouldn't fight back?" or "What if someone was going to kill your mother (or your wife, your husband, your kids, and so on) and you had a gun, would you shoot them?" These questions reflect an unnuanced understanding of pacifism. In fact, there are actually many kinds of pacifists and pacifisms.[1]

PACIFISTS AND PACIFISMS
ABSOLUTE PACIFISM

This belief holds that all forms of violence and war are always wrong, no exceptions. This form of moral absolutism is a deontological ethic (see chapter 1) that contends violence can never be justified or excused under any circumstances, regardless of consequences. Some forms of absolute pacifism (also known as maximal pacifism and as opposed to minimal pacifism) reject the use of any force or coercion, even in self-defense or for protecting the weak and vulnerable, or in cases of humanitarian intervention. These forms may include a rejection of abortion, capital punishment, and even eating meat.

Absolute pacifists dismiss the self-defense objection as presenting a false dichotomy. Rarely are we faced with a kill-or-be-killed scenario, they argue. Nonviolent alternatives almost always exist; they are simply not explored or are too easily dismissed as impractical.

Typically religiously based pacifists (such as Christian, Hindu, or Buddhist) are absolute. Mohandas Gandhi, Leo Tolstoy, and Martin Luther King Jr. are often cited as examples of absolute pacifists. However, some do not believe King and Gandhi were absolute, since their methods often provoked their opponents to use force, and their efforts were supported by others who used some form of coercion.[2]

UNIVERSAL PACIFISM

This belief holds that rejection of violence is a universal value, applying to everyone, everywhere, and not just to particular individuals or communities (see principled pacifism). For universal pacifists, any profession that resorts to violence or threatens violence is an inherently immoral profession (for example, soldier or police officer).

The most extreme form of pacifism, then, is absolute and universal pacifism, which argues that the use of violence, force, or coercion—or even the threat of these—is always wrong for everyone (no exceptions). Absolute and universal pacifism is often contrasted with classical pacifism.

PRINCIPLED PACIFISM

This form of pacifism is motivated out of a commitment to peace and a rejection of violence. Like absolute pacifism, it does not consider context or consequences as relevant; instead one is committed to the principle of peacemaking. Principled pacifism differs from absolute pacifism in that it is not based on an objective claim that violence is inherently wrong, rather it rejects violence out of a personal motivation or communal commitment, allowing for exceptions in limited situations. For principled pacifists, the commitment to peace and nonviolence is a personal choice, a commitment of the individual (*particular* pacifism) or a smaller group (*communal* pacifism). Although principled pacifists reject violence, they do not judge others who resort to violence (for example, police officers and soldiers) as inherently wrong or immoral. Principled pacifism also includes people whose vocation or profession is based on nonviolence (for example, clergy, physicians, and humanitarian aid workers). Principled pacifists can therefore claim, "I (we) believe that violence is wrong, but accept the right of others to use force, such as the state or those responsible for protecting the common good." Principled pacifism is contrasted with strategic pacifism.

CLASSICAL PACIFISM

Classical pacifism distinguishes between the use of force by police and the use of force by the military. Classical pacifists reject war between nations, but they can support "police actions" whereby limited force is used to restrain evil or aggression, to defend human rights, and so on. Sometimes military forces are called into "police actions" (such as humanitarian intervention), which blurs the distinction between police and military, although in many countries the military and police are the same. Classical pacifism is closely related to principled pacifism and contrasts with absolute pacifism.

STRATEGIC PACIFISM

This pragmatic commitment to peacemaking sees violence as counterproductive. Strategic pacifism is a consequentialist ethic (see chapter 1): violence is rejected because it produces bad outcomes, not because violence is intrinsically wrong. Strategic pacifism allows for the use of force as a means of conflict resolution *only* if nonviolent alternatives have been exhausted or would be ineffective. Alternatively called *contingent* pacifism, *conditional* pacifism, or *relative* pacifism, it was espoused by Albert Einstein and Bertrand Russell, both of whom generally rejected violence but thought Nazi Germany represented an exceptional case. As Russell described his position, "*Very few* wars are worth fighting. . . . The evils of war are almost always greater than they seem to excited populations at the moment when war breaks out."[3]

Similarly, *prima facie* ("on first appearance") pacifism operates with the assumption that war and violence are normally wrong, and this assumption can only be overridden when compelling evidence suggests otherwise. This places the burden of proof on those making the claim that force is necessary.

Strategic pacifism also includes *just war* pacifism (or nuclear pacifism), the belief that modern warfare (with its risk of biological, chemical, and nuclear attacks) renders all war immoral since it could produce widespread and catastrophic results. This is a *de facto* pacifism: war and violence are not inherently wrong, but the context of modern warfare renders war undesirable, illogical, and disproportionate. Others have called this *political* pacifism, because it emphasizes political solutions to conflicts. Political pacifists are often called doves (as opposed to hawks) because they view military solutions as impractical and counterproductive. Strategic pacifism shares similarities with the contemporary just war theory (discussed in chapters 4 and 5). Strategic pacifism contrasts with principled pacifism.

A further distinction can be made in these types of pacifism between separatist and politically engaged pacifism. While these two types are mutually exclusive, they can be combined with the types of pacifism just discussed.

SEPARATIST PACIFISM

This type of pacifism calls for withdrawal from the larger society, which is often viewed as inherently sinful or irredeemably ensnared in violence. Often practiced by Christians (for example, the Amish), separatist pacifism resembles communal pacifism and views the secular world as toxic to the life of discipleship and especially to one's commitment to peacemaking. It contrasts with politically engaged pacifism.

POLITICALLY ENGAGED PACIFISM

Pacifists who subscribe to this belief seek to reform or convert the larger society to pacifism. Politically engaged pacifists do not avoid the secular world as separatist pacifists do; instead they engage the world and tend to work for social, political, and economic justice.

It thus becomes clear that pacifism is not monolithic, and that not all pacifists are absolute pacifists. Nor are the types of pacifism necessarily mutually exclusive, although some are. For example, one can be both a principled and a separatist pacifist, but one cannot be both an absolute and a strategic pacifist. Just as there is a continuum of approaches to war and peace within Christianity, so too there are degrees of pacifism, as the chart on page 18 demonstrates.

CONSCIENTIOUS OBJECTION

In chapter 1 we explored the role of conscience in making moral decisions. Conscience was described as the capacity to know what is right, and the desire to pursue and then act upon it. Looking to your own conscience, could you ever use deadly force? Do you think you could serve in the military (voluntarily or if drafted) with the knowledge that you probably or even possibly would be put in a situation where you would be expected to kill another human being?

Conscientious objection refers to a refusal to participate in or support war due to deeply held religious, spiritual, or philosophical

Conscientious Objection *(continued)*

beliefs. The U.S. government's Selective Service System defines a conscientious objector (CO) as "one who is opposed to serving in the armed forces and/or bearing arms on the grounds of moral or religious principles." It recognizes two types of CO: (1) persons who are "opposed to any form of military service" and who in instances of a draft would then be assigned to alternative service such as working in a hospital or in conservation efforts, caring for youth or the elderly, or working in education; and (2) a person "whose beliefs allow him to serve in the military but in a non-combatant capacity." Such an individual "will serve in the Armed Forces but will not be assigned training or duties that include using weapons."[4]

Selective Conscientious Objection (SCO) refers to a refusal to participate in or support a particular military action because one has concluded that it is unjust. Currently, the U.S. military does not recognize SCO status; it only grants CO status and does that only after a rigorous examination, which has at times been demeaning to the applicant. Stories of those seeking CO status being called cowards and having their mental health or patriotism called into question are not uncommon. One of the primary reasons for refusing to recognize SCO status is pragmatic. A military relies heavily on having ready-to-deploy troops. If soldiers could "opt out" of particular wars or even particular military actions on grounds of conscience, this could seriously hamper military effectiveness. But note this is a practical argument, not an ethical one.

The Catholic Church has long recognized the legitimacy of both CO and SCO status and is highly critical of the failure to recognize SCO. *The Catechism of Catholic Church* declares:

> The citizen is obliged in conscience not to follow the directives of civil authorities when they are contrary to the demands of the moral order, to the fundamental rights of persons or the teachings of the Gospel. *Refusing obedience* to civil authorities, when their demands are contrary to those of upright

Conscientious Objection *(continued)*

conscience, finds its justification in the distinction between serving God and serving the political community.[5]

The Catholic Peace Fellowship works with military personnel interested in applying for CO status and educating youth on how to build a CO file that could be used to apply for CO status in case a draft were ever reconstituted. For more information on their work, visit *http://www.catholicpeacefellowship.org/nextpage.asp?m=2003.*

PACIFISM AND SCRIPTURE

The Bible does not give us a single treatise on war or peace, but instead addresses questions of violence, war, reconciliation, and peacemaking in many places and through many authors. These multiple perspectives make defining a single biblical concept of peace difficult. Nevertheless, peace is a predominant theme in both the Hebrew Scriptures and the New Testament.

HEBREW SCRIPTURES

The Hebrew word for peace is *shalom*. From ancient to modern times, this word has been used as a greeting (similar to "hello"), but it also has theological significance. The two most prominent understandings, types, or senses of peace in the Hebrew Scriptures are covenantal peace and eschatological peace.

Covenantal peace is seen primarily as a gift from God. It is the fruit of living in right relationship with God and with others. Recalling the biblical themes discussed in chapter 1, covenantal peace is based on the notions of (1) covenant (that is, the special relationship between God and Israel); (2) the importance of the Torah (the instructions, commandments, and laws) in safeguarding the covenant and living in right relationship; and (3) justice (fidelity to the terms of relationship); with special attention to (4) the needs of the poor (preferential option for the poor).

According to the Scriptures, when the Israelites live in right relationship with God and one another, peace and prosperity result. God promises:

> I will make with them a covenant of peace; it shall be an everlasting covenant with them, and I will multiply them, and put my sanctuary among them forever. My dwelling shall be with them; I will be their God, and they shall be my people. (Ezek 37:26–27)

> If you would hearken to my commandments, your prosperity would be like a river, and your vindication like the waves of the sea. (Isa 48:18)

> If you live in accordance with my precepts and are careful to observe my commandments, I will give you rain in due season, so that the land will bear its crops and the trees their fruit . . . and you will have food to eat in abundance, so that you may dwell securely in your land. I will establish peace in the land, that you may lie down to rest without anxiety. I will rid the country of ravenous beasts and keep the sword of war from sweeping across your land. (Lev 26:3–6)

But when Israel fails to observe the terms of God's covenant, God also threatens:

> But if you do not heed me and do not keep all these commandments, if you reject my precepts and spurn my decrees, refusing to obey all of my commandments and breaking my covenant, then I will give you your deserts. . . . You will sow your seed in vain, for your enemies will consume the crop. I will turn against you, till you are beaten down by your enemies and lorded over by your foes. . . . I will make the sword, the avenger of my covenant, sweep over you. (Lev 26:14–17, 25)

> Why do these people rebel with obstinate resistance? . . . Therefore I will give their wives to strangers, their fields to spoilers. . . . "Peace, peace!" they say, though there is no peace. . . . We wait for peace to no avail; for a time of healing, but terror comes instead. (Jer 8:5,10–11,15; see also 6:14)

The message is clear: by adhering to the terms of the covenant and the Torah, peace and prosperity will result. That is, by treating God and neighbor with respect, by actively seeking forgiveness from God and forgiving one another, by treating one another honestly and fairly, and by being generous and kind, especially to the poor, weak and vulnerable, the community can expect peace (*shalom*), which is intimately connected with justice (*tsedaqah*).

Eschatological peace derives its name from the word *eschaton*, meaning the end of time. Judaism even today lives in hopeful expectation of a time when the reign of sin on earth will end and life will return to what God originally intended—heaven on earth. It will be a time of abundance, perfect justice, and peace. Christians believe that this age has already begun in the life, death, and resurrection of Jesus Christ, to be completed in Christ's return at the end of time when God will judge the living and the dead. For Jews, Jesus is not the Messiah (the one who will usher in this age of peace and justice); thus Jews still await the coming of the Messiah. Eschatological peace refers to the hope and expectation of a perfect peace grounded in justice. The prophet Isaiah eloquently describes such an age of peace and harmony not only among humans but all living creatures. He may have originally foreseen the rule of a future Israelite king, but his vision has been extended to the eschaton:

> Then the wolf shall be a guest of the lamb, and the leopard shall lie down with the kid; the calf and the young lion shall browse together, with a little child to guide them. The cow and the bear shall be neighbors, together their young shall rest; the lion shall eat hay like the ox. The baby shall play by the cobra's den, and the child lay his hand on the adder's lair. There shall be no harm or ruin on all my holy mountain; for the earth shall be filled with knowledge of the LORD, as water covers the sea. (Isa 11:6–9)

Isaiah's image draws on the biblical understanding of sin as a disruption in the relationships between God and humankind, among humans, and between humans and nature (see biblical themes in chapter 1).

Elsewhere, eschatological peace is promised as a time of prosperity and security:

> Then will the desert become an orchard and the orchard be regarded as a forest. . . . Justice will bring about peace; right will produce calm and security. My people will live in a peaceful country, in secure dwellings and quiet resting places. (Isa 32:15,17–18)

> They shall beat their swords into plowshares [farming tools], and their spears into pruning hooks; one nation shall not raise the sword against another, nor shall they train for war again. (Mic 4:3; see also Isa 2:4)

> Surely the LORD will proclaim peace to his people, to the faithful, to those who trust in him. Near indeed is salvation for the loyal; prosperity will fill our land. Love and truth will meet; justice and peace will kiss. Truth will spring from the earth; justice will look down from heaven. The LORD will surely grant abundance; our land will yield its increase. Prosperity will march before the LORD, and good fortune will follow behind. (Ps 85:9–14)

The dominant images of peace in the Hebrew Bible are communal. The Scriptures do not emphasize peace as a sense of personal well-being or even as peace among neighbors. Instead peace is God's gift to the entire people, whether it comes as the fruit of keeping the covenant or is the peace that will come at the end of time. In addition, the Hebrew Scriptures reject the simplistic notion of peace as being merely the absence of war or violence. *Shalom* is a peace founded upon justice, which again is about living in right relationship with God and others. Thus peace in the Hebrew Scriptures is a work and by-product of social justice.

NEW TESTAMENT

The New Testament teaches that Jesus is the Messiah (the Christ) who brings the long-awaited eschatological peace. This idea saturates Jesus' preaching, particularly in his notion of the Kingdom of God (or Reign of God), which he described in the Sermon on the Mount:

> When he saw the crowds, he went up the mountain, and after he had sat down, his disciples came to him. He began to teach them, saying: "Blessed are the poor in spirit, for theirs is the kingdom of heaven. Blessed are they who mourn, for they will be comforted. Blessed are the meek, for they will inherit the land. Blessed are they who hunger and thirst for righteousness, for they will be satisfied. Blessed are the merciful, for they will be shown mercy. Blessed are the clean of heart, for they will see God. *Blessed are the peacemakers, for they will be called children of God.* Blessed are they who are persecuted for the sake of righteousness, for theirs is the kingdom of heaven. Blessed are you when they insult you and persecute you and utter every kind of evil against you [falsely] because of me. Rejoice and be glad, for your reward will be great in heaven. Thus they persecuted the prophets who were before you." (Matt 5:1–12; see also Luke 6:20–26; emphasis added)

Jesus goes on to interpret several commandments:

> "You have heard that it was said, 'An eye for an eye and a tooth for a tooth.' But I say to you, offer no resistance to one who is evil. *When someone strikes you on [your] right cheek, turn the other one to him as well.* If anyone wants to go to law with you over your tunic, hand him your cloak as well. Should anyone press you into service for one mile, go with him for two miles. Give to the one who asks of you, and do not turn your back on one who wants to borrow.
>
> "You have heard that it was said, 'You shall love your neighbor and hate your enemy.' But I say to you, *love your enemies, and pray for those who persecute you, that you may be children of*

your heavenly Father, for he makes his sun rise on the bad and the good, and causes rain to fall on the just and the unjust. For if you love those who love you, what recompense will you have? Do not the tax collectors do the same? And if you greet your brothers only, what is unusual about that? Do not the pagans do the same? So be perfect, just as your heavenly Father is perfect." (Matt 5:38–48; see also Luke 6:27–36; emphasis added)

Elsewhere Jesus counsels his followers, "Be merciful, just as [also] your Father is merciful" (Luke 6:36) and warns them, "Behold, I am sending you like lambs among wolves. . . . Into whatever house you enter, first say, 'Peace to this household.' If a peaceful person lives there, your peace will rest on him; but if not, [your peace] will return to you" (Luke 10:3–7; see also Matt 10:12–13). After his resurrection, when Jesus returns to his disciples, his greeting is "Peace be with you" (Luke 24:26).

Jesus' commitment to nonviolence can also be found in his actions. For example:

- When Judas and the soldiers come to arrest Jesus in the garden of Gethsemane, Peter draws his sword to protect him but Jesus rebukes him, saying, "Put your sword back into its sheath, for all who take the sword will perish by the sword" (Matt 26:52; see also Mark 14:43–52; Luke 22:47–53; John 18:10–11).

- After his arrest, Jesus stands before Pontius Pilate (a Roman ruler of the region), who interrogates him. When asked if he is a king, Jesus replies, "My kingdom does not belong to this world. If my kingdom did belong to this world, my attendants [would] be fighting to keep me from being handed over" (John 18:36). Some interpret this as an act of restraint on Jesus' part, an unwillingness to resort to fighting.

But Jesus' language of peace is not unequivocal, for he uses "the sword" to symbolize conflicts to come: "the one who does not own a sword, should sell his cloak and buy one" (Luke 22:36). "Do not think I have come to bring peace upon the earth. I have come not to bring peace but the sword. For I have come to set a man 'against his father, a daughter against her mother, and a daughter-in-law against her mother-in-law; and one's enemies will be those of his own household'" (Matt 10:34–36; see also Luke 12:51–53). And, "If anyone comes to me without hating his father and mother, wife and children, brothers and sisters, and even his own life, he cannot be my disciple" (Luke 14:26). Jesus also uses military images to describe discipleship (Luke 14:31–32).

Jesus' concept of the Kingdom of God includes divine judgment and violent punishment. He uses the analogy of good trees and bad trees, in which the trees represent disciples. In the end, says Jesus, "Every tree that does not bear good fruit will be cut down and thrown into the fire" (Matt 7:19; see also Matt 3:10). The parable of the talents (Matt 25:14–30; see also Luke 19:11–27) concludes with the "bad servant" (bad disciple) being cast out by his master, who says, "Throw this useless servant into the darkness outside, where there will be wailing and grinding of teeth." In the following passage on judging the nations, Jesus declares:

> When the Son of Man comes in his glory, and with all the angels with him, he will sit upon his glorious throne, and all the nations will be assembled before him. And he will separate them one from another, as a shepherd separates the sheep from the goats. He will place the sheep on his right and the goats on his left. The king will say to those on his right, "Come, you who are blessed by my Father. Inherit the kingdom prepared for you from the foundation of the world. For I was hungry and you gave me food, I was thirsty and you gave me drink, a stranger and you welcomed me, naked and you clothed me, ill and you cared for me, in prison and you visited me." . . . Then he will say to those on his left, "Depart from me, you accursed, into the eternal fire prepared for the devil and his angels. For I was hungry and you gave me no food, I was thirsty and you gave me no drink, a stranger and you gave me no welcome, naked and you gave me no clothing, ill and in prison, and you did not care for me." . . . And these will go off to eternal punishment, but the righteous to eternal life. (Matt 25:31–46)

Moving beyond words to actions, on at least one occasion Jesus resorted to force. All four Gospels recount Jesus' driving the money changers out of the temple. "He found in the temple area those who sold oxen, sheep, and doves, as well as the money-changers seated there. He made a whip out of cords and drove them all out of the temple area, with the sheep and oxen, and spilled the coins of the money-changers and overturned their tables" (John 2:14–15; see also Matt 21:12–13; Mark 11:15–17; Luke 19:45–46). While this passage is often cited to show Jesus was not a pacifist, E. P. Sanders's excellent analysis of the "cleansing of the temple" suggests that it may have been more an act of protest or a form of civil disobedience than an overt act of violence.[6]

These seemingly violent words and actions do not significantly challenge the idea that Jesus was committed to pacifism. In the language of his day, he often used hyperbole (exaggerated speech) to emphasize his point, especially the idea that the Kingdom of God is at hand and requires definitive action. Furthermore, given the context of Jesus' message about the Kingdom of God and the Jewish understanding of eschatological peace, the Gospels see Jesus' life and ministry as ushering in a new age of peace, similar to the one found in Isaiah's oracles. Nevertheless, Jesus' nonviolent preaching and actions were deemed subversive enough by the Roman and collaborating Jewish authorities as to warrant his arrest and execution.[7] Thus his pacifism is not conflict-free. The triumphal entry into Jerusalem was a deliberately confrontational show of power. He was perceived as a threat to the political power structures of his day and perhaps is better understood as an activist who confronted injustice, albeit nonviolently.

Saint Paul asserts that Jesus' death and resurrection have reconciled an alienated and sinful humanity with God, declaring, "We have peace with God through our Lord Jesus Christ" (Rom 5:1; see also 4:24–25 and 5:3–21), and "Through him [Jesus Christ], God was pleased to reconcile to himself all things, whether on earth or in heaven, by making peace through the blood of his [Jesus'] cross" (Col 1:20, NRSV). For Paul, Jesus' life, death, and resurrection marked the advent of a new age of peace, the fulfillment of the promised eschatological peace. In this new age (the Kingdom of God), many aspects of Jewish observance no longer apply, since Christ's followers are heirs to Abraham's covenant by faith (Gal 3:7–9,29), and it is a time when all earthly forms of separation are no longer valid:

> There is neither Jew nor Greek, there is neither slave nor free person, there is not male and female: for you are all one in Christ Jesus. (Gal 3:28)

CHRISTIAN PACIFISM THROUGH THE AGES

Pacifism enjoys a long history within the Christian tradition. In some periods and for some sects, a commitment to absolute pacifism has been seen as mandatory, while at other times and for other sects, pacifism has been viewed suspiciously. While today most Christians do not view pacifism as a requirement of the faith, one could make the case that pacifism is historically normative within the Christian church.

EARLY CHRISTIAN CHURCH AND PACIFISM

Jesus did not see himself as starting a new religion, nor did he leave his disciples with a blueprint for Christianity. The decades and even centuries following Jesus' death were a crucial period for Christianity. In these "infancy years" of the religion, most of the core beliefs (doctrines and dogmas) and ethics were still not formed, nor was there uniformity regarding the biblical canon (that is, not everyone agreed on what books belonged in the Bible). For example, the question of whether Jesus was divine wasn't settled until 325; the debate over the doctrine of the Trinity and the role of the Holy Spirit wasn't settled until 381; all of which means that, for the first 350 years of Christianity, there was no uniformity of belief regarding the very nature of God. Interestingly, the early Christians were fairly univocal in their stance toward the use of force and violence, however. For the first three to four centuries of Christianity, pacifism was the norm for Christians.

The early Church "grew up" under the *Pax Romano*. The Roman Empire was the superpower of the Mediterranean world that maintained order within its borders through the threat and use of tremendous military power. The Romans did not tolerate political or social instability, but they did allow their subjects to enjoy relative freedom. Typically subjects were free to practice their religion, afforded a degree of free speech, and permitted to enjoy their cultural customs as long as they did not challenge Roman authority. While it is historically anachronistic to describe the Romans as espousing religious liberty and freedom of speech as we use those terms today, uniformity in belief was not a primary objective of the Romans; law and order were. They did not tolerate interreligious persecution or sectarian violence. This relative peace, coupled with an extensive network of roads, allowed Christianity to spread fairly rapidly (mostly in urban areas). Thus, initially Christianity spread because of the protection of the Roman Empire.

Many of the early Christians (although not all), however, refused to serve in the Roman military, and many soldiers who converted to Christianity refused to fight.[8] Their commitment to absolute pacifism and the rejection of military service were based on two primary theological reasons: (1) the use of force (violence) was seen as antithetical to the teachings of Jesus, and (2) service in the Roman military required worship of the emperor as a god, which was a form of idolatry. James Turner Johnson also identifies several sociological reasons for the early Church's rejection of military service:

> First, recruitment for the army drew almost entirely on the rural population, where soldierly characteristics were more likely to be found than in urban areas; and second, many of these early Christians belonged to social groups whose members were not in any case liable for service in the legions. Furthermore, the cities where early Christianity flourished were far removed in this period from the presence of war, which was a phenomenon limited to the frontiers of the Roman

Empire. The only city- and town-dwellers who were likely to enter the army as common soldiers were volunteers, and there was no pressure to volunteer. Slaves and freedmen were in this period explicitly excluded from military service, and insofar as Christians belonged to these categories, they could not join even if they wished to. Finally, there was little reason for interaction between serving soldiers and the peaceful townspeople in normal times: they inhabited two essentially different worlds.[9]

The early Christians refused military service for a variety of reasons. Interpreted as a refusal to support the empire, however, their position contributed to the Roman suspicion and persecution of this new religious movement.

The witness of these early Christians is inspiring and challenging:

- Justin Martyr (100–165) contrasted his life before and after his conversion to Christ in terms of peace and violence:

  > We who [once] delighted in war, in the slaughter of one another and in every other kind of iniquity have in every part of the world converted our weapons into instruments of peace: our swords into ploughshares, our spears into farmers' tools [Isa 2:4], and now we cultivate piety, justice, brotherly charity, faith, and hope, which we derive from the Father through the crucified Savior. (*Dialogue with Trypho, a Jew*, 110)

- Clement of Alexandria (about 150–215) said of the Christian life:

  > If you enroll as one of God's people, heaven is your country and God your lawgiver. And what are his laws? You shall not kill; you shall love your neighbor as yourself. To him that strikes you on the one cheek, turn to him the other also [Matt 5:38]. . . . The Church is an army that sheds no blood. (*Protrepticus*, 10–11)

- Tertullian (160–220) addressed the questions, "Can a member of the faithful become a soldier?" and "Can a soldier be admitted to the faith?" by answering:

> There can be no compatibility between an oath made to God and one made to man, between the standard of Christ and that of the devil, between the camp of light and the camp of darkness. The soul cannot be beholden to two masters, God and Caesar. Moses, to be sure, carried a rod; Aaron wore a military belt and John had a breast plate. If one wants to play around with the topic, [Joshua] led an army and the Jewish nation went to war. But how will a Christian do so? Indeed how will he serve in the army even during peacetime without the sword that Jesus Christ has taken away? Even if a soldier came to John and got advice on how they ought to act, even if the centurion became a believer, the Lord, by taking away Peter's sword, disarmed every soldier thereafter [Matt 26:53; see also Mark 14:43–52; Luke 22:47–53; and John 18:10–11]. We are not allowed to wear any uniform that symbolizes a sinful act. (*On Idolatry*, chap. 19)[10]

Elsewhere Tertullian writes:

> Will a son of peace, who should not even go to court, take part in battle? Will a man who does not avenge wrongs done to himself have any part in chains, prisons, tortures and punishments? Will he perform guard duty for anyone other than Christ? . . . By looking around one can see how many other forms of wrongdoing are involved in fulfilling the duties of military camps, things which must be considered violations of God's law. Carrying the title "Christian" from the camp of life to the camp of darkness is itself a violation. . . . Once a man has accepted the faith and has been marked with its seal, he must immediately leave the service. (*On the Crown*, chap. 11)[11]

- Origen (185–254), responding to the charge that Christians were weakening the empire because of their refusal to serve in the military and government, argued that while Christians themselves were forbidden to fight, they did support the empire by providing "divine assistance," that is, prayer:

> To be sure, the more pious a man is, the more effectively does he assist the emperors—more so than the troops that go out and kill as many of the enemy as possible on the battleline. . . . The Christians fight through their prayers to God on behalf of those doing battle in a just cause and on behalf of an emperor who is ruling rightly in order that all opposition and hostility toward those who are acting rightly may be eliminated. What is more, by overcoming with our prayers all the demons who incite wars, who violate oaths and who disturb the peace we help emperors more than those who are supposedly doing the fighting. . . . We do battle on [the emperor's] behalf by raising a special army of piety through our petitions to God. (*Against Celsus*, book 8, chap. 73)[12]

Thus he forbids Christians to fight, but does not dismiss the use of force as inherently wrong. In fact, he argues that Christians can support just war efforts through prayer; they just can't directly participate in them. He is arguing for what we call principled pacifism.

- Maximilian of Tebessa (274–295) refused military service and was brought before Proconsul Dion, who opened the investigation by asking, "What are you called?"

Maximilian: Why do you want to know my name? It is not permitted to me to serve in the military since I am a Christian.

Dion: Serve so that you do not perish.

Maximilian: I will not serve; cut off my head; I do not serve the world. I serve my God.

Dion: Who has persuaded you of this?

Maximilian: My soul [conscience] and he who has called me.

Dion: Serve and accept the seal [badge of the emperor].

Maximilian: I will not accept the seal: I already have the seal of my Christ.

Dion: I will send you to your Christ right now.

Maximilian: I wish that you would do so. That is even my title to glory.

(As they tried to put the seal around Maximilian's neck, he resisted, saying,) I do not accept the world's seal, and if you give it to me, I will break it, since I value it at naught. I am a Christian. It is not permitted to me to bear the lead [seal] upon my neck after [having received] the saving seal of my Lord Jesus Christ, the Son of the Living God. . . . All of us Christians serve Him. Him we follow as the source of life and author of salvation.

Dion: Serve, and accept the seal, so that you do not suffer a terrible death."

Maximilian: "I will not die. My name is already with my Lord; I cannot serve in the military. . . . My service is for my Lord; I cannot serve the world. As I have already said: I am a Christian.

Dion: Maximilian, since you have disloyally refused the military oath, it has been decided for you to be punished by the sword.

Maximilian: Thanks be to God.

Maximilian was beheaded on March 12, 295.[13]

- Marcellus (died 298), a Roman centurion who converted to Christianity, cast away his sword during a festival in honor of the emperor with the words:

"If such be the conditions of service that men are compelled to sacrifice to the gods and emperors; then behold, I throw away the staff and belt; I renounce the standards and refuse to serve." During his trial for treason, he explained, "It is not fitting for a Christian man who serves Christ the Lord to serve human powers." He was beheaded on October 30, 298.[14]

In the early Church, a commitment to pacifism was considered a constitutive or essential element of the Christian faith. So how is it that today most Christians are not pacifists? Tradition holds that after a victory he credited to the Christian God in 312, the Roman Emperor Constantine became a supporter of Christianity, thus reducing persecution by the pagan Roman religion in which the emperor was considered a god. Shortly after, the Edict of Milan permitted Christian worship within the empire. Constantine's toleration and eventual privileging of Christianity posed serious challenges to the Christian faith. How would a once persecuted minority religion based on the teaching of a first-century Jewish rabbi adapt to being the official religion of a world superpower? It is impossible for an extended empire like that of the Romans to rule by a commitment to pacifism. By 416, only Christians could serve in the empire's military. In little more than one hundred years after Maximilian and Marcellus were beheaded for refusing military service, the Christian stance on the use of force had changed completely. What had happened?

Augustine of Hippo (354–430) is credited with providing the theological justification for the use of force within the Christian tradition. He is often called the father of the just war theory," a position that justifies the use of force when it supports a just cause (like protecting the weak and vulnerable), is used with right intention (peace), and has been legitimated by a competent authority. We will explore the just war theory at length in chapters 4 and 5. But as we saw with Origen, long before the Constantinian shift, Christian apologists rationalized that the empire's use of force could be justified, even though Christians could not participate

AUGUSTINE ON KILLING IN WAR

"For when a soldier kills a man in obedience to the legitimate authority under which he served, he is not chargeable with murder by the laws of the country; in fact he is chargeable with insubordination and mutiny if he refuses. But if he did it of his own accord, on his own authority, he would be liable to a charge of homicide. Thus he is punished if he did without orders for the same reason that he will be punished when he refuses when ordered." (*City of God*, book 1, chap. 26)[15]

in it directly. Ambrose of Milan (339–397) praised those who were willing to sacrifice themselves while protecting the vulnerable. And so a new ethic was shaped, an ethic that recast the early Christian minority's rejection of force into a mold of Christian empire. Government (the empire or state) is seen as an instrument of God and is endowed with a right to self-defense, an obligation to protect the common good, and a duty to protect the weak and vulnerable.

While many pacifists are critical of the political theology of Origen, Ambrose, and Augustine because it seems to abandon the Gospel commitment to absolute pacifism, it should not be overlooked that both Ambrose and Augustine forbade Christians to use force in self-defense. While this seems at first contradictory, Ambrose and Augustine accepted the state's right to use force because the state (and particularly the sovereign, that is, the king or prince) was responsible for securing the common good. The use of force, therefore, was a tool of statecraft (pursuing interests of the state, government, and presumably the common good). Individual Christians had to maintain a Gospel commitment to pacifism in their personal lives, but when a Christian soldier killed on the battlefield he was not acting as a "private citizen." He was a tool of the state and was acting under the sovereign's authority and responsibility to the common good. Individual Christians did not have recourse to the use of deadly force; it was an act reserved to the state alone. The context determined moral responsibility.

Interestingly, Augustine and Ambrose forbade clergy (priests and monks) to participate in military activity because they celebrated Eucharist, which required a ritual purity. Thus we see even in this early slide toward the ethics of empire (that is, an ethic that justifies certain activities in the name of state interests) an uneasiness regarding the use of force. It was something that had to be rationalized. Augustine and Ambrose did not praise the use of force, nor did they fully justify it; instead they reserved it as an instrument of statecraft.

THE MIDDLE AGES

By the Middle Ages, Christian pacifism had been almost completely replaced by the ethics of empire and the just war theory. While peace was still held as an ideal and a worthy goal, the use of force by Christian monarchs, soldiers, and popes was commonplace. The exploits of Christian knights as models of piety and selfless service were celebrated, as were many soldier-saints.

The few exceptions to this nearly unquestioned acceptance of using force include the Peace of God and the Truce of God. These were a set of Church sanctions levied against princes and lords in an attempt to limit the violence of local skirmishes between feuding lords and princes.

The Peace of God (*Pax Dei*) began in France in the late tenth century and spread throughout Western Europe through the thirteenth century. It granted noncombatant immunity to clergy and peasants (the poor, who made up the majority of the population). In other words, Church leaders forbade targeting these groups and attached ecclesiastical penalties such as excommunication to those who violated this rule. Later it was expanded to include children, pilgrims, merchants, and virgins, as well as vineyards, livestock, and church property. The Truce of God (*Treuga Dei*) prohibited violence on certain days of the year including Sundays, saints' feast days, and other holy days. It was later expanded to include from Wednesday evening until Monday morning, and the seasons of Advent, Christmas, and Easter. The aim of the Peace of God and Truce of God was to limit warfare and protect the vulnerable. Both agreements enjoyed relative, though imperfect, success.

In the thirteenth century, Francis of Assisi (about 1182–1226) started a new religious order, a reform movement of sorts, based on imitating the life of Christ. The Franciscan friars (as they are called) commit to celibacy, poverty, and obedience (since Jesus was obedient to the Father); they also are devoted to direct service

THE PRAYER OF SAINT FRANCIS

Lord, make me an instrument of Thy peace;
where there is hatred, let me sow love;
where there is injury, pardon;
where there is doubt, faith;
where there is despair, hope;
where there is darkness, light;
and where there is sadness, joy.
O Divine Master,
grant that I may not so much seek to be consoled
 as to console;
to be understood, as to understand;
to be loved, as to love;
for it is in giving that we receive,
it is in pardoning that we are pardoned,
and it is in dying that we are born to Eternal Life.

(While this prayer is often attributed to Saint Francis, the claim is doubtful; nevertheless, the prayer remains popular and is an excellent example of Franciscan spirituality and Franciscan pacifism.)

to the poor and personal pacifism, in imitation of the example set by Jesus. While the Franciscans to this day are often seen as stewards of the Catholic peace tradition due to their commitment to peace and social justice, it should be noted that Francis himself did not espouse universal absolute pacifism, but something closer to classical or principled pacifism.

While Christian pacifism was largely extinguished in the Catholic Church during the medieval period, there were attempts to limit war.[16] One medieval practice that reflects a Christian uneasiness with war and violence was the expectation that soldiers returning from war would make a religious retreat during which they would do penance for having shed blood. Their penances were often severe, reflecting the latent pacifism of the patristic early Church era, because war, even when waged for a just cause, was seen as involving evil. This idea that war needs to be limited reflects the just war tradition rather than pacifism.

THE REFORMATION

The Reformation in the sixteenth century was the second great schism in the Christian Church, after the split between the Orthodox and Catholics in 1054. The Reformation divided the Western Church again, between Catholics and Protestants. One of the principal tenets of the reformers, such as Martin Luther, John Calvin, and Ulrich Zwingli, was a return to the primacy of Scripture. Under this mantra of *sola scriptura*, they argued that Christian doctrine, morals, ethics, and practices (such as rituals and sacraments) had to have scriptural support. This was a challenge to a Catholic theology of the day that had become highly philosophical and often treated Scripture as ancillary. With this renewed interest in the primacy of Scripture, some Protestant theologians and preachers concluded what the Christians in the early centuries had concluded: Jesus was a pacifist, and the life of a disciple requires one to renounce violence.

Among these reformers were the Anabaptists (meaning re-baptizers), so named by their enemies who opposed their practice of rebaptizing adults who had been baptized as infants. The

Anabaptists were the radical reformers. Many Anabaptists called for living the Sermon on the Mount literally: a return to the beliefs and practices of the early (pre-Constantine) Church, in which Christians did not make concessions to nor cooperate with the state, and an unwavering commitment to absolute pacifism. Some Anabaptists, however, espoused principled pacifism. The Schleitheim Confession of 1527, for example, rejects the use of force by individual Christians: "Thus the devilish weapons of force will fall from us too, such as the sword, armour and the like, and all their uses on behalf of friends or against enemies; [such nonviolence is commanded] by the power of the words of Christ, 'you shall not resist evil' (Matt 5:39)." But it then goes on to recognize the right of the state (which is not part of God's Kingdom) to use force: "The [use of the] sword is ordained by God outside the perfection of Christ. It punishes and kills evil people and protects and defends the good. In the law the sword is established to punish and kill the wicked, and the secular authorities are established to use it."[17]

Menno Simons (about 1496–1561) is representative of Anabaptist theology. Simons adopted the belief that Christians are citizens of the Kingdom of God, but while in this world they live in exile:

> The Scriptures teach that there are two opposing princes and two opposing kingdoms: the one is the Prince of peace; the other the prince of strife. . . . The Prince of peace is Christ Jesus; His kingdom is the kingdom of peace, which is His church; His messengers are the messengers of peace; His Word is the word of peace; His body is the body of peace; His children are the seed of peace; and His inheritance and reward are the inheritance and reward of peace. In short, with this King, and His kingdom and reign, it is nothing but peace. Everything that is seen, heard and done is peace. . . . Peter was commanded to sheath his sword. All Christians are commanded to love their enemies; to do good unto those who abuse and persecute them; to give the mantle when the cloak is taken, the other cheek when one is

struck. Tell me, how can a Christian defend scripturally retaliation, rebellion, war, striking, slaying, torturing, stealing, robbing and plundering and burning cities, and conquering countries? . . . O beloved reader, our weapons are not swords and spears, but patience, silence, and hope, and the Word of God. With these we must maintain our heavy warfare and fight our battle. . . . True Christians do not know vengeance, no matter how they are mistreated. . . . They do not cry, Vengeance, vengeance, as does the world; but with Christ they supplicate and pray: Father forgive them; for they know not what they do [Luke 23:34; Acts 7:60].

According to the declaration of the prophets they have beaten their swords into ploughshares and their spears into pruning hooks . . . they seek nothing but peace; and are prepared to forsake country, goods, life, and all for the sake of peace.

Dear reader, behold and observe, and learn to know this kingdom and body. For if they [other Christians who use force, such as the Catholics and other Protestants] with such actions and doings were the kingdom and body of Christ, as learned ones assure them, then Christ's holy glorious kingdom, church and body would be an inhuman, cruel, rebellious, bloody, rapacious, noisy, unmerciful, and unrighteous people. This is incontrovertible! Oh, damnable error, dark blindness![18]

Simons and the Anabaptist tradition are challenging and fascinating. In their attempt to return to biblically based Christian faith, they came to the same conclusion reached by early Christians like Justin Martyr, Clement of Alexandria, Tertullian, Maximilian, and Marcellus: the gospel of Jesus Christ requires a commitment to pacifism, and resorting to force is akin to renouncing one's faith. The Anabaptist tradition and its radical commitment to pacifism survive to this day among the self-identified "peace churches": Anabaptists (Mennonites, Amish, and Hutterites), the Church of the Brethren, and the Religious Society of Friends (Quakers), as well as in a number of other Protestant denominations that have also historically espoused pacifism.

MODERN CHRISTIAN PACIFISM

In the twentieth century, the Christian pacifist mantle was worn in both Protestant and Catholic circles, but with much cross-fertilization.

The Catholic Workers are a lay Catholic movement that has no formal association with the institutional Church. Begun in New York City in 1933 by Dorothy Day (1897–1980) and Peter Maurin (1877–1949), this program for social action typically publishes a newspaper on matters of social justice, provides houses of hospitality for the poor and homeless, conducts community roundtable discussions on social justice issues, and sponsors farming communes that provide work for the unemployed and food for the hungry. Today there are hundreds of Catholic Worker communities all over the world. Like the Anabaptists, Catholic Workers adopt the Beatitudes found in the Sermon on the Mount (Matthew, chaps. 5–7) as their manifesto, espouse Christian anarchism (see "Christian Anarchism" under "Challenges to Christian Pacifism" in this chapter) and are committed to pacifism and social reform. Their pacifism is not passive. As agents of change, they seek to confront injustice, poverty, and violence through protest, writing, education, and, frequently, acts of civil disobedience that earn them jail time. They do all of this toward creating a new society that is not based on economic exploitation, nationalism, or militarism.

Day and the other early Catholic Workers enjoyed a degree of success during the Depression because they advocated for unemployed workers, but when World War II broke out, their acts of protest against the war and their counseling of workers to refuse to labor on behalf of the war effort cost them support among mainstream Catholics. Nevertheless, based on principle, Catholic Workers have consistently been a prophetic voice for pacifism within the Catholic tradition, voicing opposition to and protesting the Korean and Vietnam wars, nuclear arms, and, more recently, the two Gulf wars.

Martin Luther King Jr. is perhaps the most renowned American Christian advocate for justice and peace. Best known for his work for civil rights, especially for African Americans, King identified three great evils facing America: racism, poverty, and war, which he saw as interrelated. King famously answered the challenge that advocating for peace in Vietnam had nothing to do with the civil rights movement in America at Riverside Church, New York, on April 4, 1967, by arguing that he was fighting not simply for blacks but for the "soul of America" by calling for a "radical revolution of values."[19] He declared war an act of theft

Dr. Martin Luther King Jr. speaks at the Civil Rights March on Washington, Aug. 28, 1963.

against the poor; he lamented the fact that war disproportionately kills the poor and persons of color; he challenged Christians to be wary of nationalism because the Christian faith calls one "beyond national allegiances"; and he confessed that his conscience and fear of his own hypocrisy compelled him to speak out against the violence being done to the people of Vietnam.

Like Day, King enjoyed support when his work focused on disenfranchised Americans, but once he (like Day) questioned American foreign policy based on Christian principles, he was ridiculed. Also like Day, King's pacifism was both principled and practical. Learning from Mohandas Gandhi, King adopted civil resistance as his modus operandi. The goal of civil resistance (civil disobedience or active nonviolence) is to provoke a response. Under the logic "silence equals endorsement," civil resistance seeks to bring injustices into light in order to eliminate them. By encouraging African Americans to break laws that allowed racism to thrive (such as Jim Crow laws), they would force the hand of their oppressors. They would be arrested and offer no resistance to their abusers.

The goal of King's active nonviolent resistance wasn't simply to challenge authority or change unjust laws; it was to convert the oppressor. When images of white police officers violently attacking peaceful black protestors were broadcast on the evening news, it shocked the conscience of the nation. Seeing dogs set upon ordinary citizens and fire hoses turned on children, Americans across the land began asking themselves, "Is this what we've become?" The goal of King's nonviolent resistance was to convert those actively involved in the oppression. Participants in civil disobedience were counseled to love their enemies when they accepted the truncheon blows with the hope that this grotesque act of violence against a peaceful person would trigger their oppressor's conscience. The method of King's active nonviolence campaigns was consistent with pacifism. The objective is not to defeat the enemy, since that will only cause them to be humiliated and desire revenge. No, the goal is to end the injustice as well as the attitudes that caused it. In short, the aim is conversion: to change not only actions but hearts as well to turn enemies into friends.

More recently the work of John Howard Yoder (1927–1997), a Mennonite theologian who taught at Notre Dame University, has had a significant impact on pacifism in contemporary Christianity. Yoder espoused a pacifism that was radically rooted in faith.[20] He argued that Jesus' pacifism was not pragmatic (that is, strategic pacifism) but principled. Jesus' principled pacifism, however, was not a commitment to nonviolence per se but was based in total obedience to God, a surrendering to the will of God. This requires Christians to abandon all hope for worldly success; they are to be obediently faithful, which requires not resorting to unjust means even if the end (goal) is just. Instead, Christians are counseled to rely on God. Yoder's interpretation of the social ethic of Jesus focuses on obedience instead of objectives, even if those objectives are good, right, holy, and just. Yoder's thought grounds Christian pacifism in a radically obedient faith. Yoder also challenges just war thinkers to be more honest. While he taught his students the just war theory precisely because its categories and criteria were useful in critically thinking about war and because it is part of the Christian tradition, he also chided just war theorists as improper stewards of an ethic whose aim was purportedly to limit war, not "justify it."[21]

Yoder influenced countless contemporary Christian ethicists including Stanley Hauerwas and Michael Baxter. Yoder's influence on Hauerwas can be found in Hauerwas's suspicion of power and calls for reliance on divine providence against trusting in human efforts. Hauerwas, a United Methodist, was originally a Christian realist (discussed below) when he studied and taught at Yale University. Later he took a position at Notre Dame, where he met Yoder. He currently teaches at Duke University and in 2001 was called "America's best theologian" by *Time* magazine. Thomas Hibbs neatly summarizes Hauerwas's pacifism:

> Hauerwas's pacifism does not fit neatly with generic, secular pacifism. He readily acknowledges the nobility of war and repudiates liberal views of war as rooted in a narrow selfishness; instead, war typically involves a "moral commitment to the good of others." War is a way of "reaffirming our national history" by performing acts that render us worthy heirs to those who have made sacrifices in the past. By contrast, liberal pacifism is often cowardly, in its assumption that death is the greatest evil, and naively utopian, in its assumption that the antiwar movement will eventually issue in world peace.
>
> Far from aligning Christianity with liberalism, Hauerwas's pacifism emerges from a distinctively Christian vision of history and power. Pacifism is a way of giving witness to a higher power, which is "self-emptying and pacific." Hauerwas worries that Christians who participate in war are motivated by an idolatrous desire to "make history turn out right," a desire that denies God's providential control over history. The life of Christ embodies a model of power that eschews all coercion and falsehood. . . .
>
> But Hauerwas's pacifism gives rise to other sorts of difficulties. He puts Christianity in tension not only with war but with any notion of secular justice. The real issue here is how Christians

can support any coercive activities of the state: from soldiers to judges to policemen. Hauerwas asserts intimate links between capitalism and war and (in his anti-liberal and anti-utopian pacifism) between the modern state and war. Given these claims, it seems that Christians must be not just "resident aliens" [that is, citizens of the city of God living in the city of man, to use Augustine's imagery] but stalwart—perhaps even seditious—enemies of the state in all its economic and legal functions.[22]

Hauerwas extends Yoder's call to radical obedience and trust in divine providence to a suspicion of all forms of state-exercised power. Since many dismiss pacifists as unrealistic, both Yoder and Hauerwas address the issue of "achieving earthly success" from a theological perspective. They call for a radical trust and assert that it is God, not humans, who makes peace possible. In this they both reflect the biblical notion that peace is ultimately a gift from God, not a work of human hands.

Yoder and Hauerwas, two Protestant theologians, have had a tremendous impact on Catholic ethics of war and peace. Yoder is even footnoted in the U.S. Conference of Catholic Bishops' pastoral letter, *The Challenge of Peace*. Having both taught at Notre Dame, they have influenced a generation of Catholic ethicists, including theologian Michael Baxter, CSP.

Baxter's pacifism is also firmly rooted in faith. He sees peace as God's gift flowing from Jesus' sacrifice on the cross, which has reconciled a sinful humanity with God or, as Saint Paul expresses it, "Therefore, since we have been justified by faith, we have peace with God through our Lord Jesus Christ" (Rom 5:1). Thus peace is the fruit of having been reconciled with God by God. Second, Baxter emphasizes that peace is inherently communal; it is not a personal gift, but one bestowed on the Church (the body of Christ). Like Yoder, Baxter chides just war thinkers to be more honest in their reflections, and he laments that the just war tradition, originally conceived to limit war and intended to stress the sinfulness of it, has in practice been used to justify or rationalize violence. Hardly naïve, Baxter contends that the Christian commitment to pacifism "requires Christians to pay many costs," but it is also a litmus test of one's faith:

> Christians must, in other words, have faith in Divine Providence. . . . We should not recoil from the attempt to do the impossible because God never commands the impossible; rather what seems impossible or morally ill-advised because of deleterious consequences, such as unilateral nuclear disarmament, turns out in God's providence to be possible and good.[23]

Echoing the angel Gabriel's message announcing Jesus' birth to Mary, "nothing will be impossible for God" (Luke 1:37), and the traditional Christian maxim, "we are called to be faithful, not successful," Baxter, like Yoder and Hauerwas, casts pacifism as a choice between being faithful to the command and example of Jesus Christ or succumbing to the worldly desire to be successful, practical, or realistic, a desire that is often premised on fear.

CONTEMPORARY CATHOLIC MAGISTERIAL TEACHINGS ON PACIFISM

Pacifism enjoyed a place of prominence in the early centuries of Christianity. It was later supplanted by the just war tradition and holy war thinking, which we will explore in the following chapters. But as we have seen, pacifism never completely disappeared, and it has experienced a renaissance of sorts in recent decades within the Catholic Church.

In 1963, Pope John XXIII wrote *Peace on Earth* (*Pacem in terris*) in which he decried the destructiveness of modern warfare. This encyclical was a watershed moment in modern Catholic pacifism. After centuries of languishing under a nearly unquestioned endorsement of just war thinking by the Magesterium, Catholic pacifists found a sympathetic ear with John XXIII. Pacifism was once again upheld as normative within the Catholic faith. Two years later at Vatican II, the bishops expressed "admiration for all those who forgo the use of violence" (The *Church in the Modern World*, no. 78). The bishops defined peace in a positive and biblical fashion, as both a gift from God and the result of justice.

"Peace is more than the absence of war: it cannot be reduced to the maintenance of a balance of power between opposing forces nor does it arise out of despotic dominion, but is appropriately called 'the effect of righteousness' (Is 32:17). It is the fruit of that right ordering of things with which the divine Founder has invested human society and which must be actualized by man thirsting after an ever more perfect reign of justice" (The *Church in the Modern World*, no. 78). In their 1983 pastoral letter, *The Challenge of Peace*, U.S. bishops affirmed the pacifist tradition as valid (especially active nonviolence exhibited by people like Mohandas Gandhi, Dorothy Day, and Martin Luther King Jr.) and recognized conscientious objection and selective conscientious objection as legitimate. They defined peace as "both a gift of God and a human work" (The *Challenge of Peace*, no. 68), that is, a cooperative effort between God and humans. They declared, "The Church's teaching on war and peace establishes a strong presumption against war which is binding on all." But they do not go so far as to declare pacifism to be mandatory: "this presumption may be overridden, precisely in the name of preserving the kind of peace which protects human dignity and human rights" (no. 70). They thus reduced pacifism to a legitimate personal moral choice, but not an inherent Christian obligation (nos. 111–121).

The *Catechism of the Catholic Church* grounds peace in the life, death, and resurrection of Christ: "Earthly peace is the image and fruit of the peace of Christ, the messianic 'Prince of Peace'" (*Catechism*, no. 2305, emphasis in original), and goes on to clarify:

> Those who renounce violence and bloodshed and, in order to safeguard human rights, make use of those means of defense available to the weakest [for example, protests, demonstrations, legal proceedings, sit-ins, boycotts], bear witness to evangelical charity, provided they do so without harming the rights and obligations of other men and societies. They bear legitimate witness to the gravity of the physical and moral risks of recourse to violence, with all of its destruction and death. (*Catechism*, no. 2306)[24]

Pacifism is a legitimate and honored commitment within the Catholic tradition so long as it is a pacifism rooted in the Gospel and aimed at the common good.

CHALLENGES TO CHRISTIAN PACIFISM

Occupying the extreme left in our continuum of approaches to war and peace, pacifism garners many criticisms. Pacifists are often derided as selfish cowards. While egoism and cowardice can motivate some to use pacifism as a moral camouflage, the example of pacifists throughout history, such as Jesus of Nazareth, Francis of Assisi, Mohandas Gandhi, Dorothy Day, and Martin Luther King Jr., clearly demonstrates that pacifism is not for the self-centered or those who are afraid of violence. The pacifist route is paved with rejection and ridicule. It is not for the faint of heart. Another criticism is that pacifists are "free riders." They enjoy the benefits of living in a secure environment (such as protection of police and military) without accepting any of the burdens or obligations of citizenship. This has led some to label them as traitors. By refusing to support the mechanisms that directly provide the security they enjoy, they are said to be turning their backs on those who protect them. In response, Christian anarchists (such as Day, Yoder, and Hauerwas) call for a return to the ancient Christian rejection of military service to the state as a form of idolatry. Our first loyalty is not to nation but to God, which requires a rejection of war, violence, and militarism.

Two of the strongest criticisms leveled against pacifism are that it is hypocritical and naïve. We explore those criticisms now.

CRITICISM 1: PACIFISM AS HYPOCRITICAL AND THE CHALLENGE OF HUMANITARIAN INTERVENTION

Many argue that pacifism is hypocritical. In claiming that violence must be rejected because human life is sacred, pacifists ignore the reality that sometimes force must be used to stop the oppression of others. This is the case for humanitarian intervention, which refers to the use of force to defend those who are being

CHRISTIAN ANARCHISM

While many shrink in fear from the word *anarchism* due to its association with revolution and lawlessness, Christian anarchism is a commitment to living the gospel of Jesus Christ coupled with a refusal to swear loyalty to, derive benefits from, or support institutionalized government on the grounds that loyalty to the state, patriotism, and its more extreme cousin, nationalism, represent worship of a false god.

Catholic Worker and social activist Ammon Hennacy (1893–1970) defined Christian anarchism this way:

> Christian anarchism is based upon the answer of Jesus to the Pharisees, when He said that he [who is] without sin should be the first to cast the stone, and upon the Sermon on the Mount, which advises the return of good for evil and the turning of the other cheek. Therefore, when we take any part in government by voting for legislative, judicial, and executive officials, we make these men our arm by which we cast a stone and deny the Sermon on the Mount.
>
> The dictionary definition of a Christian is: one who follows Christ; kind, kindly, Christ-like. Anarchism is voluntary cooperation for good, with the right of secession. A Christian Anarchist is therefore one who turns the other cheek; overturns the tables of the money-changers, and does not need a cop to tell him how to behave. A Christian Anarchist does not depend upon bullets or ballots to achieve his ideal; he achieves that ideal daily by the One Man Revolution with which he faces a decadent, confused, and dying world.[25]

In a similar fashion, Daniel Smith-Christopher calls Christians to live "political atheism," whereby Christians ought to refuse facile conflations of Church and state and remain suspicious of attempts to cloak patriotism in the mantle of faith.[26]

attacked, typically by elements within their own nation. National sovereignty—the idea that nations cannot directly interfere in the internal affairs of other states—has been a long-standing principle in international affairs. Generally, international boundaries are sacrosanct, and when one nation's military crosses another nation's border without their permission it can be perceived as an act of war (an act of aggression). But what should states do when there is overwhelming evidence that a government is violating the human rights of its own citizens? This situation, after all, is not uncommon. Frequently minority groups (religious or ethnic) within a state fall victim to tyrannical and sometimes genocidal regimes. Michael Walzer defends wars of humanitarian intervention on the following grounds:

> Humanitarian intervention involves military action on behalf of oppressed people, and it requires that the intervening state enter, to some degree, into the purposes of those people. . . . Governments and armies engaged in massacres are readily identified as criminal governments and armies (they are guilty under the Nuremburg code of "crimes against humanity"). Hence humanitarian intervention comes closer than any other kind of intervention to what we commonly regard, in domestic society, as law enforcement and police work. . . . Humanitarian intervention is justified when it is a response (with reasonable expectations of success) to acts "that shock the moral conscience of mankind."[27]

Such a definition of humanitarian intervention is rather vague. While traditional notions of national sovereignty prevent outside states from intervening in the internal affairs of another state, Walzer is arguing that a state forfeits its claims to sovereignty whenever it perpetrates (by its own hand) or permits (via some other group like a local militia) a humanitarian crisis.

The United Nations has recognized the need for humanitarian intervention for several years, but its effectiveness in responding to such crises has been hindered by a lack of clear protocols defining what constitutes a humanitarian crisis worthy of intervention and protocols outlining the requisite response (that is, who should respond and how?).

More recently, in the wake of domestic wars in Somalia, Rwanda, Bosnia, and Kosovo, the U.N. International Commission on Intervention and State Sovereignty has reinterpreted the traditional understanding of humanitarian intervention by shifting away from language about the right or duty to intervene and toward a new concept called the Responsibility to Protect (R2P). This move is seen as being more proactive in the face of humanitarian crises. Instead of having to make the case for why traditional notions of national sovereignty need to be overridden, the R2P begins with the assumption that when faced with widespread human suffering coupled with the failure of the host state to adequately address the crisis, neighboring states have an obligation to act. Semegnish Asfaw observes that with this shift:

> Sovereignty is redefined as duty-bearer status, rather than as absolute power. In other words, states can no longer hide behind the pretext of sovereignty to perpetrate human rights violations against their citizens and live in total impunity. Rather sovereignty has been reconceived in such a way that states have an obligation to protect their citizens and ensure them their basic rights by preserving their dignity, well-being and safety. . . . State sovereignty implies also [that] the responsibility to protect and serve the welfare of people lies with the State itself. However, when there is egregious failure to carry out the responsibility, whether by neglect, lack of capacity, or direct assaults on the population, the international community has the duty to assist peoples and states, and in extreme situations, to intervene in the international affairs of the State in the interests of the safety of the people.[28]

Here the R2P parallels the traditional Catholic understanding of sovereignty. Thomas Aquinas, for example, vested the sovereign (the highest political authority in the land) with tremendous authority, including the right to wage war. But he also declared that the sovereign forfeits its authority when it fails to secure the common good.[29]

The International Commission on Intervention and State Sovereignty identifies three principal elements to the R2P:[30]

- The Responsibility to Prevent includes proactive steps to prevent humanitarian crises such as economic development, education, protection of human rights, good governance, widespread political participation, fair trade, arms control, transparency and accountability in political institutions, especially security forces (police, military, private security forces). This category stipulates many of the same practices endorsed by the Just Peacemaking Perspective which will be addressed in chapter 5.

- The Responsibility to React applies only after preventative measures have failed. It includes measures designed to limit violence, such as political, economic, and diplomatic sanctions (as long as they target political, economic, and military leaders and not civilians) and arms embargoes. The responsibility to react is governed by traditional just war criteria: right intention (to end or prevent human suffering); last resort; proportionality (minimal use of force necessary to accomplish the mission); probability of success; and right authority (the U.N. Security Council).

- The Responsibility to Rebuild concerns efforts to reestablish normalcy within a community once the active combat has ended and includes recovery, reconstruction, and reconciliation efforts. Rebuilding bears remarkable similarity to postwar ethics *(jus post bellum)* criteria, an emerging addendum to traditional formulation of the just war theory, which we will discuss in detail in chapter 4.

Sovereignty is not an absolute right. The R2P overrides the principle of nonintervention (Article 2.7 of the U.N. Charter) based on the obligation to protect the weak and vulnerable.

Returning to an explicitly Christian perspective, the obligation to protect the weak is well established within the Christian tradition, that is, the preferential option for the poor (see chapter 1). Augustine and Aquinas both justify the use of force when it is used for a just cause (such as to defend the weak), with right intention (such as to restore law and order), and when declared by a legitimate authority. In fact, Aquinas places his discussion on just war under the heading of "Charity" (neighbor-love). The love of neighbor can, at times, require the use of force. Wars waged for humanitarian intervention or under the R2P represent a serious challenge to Christian pacifism because they pit the Christian commitment to peace against the commandment to love our neighbor. Wars waged to alleviate the suffering and persecution of others represent "clean wars" (or at least cleaner than wars waged for selfish reasons). They are clean not because they are free of evil (killing is always evil), but because the intention (motive) is good—to rescue the vulnerable.

CRITICISM 2: PACIFISM IS NAÏVE AND THE CASE FOR REALISM

Critics observe that the claim that active nonviolence can or will stop those bent on domination and destruction simply does not match human experience. Pacifists often quickly point out that nonviolent resistance has worked in the past. Mohandas Gandhi persuaded the British (the most powerful empire in the world at the time) to leave India without firing a shot; the civil rights movement in the United States in the 1960s demonstrated that nonviolent civil disobedience could reduce decades of racial discrimination; and the apartheid regime of South Africa was eventually dismantled in the 1980s through civil resistance and worldwide political and economic pressure. While these cases illustrate that active nonviolence can be an effective tool for achieving justice, none of these examples is free of violence. The British were pressured to pull out of India while facing the threat of World War II, the civil rights movement included militant movements such as the Black Panthers and many riots, and apartheid in South Africa was opposed by both violent and nonviolent means. Instances of pacifist campaigns being the sole agent for change are indeed rare.

Furthermore, many nonviolent campaigns are effective precisely because the threat of violence is latent. For example, members of Christian Peacemaker Teams and Witness for Peace place themselves in potentially violent situations (such as war zones or potential war zones) and act as public witnesses and deterrents to violence. While they themselves are not resorting to force, the fact that many of these witnesses are Americans and Europeans helps in their effectiveness. Not wanting to draw the ire of the United States or other powerful nations, smaller armies and militias take extra steps to avoid armed conflict where these witnesses are stationed out of fear that killing a U.S. citizen or a European will provoke a deadly response or will at least stain their public image. In essence, these nonviolent groups are backed up by a potential use of force, even if it is not at their request.

History is full of examples of the powerful defeating those who offer little or no resistance. Pacifists are often asked, "Do you really think that pacifism could have stopped Hitler?" or more recently, "Do you really think pacifism would be effective against the likes of al-Qaeda and other terrorists?" Questions like these are often put forward by realists.

Realists argue that we live in a world where the use of force is necessary and pacifism is at best foolish and at worst suicidal. While there are many kinds of realism, we will examine two: political realism and Christian realism.

POLITICAL REALISM

Political realism is a prominent political philosophy among those involved in international affairs, that is, those who are actively engaged in statecraft. For political realists, international affairs are either amoral (morality and all of its related concepts, such as justice, fairness, human rights, and so on are irrelevant) or at best apply a selfish morality (a type of egoism) with only one rule: the right thing for any state or government to do is whatever advances or protects their own self-interest. For political realists, either there are no rules or the only rule is "Do what's best for you and your people."

Political realism enjoys a long history. One of the earliest proponents of this all's-fair-in-love-and-war philosophy was the Greek philosopher and historian Thucydides (about 460–404 BCE), who in his *History of the Peloponnesian War* proposed that talk of right or wrong during war is meaningless; instead, the discussion should be focused on what is feasible and necessary to achieve victory. Thomas Hobbes (whom we encountered in chapter 1) wrote *Leviathan* during the bloody English civil war of the seventeenth century. In it he argues that "man in that state of nature" is in a constant state of war, which he describes as "solitary, poor, nasty, brutish, and short." He goes on to declare: "To this warre of every man against every man . . . nothing can be Unjust. The notions of Right and Wrong, Justice and Injustice, have there no place. Where there is no common Power, there is no Law; where no Law, no Injustice."[31] According to Hobbes, we seek the protection of governments (the Leviathan) out of fear of others and self-interest precisely because our natural environment is bloody and competitive, so we make a contract with the state. We surrender some of our individual liberty for protection and security and to escape the state of nature. When war breaks out, however, it signals the breakdown of the contract. When the state is no longer willing or able to provide security, we are once again thrust back into the state of nature where there are no moral limits to our behavior. That is, once war has broken out, morality ceases to exist, since morality is nothing more than the rules of behavior established by the Leviathan in order to provide security.

More recently, Mao Tse-tung (1893–1976), the Chinese Marxist military and political leader who helped establish the People's Republic of China, dismissed placing any limits on warfare precisely because he held that victory is the only moral consideration when deciding what to do. Mao called the practice of limiting brutality in war in the name of codes of honor "asinine ethics." The purpose of war is the defeat of one's enemy, therefore, anything that leads to the defeat of one's enemy must be considered good.[32] Even more recently, during the Iraq War (2003–), one finds examples of political realism, most often in arguments asserting the U.S. invasion of Iraq was necessary for national interest or national security. As President Bush put it, "It's better to fight them there than here."[33]

Two types of political realism can be identified.[34] *Descriptive realism* is the belief that ethics do not apply to governments precisely because governments are not people and therefore lack the normal means for judging an action as right or wrong, such as conscience, free will, rationality, and so on. In other words, states are incapable of doing good or bad; only people within governments who make decisions and carry out actions can be judged as doing right or doing wrong. A similar argument is made in business ethics. Corporations are not people, they do not have the capacity to make choices (only people in companies have that ability), so one cannot use ethical terms to describe the actions of corporations (for example, "The Enron Corporation didn't steal money from my pension plan, the corporate officers stole the money."). Michael Walzer, one of the most prominent scholars on the ethics of war, dismisses descriptive realism by pointing out that just because nations lack conscience, free will, rationality, and everything else necessary for making a moral judgment does not mean they cannot behave morally or immorally. Governments (like corporations) are made up of individuals and therefore can be morally evaluated. Walzer also points out that wars rarely arise out of nowhere. They are prefaced by a variety of political events in which individuals representing governments make choices (such as negotiating, offering peace, capitulating, and so on). For this reason, states rarely face a situation in which the only options are to fight or be destroyed. That sort of situation usually arises only after several stages of political options have been exercised. In short, wars are not like hurricanes or other acts of nature; they are human inventions, and they are in large part voluntary. Wars are rarely thrust upon us unannounced; they are usually chosen.[35]

The second type of political realism, *prescriptive realism*, argues that since the arena of international affairs is a competitive dog-eat-dog world, governments ought to (for practical, not moral reasons) disregard all moral rules and limits and simply pursue self-interest. Niccolo Machiavelli (1469–1527) authored *The Prince*, perhaps the greatest and oldest treatise on prescriptive realism. It is a cold, calculating account of what many today consider to be "politics as usual." Historically, *The Prince* is one of the earliest examples of a completely areligious political philosophy. While many scholars contend that *The Prince* is a satire and was not intended to be taken seriously, it has functioned as a prescriptive realism handbook.[36] Prescriptive realists contend

MACHIAVELLI'S *THE PRINCE*

Machiavelli's *The Prince* counsels the leader with a cold rationalism. His ethic is one of pure self-interest:

> Thus a prince should have no other object, nor any other thought, nor take anything else as his art but that of war and its orders and disciplines; for that is the only art which is of concern to one who commands.[37]

> But when the prince is with his armies and has a multitude of soldiers under his government, then it is above all necessary not to care about the name for cruelty, because without this name he never holds his army united, or disposed to any action.[38]

> Thus you must know that there are two kinds of combat: one with laws, the other with force. The first is proper to man, the second to beasts; but because the first is often not enough, one must have recourse to the second. Therefore it is necessary for a prince to know well how to use the beast and the man.[39]

> A prudent lord, therefore, cannot observe faith [that is, be truthful], nor should he, when such observance turns him against him [that is, when it is not in his self-interest].[40]

that religious and philosophical ethics may be useful in governing one's personal life, but the reality of international affairs requires only one moral rule: do what is best for your own nation and assume that other nations will do the same. Prescriptive realism mirrors the free-market mentality: every nation enters the arena of international affairs seeking to maximize its own self-interest.

The implications for war and peace are obvious. Unlike pacifism, which condemns violence by appealing to moral principles, realists argue that use of force is acceptable, even desirable, whenever it is practical, namely, when it will advance national interests. This does not suggest, however, that political realists are warmongers. Political realists are pragmatic. Often peacemaking (resolving conflict through negotiations, concessions, treaties, and so on) is in the best interests of the nation. Political realists often take the long view and seek practical solutions to conflict, which may well be nonviolent solutions. In this, some political realists mirror strategic pacifism. Political realists (especially prescriptive realists) will endorse rules of war, sign treaties and conventions, and seek peace, but not for the same reasons that pacifists (or just war theorists) do. Political realists will endorse moral limits in international affairs and to war in particular, not because they see the moral rules as binding per se, but because they see them as an effective means for achieving national self-interest.

CHRISTIAN REALISM

Christian realism differs from political realism by asserting that morality and moral terms do apply to international affairs and to warfare. Political realism is an amoral theory (that is, concepts of right and wrong are irrelevant to international affairs), while Christian realism is a form of moral realism. Christian realists believe that there is an objective moral order and that we can know it or at least some of its tenets.

One of the clearest and most persuasive arguments for Christian realism comes from the American Protestant theologian Reinhold Niebuhr in his essay "Why the Christian Church Is Not Pacifist," written at the start of World War II.[41] Niebuhr, who was originally sympathetic to pacifism, dismisses Christian

MIND YOUR REALISMS!

Keeping all the kinds of realism straight can be difficult (such as political realism, descriptive realism, proscriptive realism, Christian realism, and moral realism). In chapter 1 we addressed moral realism, which refers to the belief that moral rules are real. Moral realism is the opposite of ethical relativism and some kinds of skepticism. Political, descriptive, and prescriptive realisms refer to ways of approaching political questions, especially international relations (that is, they are practical); whereas moral realism and Christian realism are moral theories based on philosophical or theological beliefs.

pacifism not simply for being naïve or impractical (as political realists would, although he does make that case) but for failing to take human sinfulness seriously. Niebuhr argues that Christian pacifists have an overdeveloped confidence in human goodness; they believe that the gospel law of love is enough to rid the world of violence and evil. For Niebuhr, such an approach is not only naïve, but heretical. The gospel also contends that sin is a fact of life in an unredeemed world. To claim that all we need is love is tantamount to saying we do not need God and that Christ's sacrifice on the cross was unnecessary.

Niebuhr contends, "Most modern forms of Christian pacifism are heretical. Presumably inspired by the Christian gospel, they have really absorbed the Renaissance faith in the goodness of man, [and] have rejected the Christian doctrine of original sin as an outmoded bit of pessimism."[42] Niebuhr's argument is thoroughly theological and not merely pragmatic. He argues that Christian pacifists labor under an overly optimistic understanding of human nature (that is, "the Renaissance faith in the goodness of man"), while the traditional Christian understanding of human nature is that we are sinful creatures living in an unredeemed world. Thus for Niebuhr, Christian pacifism is not just misguided, it denies a fundamental Christian doctrine: we live in a sinful world that will not be saved if we simply try to love one another more. Only God can save us. No amount of loving our enemies can redeem the world. It is Christ alone who saves a sinful world. Niebuhr is critical of Christian pacifists:

> [They] assert that if only men loved one another, all the complex, and sometimes horrible, realities of the political order could be dispensed with. They do not see that their "if" begs the most basic problem of human history. It is because men are sinners that justice can be achieved only by a certain degree of coercion on the one hand, and by resistance to coercion and tyranny on the other hand.[43]

REINHOLD NIEBUHR, "WHY THE CHRISTIAN CHURCH IS NOT PACIFIST"

Niebuhr's "Why the Christian Church Is Not Pacifist" is one of the clearest articulations of Christian realism, a stance that challenges Christians to take the reality of sin seriously in their political ethics. It is also a stinging critique of some kinds of pacifism.

> A theology which fails to come to grips with this tragic factor of sin is heretical, both from the standpoint of the gospel and in terms of its blindness to obvious facts of human experience. . . . The gospel is something more than the law of love. The gospel deals with the fact that men violate the law of love. . . . We have, in other words, reinterpreted the Christian gospel in terms of the Renaissance faith in man. Modern pacifism is merely a final fruit of this renaissance spirit. . . . We have interpreted world history as a gradual ascent to the Kingdom of God which waits for final triumph only upon the willingness of Christians to "take Christ seriously."[44]

Here Niebuhr stands with Augustine, who argued centuries earlier that sometimes the use of force is a necessary evil to avoid an even greater evil. For Christian realists, pacifism is an ideal, a utopian hope that is unattainable through human efforts. Christian pacifism confuses life on earth with the Kingdom of God (what Augustine called "The City of Man" and "The City of God") and fails to realize that evil and sin have not been eradicated and will not be until Christ returns in glory to establish God's definitive reign on earth. To live City of God values while in the City of Man naïvely fails to recognize the reality of sin. Pacifism suffers from an overdeveloped confidence in human goodness and an underdeveloped appreciation for human depravity. For Niebuhr, Christian pacifism runs dangerously close to the heresy that we do not need Christ, for we in fact save ourselves.

CHRISTIAN REALISM IN CATHOLIC SOCIAL THOUGHT

This exploration of Christian realism has focused on Reinhold Niebuhr, an American Protestant theologian and pastor, because he provides one of the clearest arguments for it. Christian realism is also part of the Catholic approach to war, as the following passage from Vatican II illustrates:

> Peace will never be achieved once and for all, but must be built up continually. Since, moreover, human nature is weak and wounded by sin, the achievement of peace requires a constant effort to control the passions and unceasing vigilance by lawful authority. . . . Insofar as men are sinners, the threat of war hangs over them and will continue until the coming of Christ; but insofar as they can vanquish sin by coming together in charity, violence itself will be vanquished. (The *Church in the Modern World*, no. 78)

A Response to Niebuhr—Christian Eschatological Realism: Niebuhr's realism is part of a long tradition of Christian realism, a tradition that includes Augustine, Aquinas, Martin Luther, John Calvin, and the just war tradition. Niebuhr's argument is so challenging to Christian pacifism because it is an explicitly theological argument using the doctrine of sin and redemption: Christian pacifism is heretical because it denies the depravity of human sinfulness. On the surface, I find Niebuhr's rationale convincing. Many Christian pacifists do suffer from an overdeveloped confidence in human goodness and fail to take the reality of sin seriously. Yet, ironically, it is faith in the power of the resurrection that provides a counterposition to Niebuhr.

If Christian pacifists have an underdeveloped appreciation for human sinfulness, Niebuhr has an underdeveloped confidence in the power of the resurrection. The Christian faith does not end on Calvary; it begins with Easter. The Christian faith is one of unprecedented optimism, which contends that because Jesus Christ was born, lived, died, and was raised from the dead, sin in our world has already been conquered. Jesus' preaching was primarily focused on the Kingdom of God, which is not a territory or place but an epoch, an age when God's definitive Reign on earth will be complete. Jesus declares that the Reign of God has already begun and that it is growing secretly in our midst like a seed planted in the ground or like yeast kneaded into dough (Luke 13:18–21). Thus theologians have come to describe the Reign of God as "already, but not yet." It has already begun in the life and teaching of Jesus Christ, but it is not completed and will not be firmly established until Christ's return in glory at the end of days (called the *eschaton*).

The foundational Christian belief that we are living between the resurrection of Jesus and the eschaton motivates the ethical mandate that Christians are called to live and act as if we are already participants in God's Reign. Christian ethics challenges to us to embody those values characteristic of the Reign of God (for example, mercy, humility, justice, and peacefulness; see Matt 5:3–10; 25:31–46). Acting as if we were already living in the Reign of God is called *eschatological hope*.

Eschatological hope is the height of Christian radicalism. Those who have eschatological hope firmly believe that the Reign of God is already present, so we must live in a way that encourages or nurtures it. Since the Reign of God is an era without pain, suffering, violence, war, injustice, sin, and death, any time we ease pain and suffering, stop violence and war, discourage sin, thwart injustice, and stave off death we are in fact helping to build up the Reign of God. We are in essence coworkers for the Reign of God, sharing in Christ's redemptive work.

Living with eschatological hope requires a tremendous effort. It requires living the Beatitudes (humility, meekness, peacefulness, purity, steadfastness) in a world that sees such behavior as weak, stupid, and naïve.

But some, like Niebuhr, might respond by saying those who think they are building God's Reign are essentially trying to "save themselves and others; they are trying to control what belongs to God." However, living with eschatological hope and working for the Reign of God are not undertaken because "we think it'll earn us points with God or get us into heaven." It is done out of love for God and neighbor, out of fidelity to the gospel, and regardless of outcome. A disciple is called first and foremost to be faithful; whether one is successful or effective is secondary.

Commenting on Jesus' command to "Love your enemies" (Luke 6:27), Pope Benedict XVI said:

> This Gospel passage is rightly considered the *magna carta* of Christian nonviolence; it does not consist in surrendering to evil, as a false interpretation of "turning the other cheek" [Luke 6:29] claims, but in responding to evil with good [Rom 12:17–21] and thereby breaking the chain of injustice. One then understands that for Christians, nonviolence is not merely tactical behavior but a person's way of being, the attitude of one *who is so convinced of God's love and power* that [one] is not afraid to tackle evil with the weapons of love and truth alone. Love of one's enemy constitutes the nucleus of the "Christian revolution," a revolution not based on strategies of economic, political or media power: the revolution of love, a love that does not rely ultimately on human

resources but is a gift of God which is obtained by trusting solely and unreservedly in [God's] merciful goodness.[45]

Christians are called to be peacemakers, Benedict argues, not because it is practical, but because they are animated by love, a love that extends even to enemies. According to the logic of realism, this is impossible and foolhardy. But, as the pope argues, pacifism is a real possibility precisely because it is based not on human effort alone but on the "gift of God." Thus, a Christian commitment to pacifism serves as a test of faith, a test of whether the Christian pacifist believes "for God all things are possible" (Matt 19:26).

Eschatological hope motivates opposition to every injustice and act of violence precisely because violence, sin, and greed are antithetical to the Reign of God. When I present this to my students, they roll their eyes and dismiss it saying, "Yes, this sounds great but it's totally unrealistic. I can't spend every waking moment of every day fighting for justice and defending the weak and the poor," or "What can I do, I am only one person?" Interestingly, history offers several examples of people who have lived with eschatological hope. Eschatological hope enabled Saint Paul to laugh at death precisely because he knew that he already had eternal life: "Where, O death, is your victory? Where, O death, is your sting?" (1 Cor 15:55). Eschatological hope empowered Martin Luther King Jr. to fight for civil rights even though he knew it might cost him his life. Eschatological hope enabled Archbishop Oscar Romero

Archbishop Oscar Romero

ESCHATOLOGICAL HOPE

Kenneth Melchin asserts Christians must have an "attitude of confident expectation that, in some mysterious way, God is at work both personally and socially and that we can experience this activity time and time again through our lives."[46] Thus when faced with the reality of evil, Christians ought to respond with an arrogant hope because (1) God has not abandoned the world to suffering and pain; and (2) through the death and resurrection of Jesus, the world is being healed and will one day experience the end of all pain, suffering, and injustice when Christ returns in glory. It is an eschatological hope in the Reign of God.

The Christian faith is not fatalistic, nor is it apathetic in the face of injustice. It holds that the world can be and is being transformed into the Reign of God, and that this transformation happens when individuals choose to do good, to act selflessly, and to fight injustice (all of which is enabled by God's grace). Hope, then, should be the first response of Christians when they encounter evil or injustice. This eschatological hope is grounded in the belief that Christ will come again. Eschatological hope requires living the values of the Reign of God, such as being humble, poor, meek, thirsting for justice, forgiving of enemies, and giving to all who are in need (Matthew chaps. 5 – 7 and Luke 6), knowing full well that most of the world does not accept these values and will take advantage of those who live this way. It is an attempt to live as if one were already living in the Reign of God. Thus apathy or a fatalistic attitude in the face of injustice is not simply a lack of care; it is a denial of the power of the resurrection and of God's ability to transform the world.

to defend the poor and oppressed of El Salvador against a tyrannical military and economic oligarchy, resulting in his assassination. Eschatological hope allowed Dorothy Day and Mother Theresa to devote their lives to the mundane and often filthy work of serving the poor.

While these are extra-ordinary examples, it should be recognized that they did not work alone, as each of them belonged to a community of like-minded and supportive people, making King, Romero, Day, and Mother Theresa figureheads of a larger community. Also, living with eschatological hope needn't always involve extraordinary efforts. Simple acts of kindness motivated out of a desire to make the Reign of God concrete are examples of eschatological hope. Any effort at standing up for justice is an act of eschatological hope (such as defending a person who is being treated wrongly, volunteering for organizations that combat social injustice, writing letters to Congress or local newspapers to address a social need). Those with eschatological hope recognize the connection between faith and justice. To see an injustice and do nothing about it (out of fear, apathy, or a feeling of power-lessness) is akin to denying one's faith. One may as well say, "I don't believe that the Reign of God is already here. The cross is not more powerful than sin. I don't believe Christ's sacrifice was enough to defeat sin."

Mother Theresa

The examples of eschatological hope are extreme, but they challenge Christian realists like Augustine and Niebuhr. Christian pacifists refuse to engage in violence, confident that the Reign of God has already begun and violence and force have nothing to do with it. So while Niebuhr accuses Christian pacifists of heresy for failing to take human sinfulness seriously and for having an overly developed confidence in human nature, so too Christian pacifism can claim that Niebuhr and other Christian realists have an underdeveloped confidence in the power of the resurrection and fail to believe that the Reign of God is real. Did Jesus' death and resurrection destroy sin and death or not? Is the Reign of God growing secretly in our midst or not?

Christian pacifists motivated by eschatological hope claim to be realists as well, namely *Christian eschatological realists*, based on the core of the Christian faith. The Gospel (a word that means "good news") is essentially about hope. What do Christians have hope in and for? They hope and believe that through the life, death, and resurrection of Jesus Christ, a sinful world and a sinful humanity have already been redeemed. They hope for the coming of God's Reign, a world free of sin, pain, injustice, violence, and death. They also affirm that they participate in the building up of that Reign. Thus, for a Christian eschatological realist to encounter anything that opposes or frustrates development of that Reign and do nothing about it is not simply shirking duty, but is, in essence, denying the power of Christ to triumph over sin.

For Christian eschatological realists, the realistic approach to sin and war is optimistic because the redemption of the world won by the resurrection isn't a fable. It is real, and it gives reason to hope (eschatological hope) in the face of injustice, for through his death and resurrection, Jesus Christ has defeated the power of sin, violence, injustice, and evil in this world.

WHERE DO YOU FALL?

Our exploration of Christian approaches to war and peace is presented as a continuum ranging from pacifism (the most "dovish") to holy war (the most "hawkish"). Return now to page 18 where the various approaches are displayed as an array. Based on your deeper understanding of pacifism and political realism, where would you now place yourself on the continuum and why? In other words, how has encountering the ideas, arguments, or perspectives presented in this chapter caused you to reevaluate your own ethic of war and peace?

DISCUSSION QUESTIONS

1. Would you call yourself a pacifist? If so, what kind of pacifist? If not, why not?

2. Does being a Christian require a commitment to pacifism? In other words, is pacifism a constitutive dimension of the Christian faith? If yes, what kind of pacifism? If not, why not and how do you reconcile the "justified use of force" against the Gospels' evidence and witnesses of the patristic era?

3. What is your response to the introduction of realism to Christian ethical thought? Is it consistent with the Gospel and the tradition or not?

4. What is your reaction to the idea of eschatological hope?

5. Martin Luther King Jr., speaking at a meeting of Clergy and Laity Concerned at Riverside Church, New York (April 4, 1967), delivered an eloquent, moving, and powerful speech titled, "Beyond Vietnam — A Time to Break the Silence." Read the speech (available online at *http://www.americanrhetoric. com/speeches/mlkatimetobreaksilence.htm*). While much of it addresses the Vietnam war, is there anything in it which speaks to our era? What is his thesis, and how does he support it? What is your reaction to King's message?

ENDNOTES

1 The following types of pacifism come from Andrew Fiala, "Pacifism," *The Stanford Encyclopedia of Philosophy*, ed. Edward N. Zalta (Summer 2007), *http://plato.stanford.edu/archives/sum2007/entries/pacifism/*; and from David Clough and Brian Stiltner, *Faith and Force* (Washington, DC: Georgetown University Press, 2007), 44–50.

2 See David Cortright, *Gandhi and Beyond: Nonviolence for an Age of Terrorism* (Boulder and London: Paradigm, 2006), 27, 112.

3 Bertrand Russell, "The Future of Pacifism," *The American Scholar* 13 (1943): 8.

4 Selective Service System, "Conscientious Objection and Alternative Service," available online at *http://www.sss.gov/FSconsobj.htm*.

5 *Catechism*, nos. 2242 and 2311; see Pontifical Council for Justice and Peace, *Compendium of the Social Doctrine of the Church* (Dublin: Veritas, 2005), no. 399; from Vatican II, The *Church in the Modern*

World, nos. 78-79; and three statements from the U.S. Conference of Catholic Bishops: *The Challenge of Peace*, nos. 231–33; "Statement on Registration and Conscription for Military Service" (1980); and "Declaration on Conscientious Objection and Selective Conscientious Objection" (1971).

6 E. P. Sanders, "Jesus and the Temple," in *Jesus and Judaism* (Philadelphia: Fortress, 1985), 61–76.

7 See, for example, John Dominic Crossan, *God and Empire: Jesus against Rome, Then and Now* (San Francisco: HarperSanFrancisco, 2007).

8 James Turner Johnson, *The Quest for Peace: Three Moral Traditions in Western Cultural History* (Princeton, NJ: Princeton University Press, 1987), 3–66.

9 Ibid., 32.

10 Quoted in *The Ethics of War: Classic and Contemporary Readings*, ed. Gregory M. Reichberg, Henrik Syse, and Endre Begby (Malden, MA: Blackwell, 2006), 63, from Louis J. Swift, ed. and trans., *The Early Fathers on War and Military Service* (Wilmington, DE: Michael Glazier, 1983), 41–42.

11 Quoted in Reichberg, Syse, and Begby, *The Ethics of War*, 63, from Swift, *The Early Fathers on War and Military Service*, 43–44.

12 Quoted in Reichberg, Syse, and Begby, *The Ethics of War*, 64–65, from Swift, *The Early Fathers on War and Military Service*, 54–55.

13 Excerpted and adapted from *Acta of Saint Maximillian*, found in A. A. R. Bastiaensan, et al., eds., *Atti e passioni dei martiri* (Milan: Fondazione Lorenzo Valla, 1987), 238–45 [BHL 5813], available online at *http://www.ucc.ie/milmart/Maximilian.html*.

14 Transcripts of the trial are in Albert Marrin, ed., *War and the Christian Conscience: From Augustine to Martin Luther King Jr.* (Chicago: Henry Regnery, 1971), 43.

15 Augustine, *Concerning the City of God against the Pagans*, trans. Henry Bettenson, ed. David Knowles (Harmondsworth: Penguin, 1972, 1976), 37. Aquinas addresses the same subject and draws different conclusions; see *Summa Theologica* II–II, question 64; see See Reichberg, Syse, and Begby, *The Ethics of War*, 190–91.

16 Within the Protestant tradition, some groups did espouse pacifism (for example, the Waldensians in the twelfth century and the Anabaptists starting in the sixteenth century), typically based on a close reading of Scripture and an attempt to live as closely to the biblical example of Jesus as possible. The Anabaptist traditions are addressed in Chapter 2.

17 "The Brotherly Agreement of Some Children of God Concerning the Seven Articles" in *From Irenaeus to Grotius: A Sourcebook in Christian Political Thought*, Oliver O'Donovan and Joan

Lockwood O'Donovan, eds. (Grand Rapids, MI: Eerdmans, 1999), 634–35.

18 Menno Simons, "A Reply to False Accusations," in *The Complete Writings of Menno Simons*, trans. L. Verduin and ed. J. C. Wenger (Scottdale, PA: Herald, 1956); also available in *War and Christian Ethics: Classical and Contemporary Readings on the Morality of War*, 2nd ed., ed. Arthur F. Holmes (Grand Rapids, MI: Baker, 2005), 185–88.

19 Martin Luther King Jr., "Beyond Vietnam—A Time to Break the Silence," delivered at a meeting of Clergy and Laity Concerned at the Riverside Church, New York (April 4, 1967). Available online at *http://www.americanrhetoric.com/speeches/mlkatimetobreaksilence.htm*. See also his articles "Nonviolence and Racial Justice," *The Christian Century* 74 (Feb. 6, 1957): 165–67; and "Pilgrimage to Nonviolence," *The Christian Century* 77 (Ap. 13, 1960): 439–41.

20 John Howard Yoder, *The Politics of Jesus* (Grand Rapids, MI: Eerdmans, 1972, 1990).

21 John Howard Yoder, *When War Is Unjust: Being Honest in Just-War Thinking* (Minneapolis: Augsburg, 1984).

22 Thomas Hibbs, "Stanley Hauerwas's Pacifism: The Radical Gospel" *Weekly Standard* 7.34 (May 13, 2002), available online at *http://www.weeklystandard.com/Utilities/printer_preview.asp?idArticle=1204*.

23 Michael J. Baxter, "Just War and Pacifism: A 'Pacifist' Perspective in Seven Points," *Houston Catholic Worker* 24.3 (May–June 2004), available online at *http://www.cjd.org/paper/baxpacif.html*. Baxter is describing Daniel Berrigan's position in *Isaiah: Spirit of Courage, Gift of Tears* (Minneapolis: Fortress, 1996).

24 The section immediately following, it should be noted, defends the use of force by the state in certain circumstances using just war theory criteria (see *Catechism*, nos. 2307–2317).

25 Ammon Hennacy, *The Book of Ammon* (New York: Catholic Worker Books, 1965, 2nd ed. 1994), preface.

26 Ed. Daniel Smith-Christopher, "Political Atheism and Radical Faith: The Challenge of Christian Nonviolence in the Third Millennium," in *Subverting Hatred* (Maryknoll, NY: Orbis, 2007), 171–96.

27 Michael Walzer, *Just and Unjust Wars: A Moral Argument with Historical Illustrations* (New York: Basic Books, 3rd ed., 2000), 104–107.

28 Semegnish Asfaw, "Christian Perspectives on the Responsibility to Protect (R2P)," *Bulletin of the Boston Theological Institute* 7.2 (Spring 2008): 18–19. See also Semegnish Asfaw, Guillermo Kerber, and Peter Weiderud, eds., *The Responsibility to Protect: Ethics and Theological Reflections* (Geneva: World Council of Churches Publications, 2005).

29 Thomas Aquinas, *Summa Theologica* II–II, question 42, article 2; although in *On Kingship* (chap. 6) he advises leaving the punishment of tyrants to God. See Reichberg, Syse, and Begby, *The Ethics of War*, 185–86.

30 The R2P doctrine is formally articulated in *The Responsibility to Protect* (Ottawa, ON: International Development Research Centre, 2001) and is available online at *http://www.iciss.ca/menu-en.asp*.

31 Quoted in Reichberg, Syse, and Begby, *The Ethics of War*, 446–47, from Thomas Hobbes, *Leviathan*, ed. Richard Tuck (Cambridge: Cambridge University Press, 1991), 89–91.

32 For more on Mao Tse-tung and "asinine ethics," see Michael Walzer, *Just and Unjust Wars*, 225–28.

33 Interview with Ray Suarez, *The News Hour*, Public Broadcasting System (May 24, 2007). Transcript available online at *http://www.pbs. org/newshour/bb/white_house/jan-june07/terrorism_05-24.html*.

34 Brian Orend, "War," *The Stanford Encyclopedia of Philosophy*, ed. Edward N. Zalta (Winter 2005), *http://plato.stanford.edu/archives/ win2005/entries/war/*.

35 See Walzer, *Just and Unjust Wars*, 13–16, 24, and 31–32.

36 See Garrett Mattingly, "Machiavelli's *Prince*: Political Science or Political Satire?" *The American Scholar* (1958): 482–91, available online at *http://www.idehist.uu.se/distans/ilmh/Ren/flor-mach-mattingly.htm*; and Quentin Skinner, *Machiavelli: A Very Short Introduction* (Oxford, Eng.: Oxford University Press, 1981).

37 *The Prince*, trans. Harvey C. Mansfield (Chicago: University of Chicago Press, 1998), 58 (chap. 14).

38 Ibid., 67 (chap. 17).

39 Ibid., 69 (chap. 18).

40 Ibid.

41 Reinhold Niebuhr, "Why the Christian Church Is Not Pacifist," in *The Essential Reinhold Niebuhr*, ed. Robert McAfee Brown (New Haven: Yale University Press, 1986).

42 Ibid., 104.

43 Ibid., 109.

44 *The Essential Reinhold Niebuhr: Selected Essays and Addresses*, ed. Robert McAfee Brown (New Haven: Yale University Press, 1986), 111–13.

45 Benedict XVI, "Angelus," sermon delivered Sunday, Feb. 18, 2007, at Saint Peter's Square, Rome; available online at *www. vatican.va/holy_father/benedict_xvi/angelus/2007/documents/hf_ ben-xvi_ang_20070218_en.html*; emphasis in original.

46 Kenneth Melchin, *Living with Other People* (Collegeville, MN: Liturgical, 1998), 97.

CHAPTER 3

Holy War

Initially we will define *holy war* as any war that is believed to be commanded by God or waged for religious reasons. We will come to a more nuanced understanding of holy war by the chapter's end.

Holy war is pacifism's polar opposite in regard to killing. However, in some ways, pacifism and holy war share a common foundation. Both approach war and peace out of a principled rather than pragmatic commitment. Both have their absolutists, adherents who do not allow success or failure in this world to factor into the equation and whose ethical commitments are inviolable. Some absolute pacifists would rather die than resort to the use of force (even in self-defense), while some holy warriors are equally uncompromising in their values. These warriors see the holy war as a battle of good against evil that requires total commitment, even in the face of certain defeat, in which case death is counted as a sign of faithfulness. It is no accident that both pacifists and holy warriors call those who die for their cause by the same name: *martyrs* (from Greek, meaning "witness").

While most Christians today dismiss the idea of holy war as unenlightened or archaic, even a casual review of history and current affairs quickly reveals that religion often plays a central role in war: the God of the Hebrew Scriptures is often portrayed as a warrior God; the Crusades (which literally means, "war of the cross") pitted European Catholics against Middle Eastern Muslims in a battle for the Holy Land; Europe was torn apart by the bloody Thirty Years' War, in which Christians slaughtered Christians; Japanese kamikaze pilots in World War II justified their suicide attacks by using the Shinto belief of honorable death; and the recent so-called "clash of civilizations"[1] is often cast as a battle between radicalized Islam and the secularized West.

DEMONIZING THE ENEMY

Labeling a conflict as a holy war tends to cast it as a cosmic battle between the forces of good and the power of evil. This is more than a rhetorical trick. It makes compromise nearly impossible because in a war against evil, negotiation becomes cooperation with evil. Sam Keen, in his book *Faces of the Enemy*, presents a very simple thesis:[2] the first act of war is always mental. "In the beginning we create the enemy. Before the weapon comes the image. We *think* others to death and then invent the battle-ax or the ballistic missiles with which to actually kill them. Propaganda preceded technology."[3] According to Keen, we are *homo hostilis*, enemy-making animals.

EXCERPT FROM UNESCO CONSTITUTION

"Since wars begin in the minds of men, it is in the minds of men that we have to erect the ramparts of peace" (from the preamble of the United Nations Educational, Scientific, and Cultural Organization Constitution).

Keen suggests that the image of the enemy is created through a number of dichotomies that serve to define both sides of the conflict. We construct the image of the enemy in terms of what we are not (or at least what we perceive ourselves not to be). This dichotomy is commonly called "Us versus Them" thinking, wherein a people see themselves and their enemy as opposites:[4]

US	THEM
We are good.	They are evil.
We are victims.	They are to blame.
We are honest.	They are liars.
We are heroes.	They are villains.

Keen developed this schema by studying war propaganda, particularly posters and political cartoons from a variety of nations and wars. Interestingly, he found that armies and nations use nearly identical images to portray their enemies. The enemy is most often pictured as stranger and aggressor (thereby feeding paranoia); faceless (that is, less than human); a devil, demon, or enemy of God (which makes war holy); a barbarian (therefore a threat to civilized culture); ravenous (that is, they are irrational and will never stop); a dangerous criminal, outlaw, rogue, torturer, or rapist (again feeding paranoia and the idea that compromise is not an option); a beast, insect, reptile, or germ (thus requiring extinction); or as death itself (usually in the image of the grim reaper or a skeleton, which casts the conflict as an epic battle between life-goodness-light and death-evil-darkness).[5] According to the logic of Us versus Them thinking, if the enemy is any or all of these things, then I or we are its opposites: we are virtuous, rational, noble, and have God and goodness on our side.

This thinking in dichotomies is called *dualism*, a philosophy that has infected nearly every religion, becoming dangerous because it fails to see shades of gray. President George W. Bush's rhetoric explaining why the United States needed to attack Iraq after September 11, 2001, provides a nearly perfect illustration of Keen's thesis. While the connections between Iraq (and Saddam Hussein) and the terrorist attacks of September 11 were specious even at the time, Bush nevertheless mentioned the events of 9/11 and dangers in Iraq one right after the other in many subsequent speeches, thereby linguistically linking the two. More pointedly, in several speeches he cast the war on terror in dualistic terms. For example, in his 2002 State of the Union Address (delivered January 29, 2002), the president used stereotypical categories:

US

- Bush called the United States and countries that support it "a great coalition," "a coalition of partners," and "Allies [with] . . . the responsibility to fight freedom's fight" [= *we are good*].

- "Our nation is at war, our economy is in recession, and the civilized world faces unprecedented dangers" [= *we are civilized*].

- "Our cause is just" [= *we are righteous*].

- "Our nation will continue to be steadfast and patient and persistent" [= *we are virtuous*].

- "The American people have responded magnificently, with courage and compassion, strength and resolve" [= *we are heroes*].

- "Many have discovered again that even in tragedy—especially in tragedy—God is near" [= *God is on our side*].

THEM

- Bush described Iraq as a "regime," and he called Iraq, Iran, and North Korea "an axis of evil, arming to threaten world peace" [= *they are evil*].

- "We have seen the depth of our enemies' hatred. . . . They laugh at the loss of innocent life. . . . The depth of their hatred is equaled only by the madness of the destruction they design. . . . Thousands of dangerous killers schooled in the methods of murder, often supported by outlaw regimes . . . like ticking time bombs set to go off without warning" [= *they are madmen and murderers*].

- "Our enemies believed America was weak and materialistic, that we would splinter in fear and selfishness. They were as wrong as they are evil" [= *they are evil*].

In the days following this address, Bush made frequent use of the term *evil*, often calling those who opposed the United States "the evil ones." By employing the term *evil*, Bush cast the conflict with Iraq and the larger "war on terrorism" as a cosmic battle between the forces of good and evil.[6] Bush's penchant for dualist thinking was confirmed a few weeks later when he said, "Well, you've probably learned by now, I don't believe there's many shades of gray in this war. You're either with us or against us; you're either evil or you're good."[7]

CHRISTIAN HOLY WAR

Historically the Christian idea of holy war has drawn on three principal sources: the Hebrew Bible, the Crusades, and the religious wars in the post-Reformation era. Accounts of victorious holy wars in the Hebrew Scriptures can be read as ambivalent and ironic reflections about war. They were mostly compiled after the Babylonian Empire had deported a significant portion of the Israelites from the southern kingdom of Judah around 600 BCE. After that trauma, the people were struggling to understand why God had allowed them to experience devastating attacks, loss of national autonomy and land, and exile. Early Christians rejected the earthly power that these accounts depicted (see chapter 2), but later some of these accounts served as a model for religiously sanctioned violence in Christianity.

HOLY WAR AND THE BIBLE

HOLY WAR AND THE HEBREW SCRIPTURES

The Hebrew Scriptures (Old Testament) often present God as a soldier and divinely sanctioned violence as holy. When the Israelites are being pursued by the Egyptian army, they are promised, "The LORD himself will fight for you" (Exod 14:14), and their victory song declares, "The LORD is a warrior!" (15:3). The Psalms praise God as "a mighty warrior . . . mighty in battle" (Ps 24:8) and anticipate that "God will arise for battle" (68:2). The book of Isaiah announces the exiled Israelites' release: "The LORD goes forth like a hero, like a warrior he stirs up his ardor; he shouts out his battle cry, against his enemies he shows might" (Isa 42:13). At times, the Scriptures even seem to celebrate grotesque violence. Against the Babylonians, the empire that exiled the people of Judah, the Psalms express hope of vengeance: "Fair Babylon, you destroyer, happy those who pay you back the evil you have done us! Happy those who seize your children and smash them against a rock" (Ps 137:8–9).

In the ancient Middle East, nations were thought to have their own national gods, protectors of their people. Thus religion and national identity went hand in hand. The ancient Israelites were no different in this regard. The Bible portrays the Israelites' God (Yahweh) as fiercely protective and at times even jealous. These violent images are disconcerting and seem to contradict passages that we saw in the previous chapter that extol the virtues of peace (such as Psalm 85). In the face of these contradictions, the book of Ecclesiastes concludes:

> There is an appointed time for everything, and a time for every affair under the heavens.
>
> A time to be born, and a time to die; a time to plant, and a time to uproot the plant.
>
> A time to kill, and a time to heal; a time to tear down, and a time to build.
>
> A time to weep, and a time to laugh; a time to mourn, and a time to dance.
>
> A time to scatter stones, and a time to gather them; a time to embrace, and a time to be far from embraces.
>
> A time to seek, and a time to lose; a time to keep, and a time to cast away.

A time to rend, and a time to sew; a time to be silent, and a time to speak.

A time to love, and a time to hate; a time of war, and a time of peace.

(Eccl 3:1–8)

These passages reveal that the Hebrew Scriptures are complex in their attitude toward war and violence. They don't reject violence as inherently wrong; in fact, violence against Israel's enemies is often celebrated, and the Scriptures tend toward hyperbole, which if taken literally can seem monstrous.

Holy wars *(milhelmet herem)* described in the Hebrew Scriptures are not fought to spread religion or seek converts. They are waged only for the protection of the Israelites against those who would harm them or to safeguard their existence in the land promised to them by God. Thus, holy war in the Jewish biblical tradition refers to wars fought because God has commanded them or because God is present or active in the actual battle, often subject to the condition of Israelite obedience. The narratives, it should be remembered, were compiled in a time when the Israelites were trying to explain how their warrior God could have suspended these promises and used other nations as weapons to evict them.

The Hebrew Bible contains several instances of holy war; most occur during the Israelites' long journey from oppression in Egypt to the land promised to their ancestors and their settlement there. They encounter numerous obstacles, including other peoples that seek to conquer them or that are threatened by their presence (for example, kings Sihon in Deut 2:24–37 and Og in Deut 3:1–11), and the Scriptures report divine victories on behalf of the Israelites. God's presence in battle is symbolically represented by the Ark of the Covenant (a container for the stone tablets of the Ten Commandments and symbolic throne for God's presence), which the Israelites carry before them in battle (Num 10:35–36; 1 Sam 4:4–11; 2 Sam 11:11). The lesson intended from all of this is clear. The Israelites are God's covenanted people taking possession of a land promised them by God. No opponent can thwart their efforts, and anyone who opposes them opposes God and will be defeated.[8]

In two cases, God even goes so far as to order genocide against Israel's enemies, the Amalekites and the Canaanites.

The Amalekites: During their escape from Egypt, the Bible reports that the Israelites are attacked by Amalekites.[9] In the following passage, we see illustrated two aspects of holy war: divine assistance through God's representative (Moses), and a divine promise of perpetual war against those who oppose God's people:

> At Rephidim, Amalek [ruler of the Amalekites] came and waged war against Israel. Moses, therefore, said to Joshua, "Pick out certain men, and tomorrow go out and engage Amalek in battle. I will be standing on top of the hill with the staff of God in my hand." So Joshua did as Moses told him: he engaged Amalek in battle after Moses had climbed to the top of the hill with Aaron and Hur. As long as Moses kept his hands raised up, Israel had the better of the fight, but when he let his hands rest, Amalek had the better of the fight. Moses' hands, however, grew tired; so they put a rock in place for him to sit on. Meanwhile Aaron and Hur supported his hands, one on one side and one on the other, so that his hands remained steady till sunset. And Joshua mowed down Amalek and his people with the edge of the sword.
>
> Then the Lord said to Moses, "Write this down in a document as something to be remembered, and recite it in the ears of Joshua. I will completely blot out the memory of Amalek from under the heavens." Moses also built an altar there, which he called Yahweh-nissi; for he said, "The LORD takes in hand his banner; the LORD will war against Amalek through the centuries." (Exod 17:8–16)

Hostility against the Amalekites (or singular, Amalek, for the group) and the promise to obliterate them runs throughout the Hebrew Bible:

> Bear in mind what Amalek did to you on the journey after you left Egypt. . . . Therefore, when the LORD, your God, gives you rest from all your enemies round about in the land which he is giving you to occupy as your heritage, you shall blot out the memory of Amalek from under the heavens. Do not forget! (Deut 25:17–19; see also Num 24:20; Judg 6:3,33; 7:12)

Later Samuel, a prophet who speaks on behalf of God, orders Saul, the first king of the Israelites, to continue the hostility:

> Listen to the message of the LORD. This is what the LORD of hosts has to say: "I will punish what Amalek did to Israel when he barred his way as he was coming up from Egypt. Go, now, attack Amalek, and deal with him and all that he has under the ban. Do not spare him, but kill men and women, children and infants, oxen and sheep, camels and asses." (1 Sam 15:1–3)

Saul attacks and defeats the Amalekite army, but does not fulfill the wholesale slaughter of the ban: "He took Agag, king of Amalek, alive, but on the rest of the people he put into effect the ban of destruction by the sword. He and his troops spared Agag and the best of the fat sheep and oxen, and the lambs. They refused to carry out the doom on anything that was worthwhile, dooming only what was worthless and of no account" (1 Sam 15: 8–9). The prophet Samuel executes Agag, and Saul loses God's favor and the throne. God's vengeance against the Amalekites is continued by David, the king who follows Saul (1 Samuel 30; 2 Samuel 1). Eventually, the people of Judah "destroyed the remnant of the Amalekites that had escaped, and [Judahites]have resided there to the present day" (1 Chron 4:43).

Without other (nonbiblical) evidence of Amalekites, it is difficult to determine whether these biblical references describe specific historical encounters or if the word *Amalek* is used as a symbolic umbrella term for all of the nomadic raiders that were always at the desert frontiers of Israelite territory.

The Canaanites: The other primary example of divinely ordained genocide occurs when the Israelites reach Canaan. But before they can take possession of the land promised to them, they must first deal with the people who are already living there, the Canaanites, listed as consisting of seven tribes or nations (Deut 7:1; Josh 3:10). The divine motivation for commanding the Israelites to annihilate the Canaanites is described as at least threefold: these nations are wicked (Deut 9:5), God is keeping the promise to Abraham (Deut 9:5), and it would be dangerous for the Israelites to coexist with these people because Israel might be "ensnared" to serve their gods (Deut 7:16). The Israelites are reminded repeatedly that they do not deserve this gift. They are not worthy, but God is faithful to the promise (Deut 9:1–6).

Moses instructs the Israelites:

> When the LORD, your God, brings you into the land which you are to enter and occupy, and dislodges great nations before you . . . and when the LORD, your God, delivers them up to you and you defeat them, you shall doom them. Make no covenant with them and show them no mercy. You shall not intermarry with them . . . for they would turn your sons from following me to serving other gods, and then the wrath of the LORD would flare up against you and quickly destroy you.
>
> But this is how you must deal with them: Tear down their altars, smash their sacred pillars, chop down their sacred poles [monuments to their gods], and destroy their idols by fire. For you are a people sacred to the LORD, your God; he has chosen you from all the nations on the face of the earth to be a people peculiarly his own. It was not because you are the largest of all nations that the LORD set his heart on you and chose you, for you are really the smallest of all nations. It was because the LORD loved you and because of his fidelity to the oath he had sworn to your fathers, that he brought you out with his strong hand from the place of slavery, and ransomed you from the hand of Pharaoh, king of Egypt. Understand, then, that the LORD, your God, is God indeed, the faithful God who keeps his merciful covenant down to the thousandth generation toward those who

love him and keep his commandments, but who repays with destruction the person who hates him; he does not dally with such a one, but makes him personally pay for it. You shall therefore carefully observe the commandments, the statutes and the decrees which I enjoin on you today.

As your reward for heeding these decrees and observing them carefully, the Lord, your God, will keep with you the merciful covenant which he promised on oath to your fathers. He will love and bless and multiply you; he will bless the fruit of your womb and the produce of your soil, your grain and wine and oil, the issue of your herds and the young of your flocks, in the land which he swore to your fathers he would give you. You will be blessed above all peoples; no man or woman among you shall be childless nor shall your livestock be barren. The Lord will remove all sickness from you; he will not afflict you with any of the malignant diseases that you know from Egypt, but will leave them with all your enemies.

You shall consume all the nations which the Lord, your God, will deliver up to you. You are not to look on them with pity, lest you be ensnared into serving their gods. . . . Do not be afraid of them. Rather, call to mind what the Lord, your God, did to Pharaoh and to all Egypt. . . . The same also will he do to all the nations of whom you are now afraid. . . . The Lord, your God, will deliver them up to you and will rout them utterly until they are annihilated. He will deliver their kings into your hand, that you may make their names perish from under the heavens. No man will be able to stand up against you, till you have put an end to them. The images of their gods you shall destroy by fire. Do not covet the silver or gold on them, nor take it for yourselves, lest you be ensnared by it; for it is an abomination to the Lord, your God. (Deut 7:1–26; see also Exod 23:23–33 and 34:11–16)

This passage is quoted at length because it illustrates many of the key features of the concept of holy war found in the Hebrew Scriptures:

1. Land is a sign of the covenant, which becomes political and confrontational because it involves physical territory.

2. Compromise is not permitted; the Israelites are to show no mercy.

3. Israel's God does not tolerate the Israelites' making covenants with other gods and so (a) genocide is commanded out of fear that the Israelites might intermingle and intermarry with the Canaanites, which could lead the Israelites astray, and (b) they must destroy everything associated with the other religion and may not even keep gold and silver offered to the forbidden gods.

4. This action against the Canaanites is seen as a reaffirmation of the covenant; the Israelites are God's people, therefore (a) God promises to fight for them, and (b) they are guaranteed success even though their enemy is stronger.

5. There is a threat that if they disobey, God will punish them.

6. There is a promise that if they obey, they will be rewarded with prosperity (crops, livestock, and children).

In ancient warfare, a soldier would expect to take captives (especially women) and possessions (loot) from the defeated town. The biblical descriptions of killing everyone and destroying their goods may reflect emphasis upon God's role as warrior. In holy war, these belong to God as victor, and human soldiers must not claim God's victory or God's loot. The "ban" *(herem)* reserves these things to God by destroying and burning them, so it is often translated as "doom" or "dooming." As Lawrence Boadt observes:

> It was practiced to show that Israel put all its trust in God alone during the war and sought nothing for itself. Modern people are shocked by such brutality, but it is necessary to remember that the ancient world did not share our outlook. Their ethical principles often placed national survival above any personal goods, and identified success in war or politics with the will of their god or gods.[10]

Boadt goes on to note, "we can be sure that the ban was rarely carried out in practice and only in moments of great peril," since if it were a custom, then the population of the area would have been significantly smaller.[11] While the book of Joshua records that Joshua, Moses' successor, and his army carried out God's command and annihilated the Canaanites, the book of Judges reports that the Canaanites lived alongside the Israelites for centuries, sometimes peacefully, other times not. Other passages note that they did not capture all the land of Canaan as is often claimed (Josh 13:1–5; 15:63; 16:10; 17:11–13). Scripture scholars point out that these accounts of Israel's military victories are often idealized, magnified, and exalted to emphasize the greatness of God as the one who guarantees Israel's victories, and to stress that taking possession of the land is divine activity, which explains the apparent inconsistencies: the accounts are properly understood as theological texts or even religious propaganda, as opposed to objective historical accounts.[12] Archaeological research also suggests a much longer period of resettlement in the highlands than a single military campaign.[13] These descriptions, however, were compiled after the Israelites' own experience of defeat and exile, and the stories may have been particularly ironic and instructive to later generations.

Other examples of holy war in the Hebrew Scriptures include the following:

- Exodus 14:10–31: As the Israelites flee the Egyptian army, God provides a rescue route through the water and brings the water back to overwhelm the Egyptians.

- Deuteronomy 3: The Israelites defeat the Bashanites. "And thus the LORD, our God, delivered into our hands Og, king of Bashan, with all his people. We defeated him so completely that we left him no survivor" (Deut 3:3; see also Num 21:33–35).

- Joshua 6: During the Israelite siege of Jericho, God orders that the priests should circle the city with the Ark of the Covenant while blowing ram horns. With the final blast of the horns, the city's walls collapse and the Israelites take Jericho, where they observe the ban and kill "all living creatures in the city: men and women, young and old, as well as oxen, sheep and asses" (Josh 6:21). Only the Canaanite prostitute Rahab, who had aided Israelite spies, and her family were spared (Josh 2:1–21; 6:25). The scenario is repeated twice. According to Joshua 8, God gives Joshua a strategy for defeating the defenders of Ai. Once victorious, the Israelites kill the entire army and all of the residents of the city (twelve thousand people) and then burn it to the ground. Joshua 10 describes a victory over the forces of five Amorite kings, in which God intervenes by sending a hail-storm that kills many and by preventing the sun from setting so that the Israelites can finish the task.

- Judges 20:17–29: God is consulted regarding battle strategies before other tribes wage war against the Benjaminites.

- Chronicles 20: The Israelites begin to despair in the face of the allied armies of the Moabites, Ammonites, and Meunites. Jahaziel prophesies, "Do not fear or lose heart at the sight of this vast multitude, for the battle is not yours but God's" (20:15). The next day the allied forces turn on one another and destroy each other.

At this juncture, one might believe that the Hebrew Bible is filled with nothing but violence. However, it is important to recall the *shalom* tradition, covenantal peace, and the concept of eschatological peace (addressed in the previous chapter), which dominate the Hebrew Scriptures. On the whole, the Hebrew Bible has more to say about peace and justice than it does about holy war. According to renowned scholar Gerhard von Rad, holy war thinking in the Hebrew Bible changes over time. Early on, the Israelites see God as assisting in their military exploits or fighting alongside them. Later the human contributions to military victory are deemphasized to stress God's miraculous assistance, resulting in the belief that God wins all wars for Israel (for example, Ps 136:10–22).[14] The reverse of this view, that Israel's losses were God's punishment for disobedience, is the overarching theme from Deuteronomy through 2 Kings in the Hebrew Bible, providing a model of what not to do for the community during the period after the Babylonian captivity.

HOLY WAR AND THE NEW TESTAMENT

While the Hebrew Scriptures have several examples of holy war, the New Testament appears not to have such a tradition.[15] Jesus makes reference to "my attendants" (human or divine?) when being questioned by Pontius Pilate — "If my kingdom did belong to this world, my attendants [would] be fighting to keep me from being handed over" (John 18:36) — but he chooses not to call upon them. Paul uses military language to describe the Christian life, but this is clearly a metaphor (Eph 6:11 – 17).

The book of Revelation (especially chaps. 19 – 21) speaks of the "war of the Lamb," a battle at the end of time (eschaton) when God ultimately defeats evil and Satan. Scripture scholars debate whether these passages were intended to be (or ought to be) interpreted literally (that is, this will really happen) or symbolically (allegorically). The passages draw upon the images and language of the Hebrew Scriptures. Whereas God is described as a warrior in the Hebrew Bible and as one who comes to the aid of Israelite armies, in Revelation Christ is portrayed as a warrior with heavenly armies at his command (chap. 19). He battles Satan (the dragon, chaps. 12, 20), slays beasts (chap. 17), releases a series of plagues upon his enemies (chaps. 6, 8, 9, 15, 16; similar to Exodus 7–11), honors the martyrs and saints (chap. 20), and ultimately establishes a new heaven and a new earth (chap. 21, creating order out of chaos in a manner similar to Genesis 1 and Ps 89:6–19).[16]

One possible interpretation for the absence of a robust holy war tradition within the New Testament is that in its early years, Christianity was persecuted by both the traditional Jewish leadership (which saw Christians as apostate and blasphemous) as well as by the Romans (who saw them as a threat to social stability and political order). Since they had little economic or military power, the early Christians would not have found the idea of holy war serviceable; in fact, a doctrine of holy war would have

THE ARMOR OF GOD

"Put on the armor of God so that you may be able to stand firm against the tactics of the devil. For our struggle is not with flesh and blood but with the principalities, with the powers, with the world rulers of this present darkness, with the evil spirits in the heavens.

"Therefore, put on the armor of God, that you may be able to resist on the evil day and, having done everything, to hold your ground. So stand fast with your loins girded in truth, clothed with righteousness as a breastplate, and your feet shod in readiness for the gospel of peace. In all circumstances, hold faith as a shield, to quench all (the) flaming arrows of the evil one. And take the helmet of salvation and the sword of the Spirit, which is the word of God." (Eph 6:11–17)

only rationalized further persecution of the powerless Christians by the more powerful established Jewish leadership and Roman authorities. Instead, as we saw in chapter 2, the early Christians were largely pacifists, based on the teachings and example of Jesus Christ. This is not to suggest, however, that Christianity does not have a holy war tradition. On the contrary, it does; it is just not grounded in Scripture.

THE CRUSADES

The Crusades are the best example of Christian holy war. Today the term *crusade* is often used to refer to any valiant, zealous, or righteous enterprise, often with religious overtones, or any ideologically driven military campaign. Properly speaking, it refers to a series of military raids by European Christians into Muslim-controlled territories in the Middle East and Asia Minor between 1095 and 1291. Muslim forces had conquered present-day Israel and Palestine in the seventh century. For the most part,

THE CRUSADES

The numbering and dates of the Crusades varies depending on who is doing the counting. Traditionally, there are nine principal crusades and several minor crusades.

First Crusade (1095–1101)

Byzantine Emperor Alexius I requests military aid from the Western Empire (Catholic Christian) to defend his Eastern Empire (Orthodox Christian) from Seljuk Turks (Muslim). In 1095, Pope Urban II calls for the first military attack to reclaim the Holy Land, and crusaders capture several major cities, including Jerusalem. During their long march, many atrocities are reported, including massacres, cannibalism, displaying of corpses, and so on.

Robert de Normandie at the Siege of Antioch, 1097–1098

The Crusades *(continued)*

Second Crusade (1145 – 1149)

French and German forces fail to retake Jerusalem, which had fallen back under Muslim control. En route, the armies commit acts of violence, including massive killings of Jews, who are often violently persecuted during the Crusades as part of centuries-long European anti-Semitism. Jews are targeted because they are seen as "infidels" (that is, non-Christian) and branded as "Christ killers." The Catholic Church officially condemned anti-Semitism and specifically repudiated the claim that Jews are responsible for the death of Christ in 1965 in the document *In Our Time* (*Nostra aetate*), which signaled a transformation in the relationship between Jews and Catholics.

Third Crusade (1187 – 1192)

Perhaps the most celebrated crusade, it pits King Richard I of England (Richard the Lionhearted of Robin Hood fame), King Phillip II of France, and Holy Roman Emperor Frederick I against the celebrated and talented Saladin, Sultan of Egypt, who has successfully united various Muslim groups into a unified and formidable force. The crusading armies capture several key locations along the way, but ultimately this "kings' crusade" ends in a treaty that leaves Jerusalem in Muslim hands, allowing unarmed Christian pilgrims to visit holy sites.

Fourth Crusade (1202 – 1204)

A poorly funded and mismanaged venture, this crusade never reaches the Holy Land. Instead, the crusaders turn their attention to the Byzantine Empire (Orthodox Christians) and sack the capital Constantinople. This solidifies the schism between the Eastern Orthodox and Catholic churches (and the Eastern and Western empires), an ironic twist given that the Crusades were initially launched to save the Byzantine Empire from Muslim Seljuk Turks (see the First Crusade).

Fifth Crusade (1217 – 1221)

Called for by the Fourth Lateran Council (1215), this attempt to recapture the Holy Land enjoys key victories, only to extend itself

The Crusades *(continued)*

too far, resulting in large losses of crusaders and an eight-year peace agreement.

Sixth Crusade (1228–1229)

Pope Gregory IX excommunicates Emperor Frederick II in 1228 for failing to launch a crusade. In the same year, Frederick II launches a crusade that captures Jerusalem, Nazareth, and Bethlehem, which Europeans then hold for a decade.

Seventh Crusade (1248–1254)

Begun as a response to the catastrophic defeat of Christian forces in Egypt in 1243 and the loss of Jerusalem in 1244, King Louis IX of France launches an unsuccessful attack against Muslim forces in Egypt.

Eighth Crusade (1270)

Louis IX sponsors a second crusade, this time against forces in Syria. The crusaders never reach Syria, stopping in Tunis, where Louis IX dies.

Ninth Crusade (1271–1272 CE)

The future King Edward I of England leads an unsuccessful attempt to conquer Syria.

Other crusades:

Three Swedish Crusades (1155, 1249, and 1293)

Albigensian Crusade against the Cathars in southern France (1209)

Children's Crusade, which is either fictional or a horrid catastrophe (1212)

Arogenese Crusade in Catalonia, Spain (1284–1285)

Alexandrian Crusade (1365 CE)

Several Crusades in the Balkans (1396–1456)

Crusade against the Tartars in Lithuania (1399)

Hussite Crusade in Bohemia in present-day Czech Republic (1420–1434) the Muslims allowed unarmed Christian pilgrims to visit sites considered sacred by Christians because of their association with Jesus (Jerusalem, Bethlehem, Nazareth, and so on). They also allowed Jews to return to Jerusalem to live and worship.

Historical analyses of the causes of the Crusades are often muddied by piety, political correctness, and misinformation. To devout Western Christians (especially Catholics), the Crusades are often portrayed as valiant attempts to recapture the Holy Land from the so-called infidels (that is, non-Christians, Muslims), to reopen pilgrimage routes that had at times been closed to Christians, and to protect holy sites from being profaned or destroyed by non-Christians. From a Muslim perspective, the Crusades are a form of cultural and religious imperialism, an unprovoked attack by the Christian popes and kings. Other explanations focus on social, political, and economic aspects: the Crusades were a mechanism for occupying a large number of unemployed knights and other warriors (due to decades of warfare in Europe) who had taken to infighting and thievery during a period of relative peace; they were an opportunity for the Western Empire to assert moral and political authority over the Eastern Empire; they tapped into centuries of European prejudice and anti-Semitism against anyone who was not Christian; and they fed on a spike in religious piety and a popular desire to do something active for one's faith.

Thomas Madden, an historian of the Crusades from Saint Louis University, laments these characterizations:

> Misconceptions about the Crusades are all too common. The Crusades are generally portrayed as a series of holy wars against Islam led by power-mad popes and fought by religious fanatics. They are supposed to have been the epitome of self-righteousness and intolerance, a black stain on the history of the Catholic Church in particular and Western civilization in general. A breed of proto-imperialists, the Crusaders introduced Western aggression to the peaceful Middle East and then deformed the enlightened Muslim culture, leaving it in ruins. . . .

Christians in the eleventh century were not paranoid fanatics. . . . With enormous energy, the warriors of Islam struck out against the Christians shortly after Mohammed's death. They were extremely successful. Palestine, Syria, and Egypt—once the most heavily Christian areas in the world—quickly succumbed. By the eighth century, Muslim armies had conquered all of Christian North Africa and Spain. In the eleventh century, the Seljuk Turks conquered Asia Minor (modern Turkey), which had been Christian since the time of St. Paul. The old Roman Empire, known to modern historians as the Byzantine Empire, was reduced to little more than Greece. In desperation, the emperor in Constantinople sent word to the Christians of Western Europe, asking them to aid their brothers and sisters in the East.

That is what gave birth to the Crusades. They were not the brainchild of an ambitious pope or rapacious knights but a response to more than four centuries of conquests in which Muslims had already captured two-thirds of the old Christian world. At some point, Christianity as a faith and a culture had to defend itself or be subsumed by Islam. The Crusades were that defense.[17]

While Madden's characterization of the Crusades as a defensive war is a stretch, he does mention that Muslim expansion, although sometimes welcomed by areas restless under Byzantine rule, was seen as a threat to Christendom. Keep in mind that a host of social, political, and economic factors, as well as ideological ones, contributed to the Crusades. Regardless of which explanation one chooses to accept now, the Crusades were presented and interpreted then as a holy war.

In 1095, Pope Urban II at the Council of Clermont called for the first crusade (although he did not use that term) in response to Byzantine Emperor Alexius I's request for military aid after his forces were defeated by Muslim Seljuk Turks in the Battle of Manzikert (1071) and the subsequent loss of most of Asia Minor (present-day Turkey). Significantly the Latin (Western European,

Catholic) Empire had long been considered the rival, if not the enemy, of the Byzantine (Eastern European, Orthodox) Empire. Alexius I's call for help was in fact his reaching out to his enemy, essentially saying, "In the past we have been adversaries, but we share a common faith and we face a much larger common enemy in Islam." In his speech, Urban casts this effort as a holy war (see "Christian Holy War and Muslim Jihad Side by Side" on pp. 296–302 for a copy of his speech). Urban promises financial reward to those who fight and political stability for Europe, as well as forgiveness of sins, for those who participate, and eternal life for those who die in this endeavor. The accounts of the event record that at the end of Urban's speech, the crowd spontaneously erupted, "God wills it!" signaling that they too recognized this as a holy war.

In similar fashion, Bernard of Clairvaux (1090–1153), a strong proponent of the Peace of God, appealed to the people of England to join the Crusades:

> The earth is shaken because the Lord of heaven is losing his land, the land in which he appeared to men, in which he lived amongst men for more than thirty years; the land made glorious by his miracles, holy by his blood; the land in which the flowers of his resurrection first blossomed. And now, for our sins, the enemy of the Cross has begun to lift his sacrilegious head there, and to devastate with the sword that blessed land. . . . They have cast their greedy eyes on the holy sanctuaries.
>
> What are you doing, you mighty men of valour? What are you doing, you servants of the Cross? Will you thus cast holy things to dogs, pearls before swine? . . . Could he [God] not send more than twelve legions of angels, or even just say the word and save his land? More certainly he has the power to do this whenever he wishes, but I tell you that God is trying [testing] you. . . . Do not hesitate. God is good, and were he intent on your punishment he would not have asked of you this present service or indeed have accepted it even had you offered it. . . . He puts himself under obligation to you, or rather feigns to do so, so that he can help you to satisfy your obligations

toward himself. He puts himself in your debt so that, in return for your taking up arms in his cause, he can reward you with pardon for your sins and everlasting glory. I call blessed the generation that can seize an opportunity of such rich indulgences as this. . . . O mighty soldier, O men of war, you have a cause for which you can fight without danger to your souls; a cause in which to conquer is glorious and for which to die is gain.[18]

Clairvaux presents the Crusades as an opportunity for forgiveness of sins and eternal life and fame, and later alludes to more worldly benefits as well (such as peace and profit). He also engages in enemy-making rhetoric, describing Muslims as greedy, animals (dogs and swine), rapacious, and violent. Such language pictures a war at God's invitation against evil itself. In such a war, compromise is collusion, although in practice many treatises with Muslim leaders were made during the Crusades.

Throughout the crusading era, the exploits of the knights—their chivalry, piety, and bravery—were celebrated throughout Europe, while the savagery of Muslim warriors was reviled. Likewise, the butchery of Christian warriors was recounted throughout the Muslim world. Both sides viewed "the other" as beastly, immoral, and unholy, leading them to cast this not simply as a political confrontation but as a cosmic battle of Good versus Evil, with both sides claiming to have God on their side.

John Howard Yoder, whom we encountered in the previous chapter, viewed the Crusades as an extension of the holy war tradition, with both being driven by ideology and not only the desire for political or military power. In this sense, holy wars and crusades have a perverted sincerity to them. Yoder identified five hallmarks of the holy war and crusade mentality:

- Its *cause has a transcendent validation* that blunts traditional restraints in battle.
- This *transcendent validation is known by revelation*, typically via a prophet, oracle, or religious leader.
- The *adversary has no rights*, which, often coupled with racist or ethnic hatred, in turn fuels the descent into total war.

MILITARY RELIGIOUS ORDERS OF THE CRUSADES

The Crusades gave rise to several military religious groups, mostly knight-monks who were devoted to defending the Holy Land, protecting pilgrims, and caring for the sick. These orders blurred the line between clergy and laity and allowed monks to engage in war and killing, which had traditionally been banned. Two of the more prominent orders were:

Knights Templar: Founded in Jerusalem in 1119, they guarded pilgrimage routes using a series of forts. They were disbanded by Pope Clement V in 1312 due to allegations of corruption.

Knights of Malta: Founded in Jerusalem in 1080, they originally operated a hospital that cared for sick pilgrims. Later their mission transitioned to military defense of the Holy Land. Eventually they settled on the island of Malta and are still in existence, although their mission has changed dramatically. (For more information, visit *http://www.smom.org/.*)

Other orders include Teutonic Knights, Knights of Saint Lazarus, and Knights of Saint Thomas Acon.

- The *principle that war must be a last resort does not apply* because compromise or accommodation of the enemy is cooperation with evil.

- The *war need not be winnable*: to die fighting for a holy cause is honorable and often seen as rewarded with eternal life.[19]

POST-REFORMATION RELIGIOUS WARS

The second period of holy war in the Christian tradition followed the Reformation in the sixteenth century, the second great schism in the Christian Church. The first split was between the Orthodox and Catholics in 1054. The Western Church divided again, this time between the Catholics and Protestants, in the Reformation.

The Reformation began as an attempt to reform the Catholic Church, and it centered largely on doctrinal issues such as the role of grace, forgiveness of sins, the authority of Scripture, and the authority of the papacy. It quickly became a social, political, and economic revolution that consumed all of Europe. A number of factors fueled the Reformation, among them: tremendous political turmoil; humanist philosophies that celebrated education, freedom of individual thought, a suspicion of arguments based on authority, and the objective study of ancient and biblical texts; the Renaissance, which celebrated ancient Greek and Roman art and philosophy; rapid advances in science; the "discovery" of the New World; a growing sense of national identity, a respect for local culture, and the rise of vernacular languages; the breakdown of the feudal system coupled with the emergence of mercantile capitalism and a growing middle class; and widespread corruption within the Catholic Church, compounded by an uneducated clergy and the generally lackluster faith life of Europeans at this time.

While there are many examples of religiously fueled violence from this period (for example, the Inquisition, the conquest of the New World), two are sufficient for our purpose of exploring holy war: the Thirty Years' War (1618–1646) and the French Revolution (1789–1799).

THE THIRTY YEARS' WAR

The social, political, religious, and economic turmoil of the sixteenth century led to much bloodshed, especially in Germany. Catholic and Protestant forces battled one another with passionate fervor and cruelty. The Peace of Augsburg (1555) sought to put an end to these religious wars by allowing princes to determine the religion of their respective territories, forcing those who did not share the religious convictions of their ruler to migrate or face persecution. This was a recipe for disaster. In 1606 the city of Donauwörth (near Catholic Bavaria) became Protestant. The Catholic minority was attacked during a religious procession in the streets by a mob (not uncommon in this era). A year later,

Duke Maximilian of Bavaria (a Catholic) brought his army to Donauwörth to force conversion of the Protestants. The Evangelical Union, a Protestant army, was formed in 1608 in response to the duke's attacks and a year later the Catholic League was formed to combat the Evangelical Union.

The other major Catholic military forces in this period were the Holy Roman Empire (which was in a serious state of disrepair) and the Hapsburg Dynasty (which was also in a state of flux). Catholic League and Bavarian forces, at the invitation of Holy Roman Emperor Ferdinand II, crushed the Protestant forces of Bohemia (present-day Czech Republic), and in 1626 all non-Catholics were expelled from the region. Only a few months earlier, armies from England, the Netherlands, and Denmark had joined the Evangelical Union and invaded Germany. In 1630 Swedish King Adolphus (Protestant) invaded the Empire and was successful in countering the Catholic League.

The Thirty Years' War has been called "the bloodiest and most devastating European war before the twentieth century."[20] Estimates of total loss of life range from three to twelve million people, many of them civilians, due to slaughter, dysentery, typhus, bubonic plague, and famine. For example, Bohemia experienced an estimated 50 to 80 percent loss of its population due to death and migration, while Germany lost approximately 15 to 30 percent of its population (including half of its male population) to war, famine, and disease. The Thirty Years' War ended with the Treaty of Westphalia (1648), which dramatically altered life in Europe. The treaty established the borders of modern Europe, led to a decentralized and disorganized Germany and a disintegrated and weakened Holy Roman Empire, and declared that religion is a matter of an individual's personal choice. The Treaty of Westphalia signaled the secularization of Europe, a shift in power from church to state, wherein religion came to be seen as a private choice and the concept of national sovereignty gained credence. It also marked the end of the Reformation. From this point on, the power of religion in European political affairs steadily declined.[21]

FRENCH REVOLUTION

The French Revolution offers an alternative and unconventional example of holy war. The Reformation never made inroads into France the way it did in Northern Europe, thus French Catholicism remained dominant during this period of turmoil.

France experienced a different kind of turmoil with the French Revolution. In May 1789, King Louis XVI called for an Estates-General, a meeting similar to a parliamentary meeting of the three estates: the clergy (Catholic), the nobles, and the bourgeoisie (the middle class, comprised of wealthy merchants and traders with no aristocratic title). During the assembly, the bourgeoisie maneuvered into a position of dominance. This was the beginning of a movement toward democratic rule and overthrow of the old feudal system. The bourgeoisie formed a National Assembly that issued the Declaration of the Rights of Man and the Citizen as well as a Civil Constitution of the Clergy, both of which wrested control of the state, the economy, and the church from the traditional ruling classes. Economic and foreign political pressures (such as widespread poverty and war with Austria and Prussia) increased tensions within France, which finally boiled over with

French Revolution, 1792

the French Revolution. The National Convention was formed, which abolished the monarchy and eventually tried, convicted, and executed the king. Yet life for the peasants did not improve under the leadership of the bourgeoisie, which led to a Reign of Terror orchestrated in large part by Maximilien Robespierre and the Revolutionary Tribunal, in a strong and violent reaction against the original architects of the revolution, as well as against Christianity itself (both Catholic and Protestant).[22]

Under the new leadership, Christianity was to be replaced by the Cult of Reason, wherein traditional Christian religious beliefs and practices were dismissed as superstitious, irrational, and unnecessary in the new age of reason and science. The Cult of Reason combined patriotism, atheism, and secularism. Among changes it introduced were a new calendar where traditional Christian holidays were replaced with festivals honoring France and her people; new marriage, birth, and death rituals (for example, some "baptized" their children invoking the trinity of "liberty, equality, and fraternity" instead of "Father, Son, and Holy Spirit"); and the building of temples to Reason. The Cult also included an intentional program aimed at de-Christianizing France. Churches were closed, some were ransacked, and ultimately the celebration of Eucharist was outlawed. Reception of the Cult of Reason was not uniform; it was later replaced by the Cult of the Supreme Being, a form of deism (which affirms belief in a creator, but not necessarily the Judeo-Christian God, and tends to emphasize reason and personal experience while rejecting miracles as superstitious).[23]

As Justo Gonzalez observes:

> All this would have been merely ridiculous, were it not for the suffering and bloodshed it cost. The promoters of the new religion made use of the guillotine with cruel liberality. Christian worship was supposedly permitted; but any priest who refused to swear before the altar of Freedom could be accused of antirevolutionary activity and sent to the guillotine. Thus between two thousand and five thousand priests were executed, as well as several dozen nuns and countless lay people. Many others died in prison.[24]

The French Revolution, especially the Cult of Reason and Reign of Terror, represents a war against religion itself. This was not an intrareligious war (that is, a war between factions or denominations within the same religion, as was the case in the Reformation) or an interreligious war (a war between different religions, as was the case in the Crusades). This was a war against religious belief per se. While Gonzalez calls the Cult of Reason a "new religion," it was not a religion in the sense that it involved worship of a divine being or beings or even belief in an ultimate reality or supernatural world. Instead it is better characterized as a quasi-religion. The Cult of Reason was secularism (the view that religious beliefs should be excluded from public affairs and in some cases moral reflection) wrapped in the external expressions of religion (rituals, temples, and holidays). The violence done in the name of promoting the Cult of Reason thus qualifies it as holy war—it was a secular war against religion.

CONTEMPORARY CHRISTIAN HOLY WAR

While holy war is often dismissed as archaic, the remnants can still be found today in slogans like "God bless our troops" or in the confusion of religious and national identities for example—placing the U.S. flag in church sanctuaries or singing hymns like "God Bless America" and "Onward Christian Soldiers" during Sunday worship. While these seem fairly benign when compared to events like the Crusades or the Thirty Years' War, they represent a blurring of the line between the priorities of Scripture and national interest. In the wake of the September 11, 2001 terrorist attacks, some people, particularly several conservative Christian ministers, cast the events as a holy war of sorts and made claims that God is on "our" side.[25]

Pat Robertson, a popular and divisive televangelist, gave a speech in which he declared most Muslims to be peaceful people, but then went on to characterize Islam as a religion with violent roots and a desire for world domination. He described the relationship between the United States and the Muslim world in language reminiscent of the Crusades:

This is a religious struggle we are involved in. It is a clash of cultures. It is a clash of opposing points of view. It is a clash of different ideologies. And we need to understand what we're dealing with and how to deal with it. . . . We as a nation as vulnerable as we are in a free country, we need to humbly come before Almighty God and acknowledge our sins and ask for His mercy and ask for His protection. He has graciously protected us since the War of 1812. America has prospered and flourished because God has put a hedge of protection around us. This has been a special country to Him. It's been a land of His choosing. And we need as a people to turn from the way we're going and to acknowledge His sovereignty and to humbly beseech Him for protection from what may be coming from those who are our enemies and those who wish to destroy us. And then by God's grace and by the united action of all of us, this great country is going to overcome whatever terrorism is coming against it. We may have some hits in various places that will be very painful. But we are not going to succumb to terror. We're not going to knuckle under to terror. We are going to win the battle against terror, and we'll come out of this together and stronger. And I hope and pray that out of some difficult days that may be ahead of us we can once again say, as we do in our pledge of allegiance, we are part of "one nation under God."[26]

Franklin Graham, son of evangelist Billy Graham and a popular minister himself, has made several remarks in which he depicted the response to September 11 as a holy war: "We're not attacking Islam but Islam has attacked us," and "The God of Islam is not the same God. He's not the son of God of the Christian or Judeo-Christian faith. It's a different God, and I believe it is a very evil and wicked religion."[27]

Christian evangelist Benny Hinn is reported to have said, "We are on God's side. This is not a war between Arabs and Jews. It's a war between God and the devil."[28]

ONWARD, CHRISTIAN SOLDIERS

Onward, Christian Soldiers, a traditional Christian hymn sung in Catholic and Protestant churches, uses explicit military imagery in describing the Christian life as a battle. Its popularity shows a comfort with war imagery in Christian worship.

> Onward, Christian soldiers, marching as to war,
> with the cross of Jesus going on before.
> Christ, the royal Master, leads against the foe;
> forward into battle see his banners go!
>
> Refrain:
> Onward, Christian soldiers, marching as to war,
> with the cross of Jesus going on before.
>
> At the sign of triumph Satan's host doth flee;
> on then, Christian soldiers, on to victory!
> Hell's foundations quiver at the shout of praise;
> brothers, lift your voices, loud your anthems raise.
>
> (Refrain)
>
> Like a mighty army moves the church of God;
> brothers, we are treading where the saints have trod.
> We are not divided, all one body we,
> one in hope and doctrine, one in charity.
>
> (Refrain)
>
> Crowns and thrones may perish, kingdoms rise and wane,
> but the church of Jesus constant will remain.
> Gates of hell can never 'gainst that church prevail;
> we have Christ's own promise, and that cannot fail.
>
> (Refrain)

Onward Christian Soldiers *(continued)*

> Onward then, ye people, join our happy throng,
> blend with ours your voices in the triumph song.
> Glory, laud, and honor unto Christ the King,
> this through countless ages men and angels sing.
>
> (Refrain)

(Text: Sabine Baring-Gould, 1834–1924; Music: Arthur S. Sullivan, 1842–1900)

In the wake of the September 11, 2001 attacks, President Bush, in an apparent slip of the tongue, said, "This Crusade, this war on terror, is going to take a while."[29]

THE DECLINE OF CHRISTIAN HOLY WAR

James Turner Johnson identifies several reasons for the decline of holy-war thinking since the Reformation. First, the holy war tradition is not unified. It offers competing criteria for who has the authority to declare it and what ought to be considered legitimate reasons for going to war and legitimate objectives in war. It has never been a systematic, rational, consistent, or coherent ethic of war. Second, the post-Reformation period witnessed the birth of the sovereign nation-state, in which religious control over political authority was rejected and the separation of church and state (part of the overall secularization of Western societies) became a hallmark of Western political culture. In this context, the idea of politically sanctioned religious war came to be seen as a violation of the separation of church and state. Third, a consensus emerged around an alternative ethic of war, namely the just war theory, which supplanted holy war thinking. Finally, two other experiences also led to the demise of holy-war thinking: (1) the "discovery" of the New World led to the question of whether military force could or should be used to compel the conversion of Native Americans; and (2) the bloody experience of Reformation wars, like the Thirty Years' War and later the French Revolution, left many to conclude that wars for religion are ineffective and excessively destructive. Combined, these influences led to the belief that religion and war do not mix.[30]

TEN TYPES OF HOLY WARS

In his historical survey of holy war in the Western and Islamic traditions, Johnson identifies ten types of holy wars.[31] Although Johnson's study offers both Christian and Muslim examples of holy war, our focus here is exclusively Christian. Islam's holy war tradition is addressed in the appendix of this book.

1. Wars fought at what is perceived to be God's command (for example, the holy wars in the Hebrew Bible)
2. Wars fought on God's behalf by his duly authorized representative (such as the Crusades)
3. Wars in which God actually fights (for example, God intervenes in battle to defend the righteous, such as drowning the Egyptian army after the fleeing Israelites cross the sea [Exodus 14])
4. Wars fought to defend religious beliefs and practices, a vague category (for example, protection of pilgrimage routes to the Holy Land by religious military orders)
5. Wars fought to spread a religion or to establish a divinely authorized social order (such as the conquest of the New World by the Conquistadores and the revolutionary Anabaptist Tomas Müntzer's attempt to establish a theocracy in Meuhlhausen, Germany [1524–1525])[32]
6. Wars fought to punish those who are religiously deviant, sinful, or heretical (for example, the post-Reformation Catholic-Protestant wars or Augustine's punishment of the Donatists)
7. Wars in which the combatants are ritually purified or made holy. This represents attempts to give warfare a religious or moral aura through purification rituals, ascetic practices, blessings, and so on (for example, before going on a Crusade, knights

would undergo a ritual wherein they would kneel, make a vow and receive a cross, and rise as a soldier for Christ and the Church).

8. War that is characterized as both an external struggle and an internal struggle of faith. This type of holy war employs war language and images to describe the life of faith and often couples overt warfare with a demand to "wage war" internally against sin, selfish desires, and so on (for example, the "soldier of Christ" image of 2 Tim 2:3–4 and Eph 6:11–17).

9. War led by a religiously inspired leader. This is similar to the second type of holy war except in that case the authority is usually recognized due to cultic status (priest, pope, and so on), whereas in this type the authority is based on the personal charisma of the leader and her or his ability to inspire (such as Joan of Arc).

10. War recognized as a miracle. This includes recognizing divine intervention after the fact (such as in 2 Chronicles 20).

Thus Christianity has a convoluted heritage when it comes to war and peace. While it sees itself as a religion of peace, it has not been immune from much of the violence witnessed over the centuries in the name of faith. Christianity, too, has its holy war as well as its pacifist history.

As a Christian and a Catholic theologian, I see no place for holy war within the Christian faith. I want to say that holy war represents a perversion of Christianity; that it is the manipulation of a faith for political purposes. But I must also admit that religion does not exist in a pure state, nor is it immune from corruption. Religions have always influenced and been influenced by political, economic, and social factors. I would like to say that Christianity does not have a holy war tradition; that it is a distortion of the teachings of Jesus Christ. But it would be irresponsible to ignore centuries of violence done in the name of Jesus Christ. Historically Christianity is a bloody religion; it has its holy wars.

WHERE DO YOU FALL?

Our exploration of Christian approaches to war and peace is presented as a continuum ranging from pacifism (the most "dovish") to holy war (the most "hawkish"). Return now to page 18 where the various approaches are displayed as an array. Based on your deeper understanding of holy war, where would you now place yourself on the continuum and why? In other words, how has encountering the ideas, arguments, or perspectives presented in this chapter caused you to reevaluate your own ethic of war and peace?

DISCUSSION QUESTIONS

1. In the United States, the athletic teams and bands of many Christian schools (elementary, secondary, and colleges and universities) are known as "The Crusaders." What do you think about this and why?

2. Do you see any evidence of a crusade mentality anywhere today? Where? Explain.

3. Some would argue that the phrase "holy war" is a contradiction in terms, that no war can ever be "holy." Do you agree or disagree? Explain.

ENDNOTES

1 Samuel Huntington, "The Clash of Civilizations," *Foreign Affairs* 72.3 (1993): 22–49, and *The Clash of Civilizations and the Remaking of World Order* (New York: Simon & Schuster, 1996).

2 Sam Keen, *Faces of the Enemy: Reflections of the Hostile Imagination* (San Francisco: Harper & Row, 1986).

3 Ibid., 10.

4 Adapted from video recording *Faces of the Enemy* (Berkeley, CA: Quest Productions, 1987, 2005), produced by Bill Jersey and Jeffrey Friedman based on Keen, *Faces of the Enemy*, esp. 16–23.

5 Keen, *Faces of the Enemy*, 15–88.

6 For more on Bush's dualistic thinking and his use of latent religious language, see Bruce Lincoln, *Holy Terrors: Thinking About Religion after September 11* (Chicago: University of Chicago Press, 2002), 19–32.

7 "Remarks by the President at Scott McCallum for Governor Reception" at the Pfister Hotel in Milwaukee, Wisconsin (February 11, 2002); available online at *http://www.whitehouse.gov/news/releases/2002/02/20020211-9.html*.

8 A crucial and meaningful exception is the surprising initial defeat of the Israelites at Ai, which is explained as God's punishment because an Israelite soldier disobeyed God's order to destroy everything and took loot for himself from Jericho (Joshua 7). Disobedience at the beginning of Israel's settlement story thus prefigures the defeats and exiles they experience later.

9 The Amalekites were apparently a nomadic or seminomadic group that ranged from western Sinai to the Arabian desert, but there is no archaeological evidence or mention outside the biblical accounts that corroborates their existence. Gerald L. Mattingly, "Amalek," in *Eerdmans Dictionary of the Bible*, ed. David Noel Freedman (Grand Rapids, MI: Eerdmans, 2000), 48–49.

10 Lawrence Boadt, *Reading the Old Testament: An Introduction* (New York: Paulist, 1984), 197–98.

11 Ibid., 198.

12 See Stephen L. Harris, *Understanding the Bible*, 6th ed. (Boston: McGraw Hill, 2003), 164–69; and Boadt, *Reading the Old Testament*, 196–205.

13 See Harris, *Understanding the Bible*, 166–70.

14 Gerhard von Rad, *Holy War in Ancient Israel* (Grand Rapids, MI: Eerdmans, 1991); originally published as *De Heilige Krieg im alten Israel* (Göttingen: Vandenhoek & Ruprecht, 1958).

15 As we saw in the previous chapter, "sword passages" appear in the New Testament, but they are typically metaphorical or, in the case of Jesus' overturning the money changers' tables, best interpreted as an act of protest.

16 See Raymond Brown, *An Introduction to the New Testament* (New York: Doubleday, 1997), 794–99, and Robert J. Karris, ed., *The Collegeville Bible Commentary: New Testament* (Collegeville, MN: The Liturgical Press, 1992), 1295–99.

17 Thomas F. Madden, "The Real History of the Crusades," *Crisis* 20.4 (April 2002); available online at *http://insidecatholic.com/Joomla/index.php?option=com_content&task=view&id=3463&Itemid=48*.

18 Bernard of Clairvaux, "Letter 391," in *The Letters of St. Bernard of Clairvaux*, ed. and trans. B. S. James (Chicago: Henry Regnery, 1st ed.,1953, and Collegeville, MN: Cistercian Publications, 2nd ed., 1998); also available in Arthur Homes, ed., *War and Christian Ethics* (Grand Rapids, MI: Baker, 2005), 88–90.

19 John Howard Yoder, *When War Is Unjust: Being Honest in Just-War Thinking* (Minneapolis, MN: Augsburg, 1984), 26–27. See also the revised edition (Maryknoll, NY: Orbis, 1996), 12–14.

20 Justo L. Gonzalez, *The Story of Christianity:* Vol. 2, *The Reformation to the Present Day* (New York: HarperCollins, 1985), 136.

21 Ibid., 134–41.

22 Ibid., 192–94 and 262–67.

23 Ibid.

24 Ibid., 266.

25 See "Attacks on Muslims by Conservative Protestants: Graham, Hinn, Falwell, Robertson, Swaggart & Baldwin," available online at *http://www.religioustolerance.org/reac_ter18b.htm;* and "Attacks on Islam Since 9/11" available online at *http://www.beliefnet.com/story/116/story_11688_1.html.*

26 Pat Robertson, "The Roots of Terrorism and a Strategy for Victory," available online at *http://www.patrobertson.com/speeches/Terrorism EconomicClub.asp.*

27 "Attacks on Islam Since 9/11." See also "Attacks on Muslims by Conservative Protestants," available online at *http://www.religious tolerance.org/reac_ter18b.htm.*

28 Speech given at the American Airlines Center (Dallas, TX) in July 2002: "Attacks on Islam Since 9/11." See also "Attacks on Muslims by Conservative Protestants."

29 Office of the Press Secretary, "Remark by the President upon Arrival: The South Lawn" (September 16, 2001); available online at *http://www.whitehouse.gov/news/releases/2001/09/20010916-2.html.*

30 James Turner Johnson, *The Holy War Idea in Western and Islamic Traditions* (University Park, PA: Pennsylvania State University Press, 1997), 1–15.

31 Ibid., 37–42.

32 For more on Müntzer, see Gonzalez, *The Story of Christianity*, 41–42 and 57–59.

CHAPTER 4

Just War Theory: A Third Way?

Having looked at the two opposite poles in our continuum of approaches (pacifism and holy war), we now turn our attention to the middle position, the just war theory. The just war theory holds that sometimes the use of force, even deadly force, is morally acceptable, but only in rare situations that meet strict requirements. This centuries-old and often modified set of ethical guidelines or principles has long been considered the gold standard for morally evaluating warfare.

Traditionally the just war theory is divided into two categories, known by their Latin names: *jus ad bellum* and *jus in bello*. The *jus ad bellum* category addresses when it is acceptable, permissible, or even required to go to war and includes several criteria: a war must be waged for a just cause and with right intention; it must be declared by a legitimate authority; it must be waged only after all attempts at peaceful conflict resolution have failed. The *jus in bello* category addresses behavior in battle itself and traditionally includes only two criteria: militaries must make every reasonable effort to distinguish between civilians and soldiers (noncombatant immunity), and the use of force cannot be disproportionate (militaries must exercise restraint in the amount of firepower they use). While the origin of the just war theory is often attributed to early Christian theologians like Augustine, others contributed to its development as well, including Jewish and Muslim scholars and a host of philosophers, political scientists, and military experts.

The terms *just war theory, just war doctrine, just war tradition,* and *just war thinking* are often used interchangeably, but there is a slight difference among them. *Just war theory* is the most common of the terms. It refers to a set of ethical principles or norms developed by philosophers, theologians, and political scientists and tends to be more theoretical. *Just war doctrine* refers to the official Catholic teaching on just war as found in magisterial documents like the *Catechism of the Catholic Church.*[1] *Just war tradition* refers to the historical development of just war theory, while *just war thinking* refers to the application of just war theory to real-life situations. But as John Howard Yoder observes, "It is appropriate to speak rather of a 'tradition' than of a 'doctrine' or a 'theory,' for there is not one official statement of this approach to which all would subscribe."[2] Thus our analysis begins with the just war tradition and moves to contemporary just war theory with a special focus on just war doctrine. Chapter 5 addresses some of the principal challenges to the just war theory, while the appendix explores how the just war theory has been developed and used by Jewish and Muslim scholars.

THE JUST WAR TRADITION

Although the term *just war theory* is fairly recent, rules of war or "war conventions" are not. Contrary to the saying, "There are no rules in love and war," history shows that there have always been rules for war, even if they haven't always been obeyed.

CLASSICAL CONTRIBUTIONS
TO THE JUST WAR TRADITION

The just war tradition did not begin with Christianity. In fact, it traces its origins to Greek philosophers like Plato and Aristotle and their proponents, such as the Roman Cicero.

Plato (427–347 BCE), like most Greek philosophers, was deeply concerned about politics and justice. One of the earliest just war thinkers, Plato saw war as sometimes justified in the name of pursuing peace, which he viewed as a well-ordered society, a theme later emphasized by Augustine. Plato stressed the importance of virtue and education so that soldiers would exercise restraint and courage in their service to the common good. Aristotle (384–322 BCE), a student of Plato's, also focused on virtue (particularly courage) and addressed war under the rubric of justice and obligations of individual citizens to serve and protect the common good. His discussion of justice falls under the larger umbrella of his theories of the natural law (see chapter 1) and the law of nations *(jus gentium)*, work that served as the foundation for later theories of international law that typically include the rules of war (for example, conventions and treaties).

Cicero (106–43 BCE) was a Roman philosopher and legal scholar whose ethics of war was also based in his understanding of the natural law. His writings on war address many of the basic principles that would, centuries later, become the just war theory. Concerning going to war *(jus ad bellum)*, he said: "Those wars are unjust which are undertaken without provocation. For only a war waged for revenge or defense can actually be just. . . . No war is considered just unless it has been proclaimed and declared."[3] Here we see an early version of two key principles of the just war theory: just cause and legitimate (or competent) authority.

Elsewhere, Cicero expands on this:

> There are two ways of settling a dispute: first by discussion; second by physical force; and since the former is characteristic of man [as a rational creature who naturally seeks peace], the latter of the brute, we must resort to force only in case we may

not avail ourselves of discussion. The only excuse, therefore, for going to war is that we may live in peace unharmed; and when the victory is won we should spare those who have not been bloodthirsty and barbarous in the warfare. . . . Not only must we show consideration for those whom we have conquered by force of arms but we must also ensure protection to those who lay down their arms and throw themselves upon the mercy of our generals. . . . No war is just, unless it is entered upon after an official demand for satisfaction has been submitted or warning has been given and a formal declaration made. . . . But when a war is fought for supremacy and when glory is the object of war, it must still not fail to start from the same motives which I said a moment ago were the only righteous grounds for going to war. But those wars which have glory for their end must be carried on with less bitterness.[4]

Here we see in nascent form many of the principles and norms that will make up the contemporary just war theory, such as: last resort (force is acceptable when discussion has failed); right intention ("the only excuse for going to war is that we may live in peace"); proportionality (restraint should be shown to captives "who have not been blood-thirsty and barbarous," as well as to those who surrender); and legitimate authority and public declaration ("no war is just, unless it is entered upon after an official demand . . . and a formal declaration made"). While Cicero states that glory is a just cause for going to war (glory was held as a high virtue in ancient Roman society), he clearly sees it as a weaker rationale compared to revenge, righting a wrong, restitution, and self-defense.

SCRIPTURE AND THE JUST WAR TRADITION

Scriptural support for what became the just war theory is thin. There is no explicit biblical endorsement of just war criteria. Those seeking validation for the theory tend to draw on the same biblical passages that we have already explored in the chapters on pacifism and holy war. As we have seen, the Hebrew Bible has its holy war rhetoric, but it also contains numerous exhortations to seek peace and justice. And, as we will see in the appendix, it also places several limits on war both *ad bellum* and *in bello*. In the New Testament, John the Baptist does not explicitly condemn soldiering; he only exhorts soldiers to act justly (Luke 3:14). Likewise, Jesus, in his interactions with a Roman centurion, does not condemn the centurion's profession and in fact praises his faith (Luke 7:1–10 and Matt 8:5–13). Similarly, Acts 10:1–49 presents the conversion of the centurion Cornelius, who is lauded as devout and God-fearing. Peter praises him and does not demand he abandon soldiering upon his conversion. Finally, Paul explicitly declares that the state has the authority to use force, a position we will explore in detail later in the chapter (Rom 13:1–4).

AMBROSE AND AUGUSTINE

In 312 CE, Roman Emperor Constantine endorsed Christianity, as legend proclaims, because of a dream and a victory in battle. A year later, Constantine issued the Edict of Milan, which granted Christians the freedom to publicly practice their religion. By 380, Christianity was the official religion of the most powerful empire on earth. By 416, only Christians could serve in the military. With this "overnight success" came many problems, including how the empire could maintain its dominant position while also claiming adherence to a religion that was largely seen as espousing pacifism (see chapter 2).

Two theologians of the era provided a theological justification for the use of military force by drawing from pagan predecessors. Ambrose (340–397) was a former Roman governor who became bishop of Milan in northern Italy. For Ambrose, the Roman Empire was an instrument of God's peace. The *Pax Romano* (the peace and order achieved by the Roman Empire) laid the foundation for the *Pax Christiana*, a time of peace, order, and prosperity that came from a Christian empire. Ambrose imported the Greek philosophers' concern for social justice into the Christian understanding of war. He held that Christians have a duty to fight when commanded by political leaders, who were assumed to derive their legitimate authority from God.

CHRISTIANITY AND POLITICAL POWER

Many Americans subscribe to a belief in the separation of church and state, a mantra within American politics. There is a difference between saying there ought not to be a state-sanctioned religion and saying that religiously grounded convictions have no place in the public square. There is also a danger in believing that religion has nothing to say about politics. Such arguments tend to reduce religious belief to the level of personal piety and eviscerate religion. Christianity in particular has social and political dimensions. The Hebrew prophets chided those in political power for failing to uphold social justice, and Jesus was crucified in large part because of his challenge to religious and political power.

In the Bible, one finds the idea that the power of those in government comes from God. "Hear, therefore, kings, and understand; learn, you magistrates of the earth's expanse! Hearken, you who are in power over the multitude and lord it over throngs of peoples! Because authority was given you by the LORD and sovereignty by the Most High, who shall probe your works and scrutinize your counsels!" (Wis 6:1–3). In the New Testament, one finds a similar idea expressed:

> Let every person be subordinate to the higher authorities, for there is no authority except from God, and those that exist have been established by God. Therefore, whoever resists authority opposes what God has appointed, and those who oppose it will bring judgment upon themselves. For rulers are not a cause of fear to good conduct, but to evil. Do you wish to have no fear of authority? Then do what is good and you will receive approval from it, for it is a servant of God for your good. But if you do evil, be afraid, for it does not bear the sword without purpose; it is the servant of God to inflict wrath on the evildoer. Therefore, it is necessary to be subject not only because of the wrath but also because of conscience.

Christianity and Politcal Power (continued)

> This is why you also pay taxes, for the authorities are ministers
> of God, devoting themselves to this very thing. Pay to all their
> dues, taxes to whom taxes are due, toll to whom toll is due,
> respect to whom respect is due, honor to whom honor is due.
> (Rom 13:1–7)

This notion that political leaders derive their authority from
God stems from a theological commitment: if God is all powerful
(sovereign), then anyone who exercises power on earth must do
so with God's permission. Its logic has been used to justify the
political theology of the divine right of kings (that is, the authority
of the king is absolute, and he can only be held accountable by
God). The danger in such a theory should be immediately apparent. It allows political leaders to act with impunity; anything they
do is automatically just, right, and good precisely because they are
doing it. Christianity has moved away from such thinking. As we
shall see, Aquinas challenged this idea by tying political authority
to responsibility for the common good, and he even allowed for
overthrowing tyrants. In contemporary Catholic social thought,
political leadership is interpreted as a duty. The obligation to
secure the common good is the primary vocation of those in
political office and ought to be exercised with particular attention
for the needs of the poor and vulnerable. "It is the role of the state
to defend and promote the common good of civil society, its citizens, and intermediate bodies" (*Catechism of the Catholic Church*,
no. 1910).

Ambrose's preaching directly contributed to Saint Augustine's
conversion to Christianity. Augustine (354–430)—an intelligent,
witty bishop and skilled rhetorician—is a giant in the history of
Christian thought and considered to be the father of the Christian
just war theory. Like Ambrose, Augustine believed Christians had a
duty to obey legitimate political leaders (even non-Christian ones)
and a duty to fight to defend the state. But Christians, according
to Augustine, were not simply citizens of the earthly state. They

were also citizens of the Kingdom of God. In his greatest work, *City of God*, he outlines his basic worldview: Christians have dual citizenship. By virtue of their baptism, they are citizens of the Kingdom of God, which he called the City of God. However, they live out their earthly lives in the City of Man—a city overrun by sin, greed, lust, and fear. The role of government in a sinful world is to restrain the power of sin, by force if necessary. Thus, governmental authority and power are instruments God uses to frustrate the power of sin.

Augustine lived when the Roman Empire was in a state of decline. The empire had expanded to the point that it could no longer defend its borders, and it was in political turmoil. In 410, German tribes (Visigoths) sacked the capital, Rome. This colored Augustine's theology of war and peace. For Augustine, peace is the fruit that comes from law, order, and obedience.

> The peace of body and soul is the duly ordered life and health of a living creature; peace between mortal man and God is an ordered obedience, in faith, in subjection to an everlasting law; peace between men is an ordered agreement of mind with mind; the peace of a home is the ordered agreement among those who live together about giving and obeying orders; the peace of the heavenly City is a perfectly ordered and perfectly harmonious fellowship in the enjoyment of God, and a mutual fellowship in God; the peace of the whole universe is the tranquility of order.[5]

For Augustine peace is the *tranquillitas ordinis*, the tranquil order or "the harmony that comes from order" or "the peace that comes from justice." While some reduce Augustine's *tranquillitas ordinis* to its political dimensions, it is actually much richer. Order for Augustine begins in the human heart. It is about loving God for God's own sake and loving everything else inasmuch as it leads us to God. This should, according to Augustine's theology, lead to *concordia* (oneness of heart), in which human relationships are arranged harmoniously based on authority, obedience, and love. The result should be a peaceful, ordered, and harmonious political community—what we today might call a just and lasting peace. For Augustine, peace is the primary objective (*telos*) of war.

> Just as there is no man who does not wish for joy, so there is no man who does not wish for peace. Indeed, even when men choose war, their only wish is for victory; which shows that their desire in fighting is for peace with glory. . . . Hence it is an established fact that peace is the desired end of war. For every man is in quest of peace, even in waging war, whereas no one is in quest of war when making peace.[6]

While the idea of "fighting for peace" seems oxymoronic, Augustine sees it as a concession made to a world in which sin, greed, anger, fear, and the desire for revenge often eclipse our rational and natural desire to live in peace. Augustine also noted that war is both a sign of sin and a necessary but lesser evil used to prevent a greater evil.

Augustine was a Christian realist. He believed that sin was real and that violence was a sign of a depraved world. He argued that force can be a form of "love of neighbor" (Matt 22:36–40 and Luke 10:25–37), but only if used to thwart a greater evil and without any desire for revenge or pleasure. Punishing sinners and preventing the spread of evil is a form of neighbor-love. For Augustine, Christians have a duty to protect the vulnerable and innocent and sometimes must use force to do so. Augustine's just war theory does not treat war cavalierly. War is about killing, and killing is a sin. Nevertheless, we must sometimes engage in the evil of war to thwart greater evils.

Augustine's point can be illustrated quite easily. Imagine you are sitting in your apartment with ten friends from your self-defense or martial arts class (including several black belts), when you hear an argument between the couple next door. The argument escalates. You hear dishes breaking against the wall and furniture being broken. Then the man screams, "That's it, I'm going to kill you." Now suppose you are living in a part of town where it typically takes the police thirty to forty-five minutes to respond. What is the "Christian" response? Clearly you can't just ignore the situation. The man is so enraged that reasoning with him isn't going to work, nor do you have time to talk him down. Many would say that the Christian response in this situation is for you and your friends to intervene—go over, kick in the door, and physically stop the man from killing his girlfriend. Augustine's point is similar—that sometimes we have to use force, which he admits is always sinful, to prevent a greater sin. He says we have an obligation as Christians to practice charity (love of neighbor) and that extends particularly to the weak and vulnerable.

Augustine is often credited as the father of the just war theory because he organized the tradition into three principles that form the core of the theory today:

1. Just cause—a war is just if and only if it is waged for a just cause (such as national self-defense or protecting the weak and vulnerable).

2. Legitimate authority—a war is just if and only if it is declared by the proper political authority (emperor, king, and so on). For Augustine, war and the killing it involves are an instrument of statecraft. Individuals do not have the right to kill, even in self-defense. Instead, under the presumption of pacifism, one ought to accept death instead of resorting to violence. But the rules for states are different than the rules for individuals. When soldiers kill in battle (even when defending themselves on the battlefield, where one might be tempted to see killing as a form of self-defense), they are not acting as private citizens; they are instruments or delegates of the state, thus the action of killing is not their own.[7]

   As we saw in chapter 2, Augustine rejects the use of violence in personal self-defense (he espoused a personal principled pacifism) because it would be a form of hatred. Violence is permitted only when authorized by a legitimate authority (that is the sovereign, king, or political leadership); thus he endorsed publicly justified warfare in the name of the common good. Augustine illustrated this point using two biblical examples: Moses' killing an Egyptian who had struck an Israelite laborer (Exod 3:11–12) and Peter' cutting off the ear of the high priest's slave when soldiers come to arrest Jesus (John 18:10–11).

> It might be shown that, though Moses slew the Egyptian, without being commanded by God, the action was divinely permitted, as, from the prophetic character of Moses, it prefigured something in the future. Now however, I do not use this argument, but view the action as having no symbolic meaning. In the light, then, of the eternal law, it was wrong for one who had no legal authority to kill the man, even though he was a bad character, besides being the aggressor. . . . Peter, when he took his sword out of its sheath to defend the Lord, and cut off the right ear of an assailant, when the Lord rebuked him with something like a threat, saying, 'Put up your sword into its sheath; for he that takes the sword shall perish by the sword' [Matt 26:51–52]. To take the sword is to use weapons against a man's life, without the sanction of the constituted authority. The Lord, indeed, had told His disciples to carry a sword; but He did not tell them to use it.[8]

Both Moses and Peter, argued Augustine, used force in "hasty zeal" out of "resentment against injury," even if motivated also by love. For Augustine, only those in positions of political leadership have the right or duty to resort to force because they are charged with the responsibility of securing order and seeking the common good. Furthermore, they can only use force as a last resort and with right intention.

3. Right intention—a war is just if and only if those waging the war are motivated by good intentions. The *tranquillitais ordinis* (the peace that comes from order or a just peace) is the only legitimate end that one can seek, since peace is the goal of war. Augustine's definition of peace as "the tranquility that comes from order" reflects his reliance on the Greek

and Roman philosophers and his own social-political context. Plato, Aristotle, and Cicero saw peace as related to a well-ordered society, and Augustine, writing during the collapse of the Roman Empire, also has a strong prejudice in favor of social order, thereby reducing peace to social stability. Those of us today who live in relatively stable social-political environments (for example, the United States, Europe, Japan, and Australia) do not fully appreciate the fear of social chaos and anarchy that colored these authors' perceptions.

For Augustine, soldiers in battle must be motivated by charity, love of neighbor, and even love of enemies. They must not delight in the blood sport of war or be motivated by revenge. "The real evils in war are love of violence, revengeful cruelty, fierce and implacable enmity, wild resistance and the lust of power."[9] At first blush, Augustine seems hypocritical. He decries violence in the name of self-defense but allows killing in battle and says it is not murder. For Augustine, intention and authority are key. When an individual sheds blood with vengeance (motive) or without permission (authority), that person commits a sin; but as a tool or delegate of the state, the soldier can kill without sinning, so long as the soldier does so dispassionately (without taking delight) and in service to the common good.

All three principles must be met for a war to be considered just. A fourth principle could be added to Augustine's just war criteria: last resort. Since he views war as sinful, it should only be used after all peaceful means of resolving a conflict have been exhausted.

Augustine was no hawk, but certainly he was no dove either. He allowed the use of force, but only when certain conditions were met. Augustine himself authorized the use of force against heretics (see "Augustine, the Donatists" pp. 170–171). His aim was not to glorify war, but to limit it. He had a strong presumption in favor of peaceful conflict resolution and saw the resort to force as a grotesque concession to a sinful world.

AUGUSTINE, THE DONATISTS, AND THE "STERN NECESSITY" OF WAR

The Donatists were a sect of North African Christians who claimed they were the purer or truer Christian church. They traced their origins to Christians who refused to deny their faith in the face of persecution and held theological beliefs that were contrary to the mainstream (Roman) Church (such as questions concerning church leadership, the validity of sacraments, and concepts about forgiveness and salvation). The Donatists opposed the mainstream Christian Church by electing alternative bishops, harassing people, laying claim to church properties, and in some instances resorting to force. Augustine, as a bishop of the mainstream Church, tried to settle the dispute peacefully through conversation and debate over practical and theological differences. When this proved ineffective, he called upon Roman authorities (the state), which seized property and fined Donatists who refused to recognize the conventional Church. Augustine resorted to the use of force by the state in the name of theological orthodoxy.

Augustine expresses well the ambivalence Christians should have toward using force, even in a good cause:

> To make war and to extend the realm by crushing other peoples is good fortune in the eyes of the wicked; to the good, it is a stern necessity. But since it would be worse that the unjust should lord it over the just, this stern necessity may be called good fortune without impropriety. Yet there can be no shadow of doubt that it is greater good fortune to have a good neighbor and live in peace with him than to subdue a bad neighbor when he makes war. It is a wicked prayer to ask to have someone to hate or to fear, so that he may be some-one to conquer.[10]

Augustine, the Donatists *(continued)*

> For it is the injustice of the opposing side that lays on
> the wise man the duty of waging wars; and this injustice is
> assuredly to be deplored by a human being, since it is the
> injustice of human beings, even though no necessity for
> war should arise from it. And so everyone who reflects with
> sorrow on such grievous evils, in all their horror and cruelty,
> must acknowledge the necessity of them.[11]

THE MIDDLE AGES

Augustine's principles remained the bedrock of Christian thought
on war for centuries and became the mainstream approach
to the moral evaluation of war for Catholicism. In the Middle
Ages, books called *penitentials* emerged to help priests with the
sacrament of reconciliation. They discussed the theology of sin and
forgiveness and ascribed penances for particular sins, including
sins committed in war. Penances lasting forty days to a year were
common for killing another person in battle. What is interesting
for our discussion is that war (even when waged for a just cause)
continued to be seen as inherently sinful. In other words, in the
Augustinian tradition, war was not seen as virtuous, only as a
lesser evil. As a sin, it required confession, penance, and absolution. Likewise, in the medieval tradition, soldiers returning from
war needed to make a religious retreat before returning to civilian
life and the sacramental life of the Church. This was a time of
psychological and spiritual healing but also a period to repent
for having shed blood.

The greatest theologian of the Middle Ages was Thomas
Aquinas (1225–1274), a Dominican priest and professor at the
University of Paris. Aquinas's crowning work was his *Summa
Theologica*, a comprehensive encyclopedia addressing nearly every
theological concept in a systematic and detailed fashion in a
question-and-answer format. His impact on Christian thought
equals that of Augustine.

Aquinas addresses war in his *Summa Theologica* in the section on charity because (like Augustine before him) he saw the justified use of force as a form of neighbor-love (defending the weak and vulnerable). Drawing on Augustine, Aquinas reiterates the same three principles regarding a just war. A war is just when it is declared by a legitimate authority, waged for a just cause, and fought with right intention. He also agrees that peace is the primary objective of war. However, since peace is a form of love of neighbor, war represents a failure to love.

On one key point, however, Aquinas subtly departs from Augustine. Answering the question, "Is war always sinful?" Aquinas responds, "No," because the state has an obligation to defend the common good, and each citizen has his or her obligation to the common good as well. Thus, killing in war is no longer seen as *inherently* (always) evil, although Aquinas doesn't go so far as to call it good or virtuous. Rather it is a nonmoral evil (an evil that is not the result of the individual's choice, such as the death of innocent people due to an earthquake), as opposed to a moral evil (evil which results from the exercise of one's free will, such as premeditated murder). A soldier killing another soldier in battle is not the same as murder. It is a tragic situation, a sign of human sinfulness, but a soldier is not morally culpable (responsible) when he takes the life of his enemy on the battlefield, unless he does so "moved by private animosity."[12]

Aquinas modified the just war principles in two other ways as well. First, whereas Augustine had a strong presumption in favor of law and order and argued for obedience to political authorities (even unjust tyrants and non-Christian rulers), Aquinas argues that the people have a right to overthrow unjust rulers, although it is a rare occasion and the results must be better than rule by the tyrant. This argument for insurrection embodies early versions of the last resort principle and what will become the proportionality principle. Recognizing that war is evil (a nonmoral evil, a failure of charity, and a sign of the reality of sin), it should not be sought unless there are no other choices and only if life under the rule of

AQUINAS'S JUST WAR THEORY

Aquinas's *Summa Theologica* is written in question-answer format. In response to the question, "Is it always a sin to wage war?" he answers:[13]

> Three things are required for any war to be just. The first is the authority of the sovereign on whose command war is waged. Now a private person has no business declaring war; he can seek redress by appealing to the judgment of his superiors. Nor can he summon together whole people [that is, assemble an army], which has to be done to fight a war. Since the care of the commonweal [commonwealth or common good] is committed to those in authority they are the one to watch over the public affairs of the city, kingdom or province in their jurisdiction. And just as they use the sword in lawful defense against domestic disturbance when they punish criminals, as Paul says, "He beareth not the sword in vain for he is God's minister, an avenger to execute wrath upon him that doth evil" [Rom 13:4], so they lawfully use the sword of war to protect the commonweal from foreign attacks. Thus it is said to those in authority, "Rescue the weak and the needy, save them from the clutches of the wicked" [Ps 81:4]. Hence Augustine writes, "The natural order conducive to human peace demands that the power to counsel and declare war belongs to those who hold the supreme authority" [*Against Faustus*, 22, 75].
>
> Secondly, a just cause is required, namely that those who are attacked are attacked because they deserve it on account of some wrong they have done. So Augustine [says], "We usually describe a just war as one that avenges wrongs, that is, when a nation or state has to be punished either for refusing to make amends for outrages done by its subjects, or to restore what it has seized injuriously [taken wrongly]" [*Quaest. In Heptateuch*; in *Josue* 10].

Aquinas's Just War Theory *(continued)*

> Thirdly, the right intention of those waging war is required, that is, they must intend to promote the good and to avoid evil [*Summa Theologica* II-II, question 66, article 8]. Hence Augustine writes, "Among true worshippers of God those war are looked on as peacemaking which are waged neither for aggrandisement nor cruelty, but with the object of securing peace, of repressing the evil and supporting the good" [This is actually a quote from Gratian, *Decretum* II, 23, I, can. 6]. Now it can happen that even given a legitimate authority and a just cause for declaring war, it may yet be wrong because of perverse intention. Hence Augustine says, "The craving to hurt people, the cruel thirst for revenge, the unappeased and unrelenting spirit, the savageness of fighting on, the lust to dominate, and suchlike — all these are rightly condemned in war" [*Against Faustus* 22, 74].

Aquinas goes on to make the distinction between killing as a private citizen and as a soldier, who is an instrument or tool of the state who kills in battle. The soldier, according to Augustine and Aquinas, vicariously exercises the authority of the sovereign (that is, he is not killing by his own authority, but exercises the authority of the sovereign, which has granted him permission to do so). So too, Aquinas argues political leaders (public persons) pursuing justice vicariously exercise the authority of God when they call for the use of force in pursuit of justice:

> If a private person uses the sword by the authority of the sovereign or judge, or a public person uses it through zeal for justice, and by the authority, so to speak, of God, then he himself does not "draw the sword," but is commissioned by another to use it, and does not deserve punishment.

the tyrant is worse than the harm that will come with the insurrection.[14] Second, Aquinas introduces the "principle of double effect," which has proven to be extremely helpful in ethically evaluating wartime activities.

Aquinas's treatment of the principle of double effect arises in his response to the question, "Is it permissible to kill in self-defense?" While Augustine denied Christians the right to use force in personal self-defense, Aquinas argues differently:

> Nothing hinders a single act from having two effects, only one of which is intended, while the other is beside the intention. Now moral acts get their character in accordance with what is intended, but not from what is beside the intention since the latter is incidental. . . . Accordingly, the act of self-defense may have a double effect: the saving of one's life, on the one hand, and the slaying of the attacker, on the other. Since saving one's life is what is intended, such an act is not therefore illicit, seeing that it is natural to everything to keep itself in existence as far as possible.[15]

In other words, while a single action may produce more than one effect, we are morally responsible only for those effects (outcomes) we intend. Aquinas goes on to say that self-preservation is natural, and therefore anyone who kills another in self-defense does not sin, but only if their use of force is proportionate to the end intended. This is why it is not allowed to use more force than necessary to defend one's life. For example, imagine you are walking down a lonely street and a robber comes up to you with a knife. Now if you had a gun in your pocket you might be tempted to pull it out and shoot the robber in the head, but that would be a disproportionate (excessive) use of force. You could simply pull out the gun and point it at the robber without pulling the trigger to scare him off, or you could shoot him in the leg to stop him. To shoot him in the head when your own life is not immediately threatened is excessive. But suppose he lunged at you, and you did pull the trigger and kill the robber. According to Aquinas, you have not sinned since your intention was self-preservation and not to kill. While Aquinas engages the principle of double effect in reference to personal self-defense (not war), it was later incorporated into just war thinking. The principle of double effect weighs the range of options (what are the choices, and which are proportionate and which are excessive), effects (outcomes), and motivation (intention).

The principle of double effect has four conditions that must be met:

1. The action cannot be intrinsically evil, that is, wrong by definition (for example, rape, genocide, the intentional killing of an innocent person).

2. The evil effect cannot be intended, even if it is foreseeable. In other words, you can know about the evil secondary effect of your action, but you cannot desire it. An easy way to evaluate one's motive is to ask, "If there were another course of action that would produce the same good effect without the bad effect would you choose it?" If you say "yes," then your intention is good; but if you say "no," then clearly you are intending (desiring) the bad effect.

3. The good effect cannot be a direct result of the bad effect. In other words, you can't get good directly from evil.

4. There has to be a very good or proportionate reason (for example, human dignity, life, freedom) for pursuing this action that has both good and bad effects. Recognizing that this course of action will result in bad effects, it has to be worth it.

While these four conditions are abstract, the principle of double effect has proven to be helpful in the moral evaluation of real-life moral problems, especially in medical ethics and in evaluating wartime activities such as war crimes.

THE MODERN PERIOD

SIXTEENTH AND SEVENTEENTH CENTURIES

European civilization remained fairly constant throughout the Middle Ages. Political power was concentrated in the hands of emperors, kings, and noblemen; the Roman Catholic Church had a religious monopoly throughout the continent and exercised tremendous religious, political, and economic power; the vast majority of the population was poor, and the economy was

THE PRINCIPLE OF DOUBLE EFFECT: TWO CASE STUDIES

The principle of double effect can seem fairly abstract at first, but it has real-life applications. It is best understood through case studies. Consider the scenarios below and ask yourself, "What would I do?" (One option is to do nothing.) As you deliberate, use the four conditions of the principle of double effect:

1. The action cannot be intrinsically evil.
2. The evil effect cannot be intended, even if it is foreseeable.
3. The good effect cannot be a direct result of the bad effect.
4. There has to be a very good or proportionate reason for pursuing this action that has both good and bad effects.

Case 1

During a just war you discover that your enemy has a munitions factory located in a city. The only way to destroy the factory is through a series of missile launches, but the missiles are not 100 percent accurate and some will probably hit a nearby nursing home and apartment complex, thus killing and injuring civilians. Do you launch the missiles?

Consider this. What is your intention? What are your options? What if the factory was making chemical or biological weapons that would most likely be used on your troops in battle? What if there was a risk that in destroying the factory a cloud of chemical dust would kill thousands of civilians in the city and neighboring towns? What percentage of accuracy would you consider necessary for you to order the strike (25 percent, 50 percent, 75 percent, 100 percent)? What is an "acceptable" loss of civilian life? What if the weapons might be used in a terrorist attack against civilians?

Case 2

During a military campaign in Afghanistan, you discover a cell of ten to fifteen terrorists is operating in a remote town (population ten thousand) that is only accessible by a bridge over a large river.

The Principle of Double Effect *(continued)*

The only way you can ensure the capture of these terrorists is to bomb the bridge and trap them in the town and then send in commandos by air drop. Even if the mission is a success, however, the civilians in the town will be cut off from all food, medicine, and fuel for the entire winter, and many will die, starving or freezing to death. If bombed, the bridge will take months to rebuild. Relocating the entire town is not an option, nor is providing the innocent civilians with food, fuel, and medical supplies for the entire winter. Do you carry out the mission?

Consider this. What if this was a village with a population of only one thousand? What if this was a city with a population of one hundred thousand? What if intelligence reports indicated that these particular terrorists were either (1) responsible for an attack that killed one hundred fifty civilians from your country or (2) were planning an attack in the next year on your own civilians that could result in one thousand or more deaths?

primarily based in agriculture. In contrast, the Modern Period was marked by political, economic, social, and religious upheaval. On the political front, nationalism was emerging along with ideas of democratic rule that challenged traditional feudal society. This was also the period of the "discovery" of the New World and a time of expansion for many European nations into the colonies in the Americas. Economically there was a transition toward capitalism with the emergence of national economies, modern banking, insurance companies, investment opportunities, several technological advances in transportation and communication, and a growing middle class whose economic and political power was not based on land or inherited title but on profit making through business enterprises, including opportunities in the New World. Socially the humanist movement emerged, which emphasized freedom of thought, rational inquiry, the scientific method, and study of ancient texts (especially ancient Greek and Roman philosophers and the Bible), with a deep suspicion for arguments based on authority and religious superstition. Religiously there was the Reformation (1517–1648). This movement began with Martin Luther's challenge to the Roman Catholic theology of grace and reconciliation (as well as the practice of selling indulgences) and was fueled by a growing sense of national identity and the humanist emphasis on freedom of inquiry and individual thought, as well as by the Renaissance. The result of this upheaval was a schism within the European Christian church, with Europe divided between Catholic and Protestant Christians. These factors combined to produce one of the most tumultuous periods in European history, involving social, political, economic, and religious turmoil, including the bloody Thirty Years' War (1618–1648).

Despite their vehement debate over many core Christian doctrines (such as the authority of Scripture, clerical authority, grace and redemption, Eucharist, and baptism), Martin Luther, John Calvin, and most of the Protestant reformers accepted a just war theory similar to Augustine's. They saw war as part of the secular authority's right to rule. The peace churches of the Anabaptist tradition (Mennonites and Church of the Brethren, plus the Quakers later in the 1600s) were the obvious exception (see chapter 2). The Protestant Reformation strengthened the just war position within Christianity. The concept of a just war was not simply incorporated into Protestant theology; it was elevated to a place of prominence. As John Howard Yoder summarizes, "The Protestant Reformation took what was previously an exceptional concession made to the sovereign and his employees and made it the norm for all citizens."[16] The reformers relied heavily on state support, which resulted in a symbiotic relationship between church and state. The state (princes and the emerging concept of national sovereignty) sanctioned or protected the emerging Protestant churches, and the churches blessed the state, vesting it with moral legitimacy. Luther, for example, endorsed the use of force against the Peasant Revolt by relying heavily (almost exclusively) on Romans 13:1–7 (see "Christianity and Political Power" pp. 163–64).

In this context, the just war theory was refined to meet changing circumstances. Francisco de Vitoria (about 1486–1546), a Spanish Dominican priest, defended the rights of Native Americans against those who believed they were less human and less worthy of respect since they were neither European nor Christian. He argued for an early version of international law that fit well with the emerging nation-state model of governance: noncombatant immunity. That is, it is immoral and illegal for soldiers to intentionally kill civilians, and when conducting military operations soldiers must make efforts to ensure civilians are not harmed. Vitoria also made cases for the proportionate (restrained) use of force and against using religion as a justification for war.

Francisco Suárez (1548–1617), a Spanish Jesuit, studied Vitoria. Suárez was an early theorist of international law, which he saw as largely based in custom and different from the natural law, and he contributed to just war theory with a high degree of sophistication through nuance. In his *The Three Theological Virtues: Charity*, Suárez argued that war is not intrinsically evil and may at times even be required. This is true not only in cases of national defense, he said, but also at times in wars of aggression "in order to ward off acts of injustice and to hold enemies in check"[17] and as a form of neighbor-love—but only when the following criteria are met:

1. *Legitimate authority:* For war, Suárez required the supreme authority of the state.

2. *Just cause:* Suárez expanded this principle to include seizure of property by another head of state, interruption of trade and travel, injury done to reputation or honor and in the name of restitution and reparations. He also included as just cause defense of the weak or what today is commonly termed humanitarian intervention. He cautioned, however, that not all injuries done to a state constitute just cause and that waging war in the name of religion is not a just cause.

3. *Macro-proportionality:* The sovereign must consider the big picture, including costs of war on his own subjects for whom he is responsible.

4. *Probability of success:* Suárez admitted the difficulty in determining this with certainty.

Concerning *in bello* criteria, Suárez expanded on the traditional categories of micro-proportionality (by counseling the use of force ought to be restrained to the least necessary) and noncombatant immunity. Finally, Suárez also addressed a number of *jus post bellum* concerns such as compensation, the taking of war booty, execution of war criminals, and punishment of civilians from aggressor nations.

Hugo Grotius (1583–1645) is considered the "father of international law." A Dutch Protestant lawyer, he placed the Christian ideas of divine law and natural law in conversation with international relations (treaties, agreements, different national laws) to form a coherent body of international law. He defended the idea of the nation-state and argued for democratic rule and restrictions on governmental power. Writing in the context of the bloody Thirty Years' War in his greatest work, *On the Law of War and Peace*, he observed:

> Throughout the Christian world I observed a lack of restraint in relation to war, such as even barbarous races should be ashamed of. Men rush to arms for slight causes, or no cause at all, and when arms have once been taken up there is no longer any respect for law, divine or human, as if, in accordance with a general decree, frenzy had openly been let loose for the committing of all crimes.[18]

Grotius went on to argue that war can be justified according to the natural law when it is waged in self-defense, for restitution (compensation for injury), or for punishment of wrongdoing, but he adds that war has rules that all sides must obey. His distinction between when it is or is not acceptable to go to war and what is right conduct in battle became the two overarching categories of just war theory: *jus ad bellum* and *jus in bello*.

THE TWENTIETH CENTURY

The just war tradition enjoyed nearly unquestioned support within the Catholic and Protestant churches and remained fairly static from the time of the Reformation up until the twentieth century, when the pacifist movement regained some strength and began to challenge the just war theory's place of dominance in Christian thinking about war (see chapter 2).

Pius XI: Pope Pius XI (1857–1939; pope, 1922–1939) departed from his predecessors who, in the tradition of Augustine, had a strong bias in favor of social order, often seeming to equate peace with order. He faced a world in which communism and right-wing fascism posed serious threats. In Mexico, a socialist regime began an anticlerical campaign. Pius XI responded in his encyclical *On the Religious Situation in Mexico* (1937) by declaring that one could make a case for overthrowing unjust government, in a manner similar to Aquinas's argument for insurrection.

> It is quite natural that when the most elementary religious and civil liberties are attacked, Catholic citizens do not resign themselves passively to renouncing those liberties. Notwithstanding, the revindication of these rights and liberties can be, according to the circumstances, more or less opportune, more or less energetic. . . . The Church protects peace and order, even at the cost of grave sacrifices. . . . It condemns every unjust insurrection or violence against constituted powers. On the other hand, among you it has also been said that, whenever these powers arise against justice and truth even to destroying the very foundations of authority, it is not to be seen how those citizens are to be condemned who unite to defend themselves and the nation, by licit and appropriate means, against those who make use of public power to bring it to ruin. (nos. 26–27)

In other words, the use of force can be justified in the face of an unjust government if it is "licit and appropriate." Catholics have a just cause to defend their rights "with all legitimate means according as the common good requires" (no. 28). He then lists "some general principles, always to be kept in mind" when resorting

FRANZ JÄGERSTÄTTER

Franz Jägerstätter (1907–1943) provides a compelling example of just war thinking. Jägerstätter, an Austrian Catholic and father of three, refused service in the German Third Reich because he thought its military aims were unjust. Citing his conscience and going against the advice of priests and bishops, he accepted imprisonment and later death by beheading instead of participating in an unjust war on the grounds that it was better to lose one's life in order to gain eternal life than to put one's salvation at risk by denying one's conscience and cooperating with evil.

to such means, including: right intention (vengeance cannot be an end in itself); the good expected to result from insurrection must be better than conditions under the current regime, and the response cannot include intrinsically evil acts.

Pius XII: In the wake of World War II, Pope Pius XII (1876–1958; pope, 1939–1958) further modified Catholic just war theory by declaring all wars of aggression or expansion to be unjust and claiming that the "just cause" principle is limited only to wars of self-defense. Thus, wars for punishment, redress, or restitution were no longer considered just causes.

John XXIII: Pope John XXIII (1881–1963; pope, 1958–1963) is often credited with reviving the pacifist tradition within mainstream Catholicism and especially the Magisterium with his encyclical *Peace on Earth* (1963). John XXIII was keenly aware that in less than fifty years, Europe had seen a new era in warfare: two world wars (with a death toll that is estimated to be between fifty and seventy million people); the rise of fascism in Italy, Germany, and Spain; a genocide that claimed between six and eleven million people; and the advent of nuclear weapons. In his opinion, the world had entered a new epoch of both tremendous peril and promise.

Regarding the just war tradition, what is significant about *Peace on Earth* is not what John XXIII said, but what he did not say. There is no mention of just war theory at all in the document, including the right to self-defense. In a form of benign rejection, the beloved pope simply ignored just war theory. He didn't repudiate it (which would put him at odds with centuries of tradition); he simply abandoned it, as if to say that in an age of weapons of tremendous destructive capacity, the just war theory was simply no longer viable.

After decrying the "terrifying destructive force of modern weapons," John XXIII writes, "In this age which boasts of its atomic power, it no longer makes sense to maintain that war is a fit instrument with which to repair the violation of justice" (*Peace on Earth*, no. 127). He marks a new era in Church teaching on war. He calls into question the very legitimacy of just war thinking in an era of weapons of mass destruction (WMDs), but at the same time he does not go so far as to explicitly endorse pacifism either.

Vatican II: The Second Vatican Council distilled centuries of just war thinking into a coherent position. Writing in the midst of the Cold War between the two behemoths (the United States and Soviet Union), the Council began its teaching on war by noting, "Peace is more than the absence of war; it cannot be reduced to the maintenance of a balance of power between opposing forces nor does it arise out of a despotic dominion (*The Church in the Modern World*, no. 78)." In the tradition of Augustine, the Council declared that peace is related to order, calling it "the fruit of that right ordering of things." They tempered this with a dose of realism and hope:

> Peace will never be achieved once and for all, but must be built up continually. Since, moreover, human nature is weak and wounded by sin, the achievement of peace requires a constant effort to control the passions and unceasing vigilance by lawful authority. . . . Insofar as men are sinners, the threat of war hangs over them and will continue until the coming of Christ; but insofar as they can vanquish sin by coming together in

charity, violence will [ultimately] be vanquished. (*The Church in the Modern World*, no. 78)

But the "peace as order" of which they speak is not order at any cost. It is a just peace that respects the rights of all and earnestly seeks the common good. The Council reiterated just war teachings, including that war is a legitimate option only after peaceful attempts at conflict resolution have failed, that self-defense is a legitimate just cause, and that legitimate authority bears responsibility for declaring a war.

They also took seriously Pope John XXIII's challenge to "undertake a completely fresh reappraisal of war" in light of modern scientific developments, which have "immeasurably magnified the horrors and wickedness of war" (*The Church in the Modern World*, no. 80. In particularly strong language, they condemned indiscriminate and disproportionate uses of force wrought by modern warfare. "Every act of war directed to the indiscriminate destruction of whole cities or vast areas with their inhabitants is a crime against God and man, which merits firm and unequivocal condemnation" (no. 80). The Council also addressed other issues: it strongly condemned genocide, called for allowing conscientious objection, cautioned that the mere "possession of war potential does not justify the use of force for political or military objectives" (no. 79), and denounced the arms race as "one of the greatest curses on the human race" (no. 81).

Paul VI: Pope Paul VI (1897–1978; pope, 1963–1978) helped solidify the renewed interest in pacifism within the Catholic Church, but he did not reject just war theory. Paul VI tempered his optimism for peacemaking with a dose of realism and explored the connection between war and development by interpreting the vast sums of money spent on national defense as a form of theft from the poor. In his famous 1965 address to the U.N. General Assembly, he cried out:

No more war, war never again. . . . If you wish to be brothers, let the weapons fall from your hands. One cannot love with offensive weapons in hand. Those weapons, especially those terrible weapons that modern science has given you . . . demand enormous expenditures; they obstruct projects of solidarity and useful work. . . . As long as man remains that weak, changeable and even wicked being that he often shows himself to be, defensive arms will, unfortunately, be necessary. As for you, however, your courage and your work impel you to study ways of guaranteeing the security of international life without recourse to arms.[19]

Despite this heartfelt plea for peace, he felt it necessary to declare defensive arms an unfortunate necessity. Paul VI shared John XXIII's optimism that the twentieth century could be a time of tremendous development and prosperity for humankind, especially the poor, but he saw the arms race as one of the chief obstacles to eradicating global poverty, a sentiment best expressed in two of his most famous quotations: "If you want peace, work for justice" and "Development is the new name for peace."[20]

PEACE AND SOCIAL INEQUALITY

Pope Paul VI had a deep concern for the needs of the world's poor and a sophisticated understanding of global political and economic relations. He stressed the link between war and poverty as evidenced in his 1967 encyclical on social and economic development:

Excessive economic, social, and cultural inequalities among peoples arouse tensions and conflicts, and are a danger to peace. . . . Peace cannot be limited to a mere absence of war, the result of an ever precarious balance of forces. No, peace is something that is built up day after day, in the pursuit of an order intended by God, which implies a more perfect form of justice among men. (*On the Development of Peoples*, no. 76)

John Paul II: Pope John Paul II (1920–2005; pope, 1978–2005) served as pope during a period of tremendous social, political, and economic upheaval that included the end of the Cold War, the fall of Soviet communism, and the most recent wave of economic globalization. He wrote fourteen encyclicals, but none were devoted to the topic of war and peace. Instead, John Paul II chose to advance his understanding of the Church's teaching on war primarily through

Pope John Paul II

his World Day for Peace messages, which he delivered every New Year's Day. John Paul II advocated a restrictive interpretation of just war theory. He linked peace to defense of human rights and economic development in a manner similar to Paul VI and demonstrated a strong support for pacifism similar to John XXIII. He injected realism into his affinity for nonviolence in a thoroughly theological manner:

> Christian optimism, based on the glorious Cross of Christ and the outpouring of the Holy Spirit, is no excuse for self-deception. For Christians, peace on earth is always a challenge, because of the presence of sin in man's heart. . . . Although Christians put all their best energies into preventing war or stopping it, they do not deceive themselves about their ability to cause peace to triumph, nor about the effect of their efforts to this end. They therefore concern themselves with all human initiatives in favour of peace and very often take part in them; but they regard them with realism and humility. . . . Christians know that in this world a totally and permanently peaceful human society is

unfortunately a utopia, and that ideologies that hold up that prospect as easily attainable are based on hopes that cannot be realized, whatever the reason behind them. It is a question of a mistaken view of the human condition, a lack of application in considering the question as a whole. . . . But this realistic view in no way prevents Christians from working for peace; instead, it stirs up their ardour, for they also know that Christ's victory over deception, hate and death gives those in love with peace a more decisive motive for action than what the most generous theories about man have to offer; Christ's victory likewise gives a hope more surely based than any hope held out by the most audacious dreams.

This is why Christians, even as they strive to resist and prevent every form of warfare, have no hesitation in recalling that, in the name of an elementary requirement of justice, peoples have a right and even a duty to protect their existence and freedom by proportionate means against an unjust aggressor.[21]

He adds a crucial caveat to his endorsement of the right to self-defense.

However, in view of the difference between classical warfare and nuclear or bacteriological war, a difference so to speak of nature, and in view of the scandal of the arms race seen against the background of the needs of the Third World, this right, which is very real in principle, only underlines the urgency for world society to equip itself with effective means of negotiation. In this way the nuclear terror that haunts our time can encourage us to enrich our common heritage with a very simple discovery that is within our reach, namely that war is the most barbarous and least effective way of resolving conflicts. More than ever before, human society is forced to provide itself with the means of consultation and dialogue which it needs in order to survive, and therefore with the institutions necessary for building up justice and peace.

May it also realize that this work is something beyond human powers![22]

Like John XXIII and Paul VI, John Paul II saw the destructive nature of modern weaponry as posing a serious challenge to just war thinking. He was willing to admit that conventional warfare might be justified under certain circumstances, but for him, the possibility that biological, chemical, or nuclear weapons might be used automatically makes war a disproportionate and indiscriminate option to conflict resolution.

John Paul II's optimism for peace is not based on human efforts, but on the triumph of the cross. In a manner similar to the Hebrew prophets and Augustine, he sees true and lasting peace as a gift from God. He is wary of human claims to bring peace because human sinfulness (selfishness, greed, pride, desire for revenge) always makes human attempts at peace temporary and incomplete. In this, John Paul II echoes the concept of Christian eschatological hope (see chapter 2). True peace will come when Christ returns to earth and fully establishes the Reign of God.

U.S. Conference of Catholic Bishops: After the Second Vatican Council, many national councils of bishops worked to implement the teachings of Vatican II. The U.S. Conference of Catholic Bishops issued a pastoral letter on peace in 1983.[23] *The Challenge of Peace* addressed the unique American Catholic

JOHN PAUL II: "WE ARE NOT PACIFISTS"

Pope John Paul II made the following impromptu remark outside of Saint Dorothy Parish in Rome on February 17, 1991. While far from an official statement or doctrine, it reflects his theology of war and peace:

> We are not pacifists, we do not want peace at any cost. A just peace. Peace and justice. Peace is always the work of justice. . . . But on the other hand it is also the fruit of charity and love. We cannot achieve peace except through love.[24]

position on peacemaking and war. While we have already addressed how pacifism enjoyed a revival during this period and how *The Challenge of Peace* defends pacifism as a legitimate approach, the pastoral also went to great lengths to defend the just war theory alongside pacifism:

> Catholic teaching sees these two distinct moral responses as having a complementary relationship, in the sense that both seek to serve the common good. They differ in their perception of how the common good is to be defended most effectively. (*The Challenge of Peace*, no. 74)

> While the just-war teaching has clearly been in possession for the past 1,500 years of Catholic thought, the "new moment" in which we find ourselves sees the just-war teaching and non-violence as distinct but interdependent methods of evaluating warfare. They diverge on some specific conclusions, but they share a common presumption against the use of force as a means of settling disputes.
>
> Both find their roots in the Christian theological tradition; each contributes to the full moral vision we need in pursuit of a human peace. We believe the two perspectives support and complement one another, each preserving the other from distortion. (*The Challenge of Peace*, nos. 120–121)

The Challenge of Peace represents the mainstream post–Vatican II Catholic position on war and peace: both pacifism and just war are legitimate approaches. But this begs the question: How can the Church defend both positions? Isn't it hypocritical to claim that violence is unjustified and that there is such a thing as a just war? The bishops readily admit this seeming contradiction:

> We believe work to develop non-violent means of fending off aggression and resolving conflict best reflects the call of Jesus both to love and to justice. . . . But, on the other hand, the fact of aggression, oppression, and injustice in our world also serves to legitimate the resort to weapons and armed force in defense of justice. (*The Challenge of Peace*, no. 78)

The bishops rationalize the legitimacy of both approaches to conflict resolution by reducing the differences between pacifism and just war to a disagreement about the best means to the same goal — peace. Pacifists and just war theorists seek the same end *(telos)*; they disagree on what is the best way to achieve it.

The bishops are able to defend both positions as "complementary" by interpreting the criteria of the just war theory as a set of rigorous conditions that must be met if the decision to go to war is to be morally permissible. "Such a decision, especially today, requires extraordinarily strong reasons for overriding the presumption *in favor of peace* and *against* war" (*The Challenge of Peace*, no. 83; emphasis in original). The bishops do this by conservatively interpreting the "just cause" and "last resort" principles and by insisting that all the criteria of the just war theory must be met before a war can be called just. They reiterate the right to self-defense, but go on to limit just cause. "War is permissible only to confront 'a real and certain danger,' i.e., to protect innocent life, to preserve conditions necessary for decent human existence, and to secure basic human rights" (*The Challenge of Peace*, no. 86).

They also introduce a seventh criterion to the *jus ad bellum* category — *comparative justice*:

> Questions concerning the *means* of waging war today, particularly in view of the destructive potential of weapons, have tended to override questions concerning the comparative justice of the positions of respective adversaries or enemies. In essence: which side is sufficiently "right" in a dispute, and are the values at stake critical enough to override the presumption against war? The question in its basic form is this: do the rights and values involved justify killing? . . . The category of comparative justice is designed to emphasize the presumption against war which stands at the beginning of just-war teaching. . . . comparative justice stresses that no state should act on the basis that it has "absolute justice" on its side. Every party to a conflict should acknowledge the limits of its "just cause" and the consequent requirement to use only limited means in pursuit of its objectives. (*The Challenge of Peace*, nos. 92–93; emphasis in original)

The comparative justice principle makes a key but subtle distinction; nevertheless, it has largely been absorbed into the macro-proportionality and just cause criteria in most contemporary versions of the just war theory.

The introduction of comparative justice, along with a rigorous interpretation of the other criteria, signal a shift in the interpretation of Catholic just war doctrine. Some have labeled this as a shift away from "The Classical Just War Tradition" toward "The Contemporary Just War Tradition."[25] The difference between the two traditions centers primarily on the interpretation of just cause and last resort. Contemporary just war thinkers are closer to pacifism. They believe the destructive nature of modern weaponry, including WMDs, renders the recourse to force as a rare option and thus places "last resort" as the primary criterion. They also limit just cause to legitimate defense and reinterpret legitimate authority to include international authorization (for example, by the United Nations). Classical just war theorists have a broader interpretation of just cause (legitimate defense, restitution, redress, and punishment) and see legitimate authority as primarily resting with the leadership of nation-states (for example, a congress, parliament, president, king). This shift toward the contemporary just war tradition within Catholicism began with John XXIII's *Peace on Earth*, the Second Vatican Council's teaching on war, the U.S. bishops' *The Challenge of Peace*, and Pope John Paul II's teachings on war.

Contemporary just war thinking finds its clearest articulation in the *Catechism of the Catholic Church*, which defends the right to legitimate defense as a just cause, but cautions "The strict conditions for *legitimate defense by military force* require rigorous consideration. The gravity of such a decision makes it subject to rigorous considerations of moral legitimacy" (*Catechism*, no. 2309; emphasis in original). The *Catechism* identifies these considerations as the traditional *ad bellum* criteria (macro-proportionality, last resort, probability of success, and comparative justice in no. 2309; and legitimate authority in nos. 2310, 2311, and 2239) and *in bello* criteria (discrimination in no. 2313 and proportionality in no. 2314), as well as a condemnation of arms races (nos. 2315–2317).

CATECHISM OF THE CATHOLIC CHURCH ON JUST WAR

2309 The strict conditions for *legitimate defense by military force* require rigorous consideration. The gravity of such a decision makes it subject to rigorous conditions of moral legitimacy. At one and the same time:

- the damage inflicted by the aggressor on the nation or community of nations must be lasting, grave, and certain;
- all other means of putting an end to it must have been shown to be impractical or ineffective;
- there must be serious prospects of success;
- the use of arms must not produce evils and disorders graver than the evil to be eliminated. The power of modern means of destruction weighs very heavily in evaluating this condition.

These are the traditional elements enumerated in what is called the "just war" doctrine.

The evaluation of these conditions for moral legitimacy belongs to the prudential judgment of those who have responsibility for the common good.

2310 Public authorities, in this case, have the right and duty to impose on citizens the *obligations necessary for national defense.*

Those who are sworn to serve their country in the armed forces are servants of the security and freedom of nations. If they carry out their duty honorably, they truly contribute to the common good of the nation and the maintenance of peace.

2313 Noncombatants, wounded soldiers, and prisoners must be respected and treated humanely.

Actions deliberately contrary to the law of nations and to its universal principles are crimes, as are the orders that command such actions. Blind obedience does not suffice to excuse those who carry them out. Thus the extermination of a people, nation, or ethnic minority must be condemned as a mortal sin. One is morally bound to resist orders that command genocide.

Catechism on Just War *(continued)*

2314 "Every act of war directed to the indiscriminate destruction of whole cities or vast areas with their inhabitants is a crime against God and man, which merits firm and unequivocal condemnation" [*The Church in the Modern World*, no. 80]. A danger of modern warfare is that it provides the opportunity to those who possess modern scientific weapons—especially atomic, biological, or chemical weapons—to commit such crimes.

2315 The *accumulation of arms* strikes many as a paradoxically suitable way of deterring potential adversaries from war. They see it as the most effective means of ensuring peace among nations. This method of deterrence gives rise to strong moral reservations. The *arms race* does not ensure peace. Far from eliminating the causes of war, it risks aggravating them. Spending enormous sums to produce ever new types of weapons impedes efforts to aid needy populations; it thwarts the development of peoples. *Over-armament* multiplies reasons for conflict and increases the danger of escalation.

2316 *The production and the sale of arms* affect the common good of nations and of the international community. Hence public authorities have the right and duty to regulate them. The short-term pursuit of private or collective interests cannot legitimate undertakings that promote violence and conflict among nations and compromise the international juridical order.

SUMMARY

A remarkable shift in Catholic teaching on war and peace has happened since World War II. Beginning with John XXIII, the place of prominence of just war thinking within the Church's teaching has been called into question. All popes since John XXIII, along with numerous national conferences of bishops, have established pacifism as an ethically valid approach to conflict resolution. Several factors have contributed to this development:

- the increasing destructive and indiscriminate nature of modern weaponry (chemical and biological)

- the horrific bloodshed of the last century, particularly in Europe
- the advent of the Cold War and the very real prospect of planetary annihilation due to nuclear weapons and
- a renewed interest in biblical studies and in early Christianity, prompted by Vatican II's call for the Church to renew itself by looking to those centuries as normative, a time when pacifism was seen as the appropriate response to conflict

Having outlined the just war *tradition*, we now turn our attention to the just war *theory* itself by exploring each criterion and the strengths and weaknesses of each.

THE JUST WAR THEORY

The just war theory's (JWT) division of its criteria into two principal categories—*jus ad bellum* (when is it permissible to go to war?) and *jus in bello* (what is right behavior in battle?)—enjoys near universal recognition. The criteria are to be conservatively or restrictively interpreted. *All six must be fully met before a war can be declared justified.* Failure to meet all six criteria constitutes an act of aggression or what the Nuremburg prosecutors called a "crime against peace."

JUS AD BELLUM

The six *jus ad bellum* criteria are:

1. ***Just Cause:*** War is legitimate if it is waged in self-defense (response to an act of aggression), to protect the innocent (defending others from aggression), in defense of human rights, or to regain what has been wrongfully seized (restitution) or withheld (redress). By the very act of unjust aggression (using force to violate the rights of another), states forfeit their right to peace; by invading another country or violating the rights of its own citizens, the state gives up its claims to sovereignty.

   - Critique: While in theory all six *ad bellum* criteria have to be met before a war can be considered just, in practice the just cause principle reigns supreme. Political rhetoric and popular opinion often reduce the entire JWT to the just cause principle. This has led critics of the JWT to claim that it serves as a rationalization or moral "cover story" for the rush to war. Political leaders often decide to go to war for self-serving interests (*Realpolitik*) and then craft their rationalization for waging war by using the JWT to make their political moves appear altruistic. This has led many to claim that the mere existence of a JWT provides a justification for the use of violence and may actually contribute to war. As Professor Susan Thistlethwaith observes:

> It is inevitable that the existence of a set of criteria for considering whether war is just under any circumstance will offer ample opportunities for human beings who wish to wage war to rationalize their reasons for doing so are just. This is demonstrably the way the just war theory has functioned in human history. No war has been just by all the criteria of the just war theory during the whole of a conflict; every war has been called a just war by the leaders on both sides of the conflict. It is certainly worth considering then whether the existence of just war theory . . . is itself one of the reasons Western culture has so readily accepted war as one of its social mores.[26]

The JWT assumes we live in a sinful and violent world, and thus it never fully explores alternative ways for resolving conflict. It limits our imagination by presuming nonviolent conflict resolution is impractical.

Furthermore, the judgments about what is or is not a just cause often depend on one's vantage point. What looks like a just cause to one may look like an act of aggression to another. Finally, there is considerable debate about whether a preventative war or preemptive war can be justified under just cause, as well as whether a state is justified in violating the territory of another state in the name of humanitarian intervention (such as to stop a government-led genocide). We will address preventative and preemptive war and humanitarian interventions in the following chapter.

2. *Legitimate (or Competent) Authority and Public Declaration:* The use of force is permissible if a legitimate political authority (a congress, parliament, president, king, depending on the law of the nation-state) engages in due process and publicly declares their intention to go to war. This principle concerns the process of declaring war.

- Critique: Who is the competent or legitimate authority? What about political rulers who are tyrants or aggressive megalomaniacs? What about civil war—who is the competent authority when a large portion of the population wants to overthrow the government or secede? While Aquinas allowed for insurrection against a tyrannical king, because he saw the role of sovereign tied to the common good (a king who is a tyrant forfeits his right to rule), Augustine saw the ruler's power as absolute. Augustine also operated under a much different political system than we have today. In most countries today, laws explicitly state the rules governing who can declare war. (Not that having such laws is without complications. For example, in the United States, Congress has not issued a formal declaration of war since 1942, yet the United States has fought in the Korean, Vietnam, and two Gulf wars since that date, as well as other smaller conflicts.) Finally, the fact that all wars have global ramifications forces the question, "Who is the legitimate authority?" Must a nation get permission from the United Nations or a coalition of other states to go to war, or can nations go to war unilaterally and still be justified? The highest form of public authority in our world today is the nation-state, which leaves the area of international relations in a state of anarchy, although not chaos. While there exists no global government per se (the United Nations does not have sovereignty over nation-states), there is a growing body of international law, countless treaties, and other global regulatory bodies.

3. **Right Intention:** The only just motives for waging war are those prescribed by the just cause principle. For Augustine, peace was the only right intention that could justify what would normally be considered a sin. Ulterior motives (revenge, geopolitical power plays, seizure of natural resources, hatred) cannot be rationalized under the JWT.

- Critique: This principle is far too subjective, as it addresses an interior disposition. How can one evaluate the intent of a state? For this reason, international law excludes talk of intention.

4. **Last Resort:** All reasonable peaceful alternatives to war must be fully exhausted before going to war. In many respects, this principle should be listed first. The *jus ad bellum* criteria apply only when "all other means" of putting an end to conflict "have been shown to be impractical or ineffective" (*Catechism*, no. 2309). Diplomacy, sanctions, third-party negotiations, and other peaceful means must fail before a state can resort to war. This reflects the serious and regrettable nature of warfare.

- Critique: This principle is often derided as being vague. How does one know when *all reasonable* means have proven *impractical* or *ineffective*? Certainly one can always go back to the negotiating table "one more time," yet strategically this might prove perilous because it gives one's enemy time to prepare for battle and, in the long run, may result in more casualties. Military success often depends on quick action. At the time of the 2003 U.S. invasion of Iraq, for example, President Bush was criticized for rushing to war and not allowing diplomacy to work. His response was that twelve years of U.N. sanctions against Iraq had proven impractical and ineffective. Others, however, argued that negotiations ought to continue, especially since international inspectors were still working to locate any WMDs.

5. *Probability of Success:* A war cannot be considered just if it will have no positive influence on the situation. Here the intent is to prevent futile conflict, such as occurs when one side has a substantial advantage or when engaging in conflict is the equivalent of mass suicide. The probability of success criterion also prohibits engaging in wars that will be protracted.

- Critique: This requirement is biased against smaller states. In a world of military and economic superpowers (such as the United States, China, Russia, and England), this principle essentially prohibits less powerful nations from ever resorting to armed force, thereby reducing their ability to negotiate on equal footing with the superpowers. It's a bully principle that smothers the national sovereignty of smaller nations. Only the strong have recourse to war. Weaker nations must submit to the powerful because they can never succeed militarily.

6. *Macro-proportionality:* The damage inflicted and costs incurred by going to war must be proportionate to the good expected to come from it. In other words, the war has to be worth the cost in terms of lives lost and damage done to people, the environment, and infrastructure. The benefits that result from defeating the aggressor must proportionally outweigh the inherent evils of war.

- Critique: It is impossible to forecast the outcomes of any war, therefore it is impossible to accurately measure whether a war is truly "worth it." For example, the 2003 U.S. invasion of Iraq was "justified" by some in the Bush administration by claiming that once Saddam Hussein was deposed, the U.S. soldiers would be welcomed as liberators and a new democratic regime would rise to power. Instead, a protracted war ensued, involving insurgents, sectarian religious conflict, criminal behavior, local power struggles, and al-Qaeda violence and claiming tens of thousands of civilian lives as well as thousands of military deaths and casualties.

JUS IN BELLO

The *jus in bello* category of the JWT concerns ethical behavior in combat. These "rules of war" enjoy international legal status in a host of war conventions (for example, the Geneva Convention) that address such things as treatment of prisoners of war, surrender in battle, and what are legitimate and illegitimate targets. Whereas responsibility for adhering to the *jus ad bellum* criteria falls to political leaders, responsibility for *jus in bello* criteria belongs to military leaders, commanding officers, and soldiers. Christianity has traditionally identified two basic *in bello* criteria: discrimination and micro-proportionality. But these two categories do not sufficiently cover all the *in bello* requirements of the JWT. Brian Orend offers a more nuanced parsing of *jus in bello* standards:[27]

1. *Discrimination (or Noncombatant Immunity):* The discrimination principle is about distinguishing between soldiers (combatants) and civilians (noncombatants), who have different status in war. While civilians have a right to life (and therefore a right not to be deliberately targeted), soldiers, because they are armed and in battle for the purpose of killing an enemy, have surrendered their right to life either voluntarily (by enlisting) or involuntarily (by conscription or draft). In surrendering their right not to be killed, they have gained the right to kill.[28] As Augustine noted centuries ago, however, the intentional targeting of civilians is never justified and is rightly condemned as murder. While civilian casualties are probably inevitable, this principle hinges on intentionality (motive).

    -   Critique: There are two main questions regarding the combatant and noncombatant distinction. First, many of the traditional rules of war were developed at a time when chivalry codes and concepts of honor governed warfare or were written with conventional warfare in mind. In conventional warfare, armies line up against each other, wearing uniforms. But as the U.S. involvement in Vietnam and in Iraq illustrates, it is difficult to distinguish between combatants and noncombatants when the enemy engages in guerilla warfare or terrorism. In guerilla warfare and terrorism, combatants can include children, the elderly, and women who hide among the civilian population, not wearing uniforms that readily identify them. This difficulty in identifying combatants can lead to a large number of civilian deaths. We address how guerilla warfare and terrorism challenge the JWT in more detail in the following chapter.

The second critique stems from the question, "Does the nature of modern weaponry render the discrimination criterion useless?" Nearly every war in the last hundred years has had more civilian casualties than military casualties. This is due to developments in warfare technology. Weapons today are simply far more potent than they were a century ago, and contemporary warfare is often fought at great distances (missiles launched from ships hundreds of miles away or bombs dropped from high altitude) instead of at close range (in hand-to-hand combat and trench warfare), as was the case prior to the Industrial Revolution. These civilian casualties are often dismissed as "collateral damage" (unintended or unforeseen injury and destruction that accompanies military action, often used as a euphemism to hide the fact that civilian casualties most often involve the death or dismemberment of children, women, and the elderly).

2. *Legitimate or Illegitimate Targets:* Just as soldiers must discriminate between soldiers and civilians, so too commanders in the field must distinguish between military targets and infrastructure necessary for life (water supplies, electrical grids, sewage treatment facilities, hospitals, crops, and so on). The deliberate targeting of such infrastructure can be justified

only if it is also used for military purposes. The principle of double effect is often invoked to justify targeting life-sustaining infrastructure.

- Critique: What about targets that are used by both the military and the civilian population? In both U.S. invasions of Iraq (1991 and 2003), the United States destroyed vital infrastructure such as power plants, sewage and water treatment facilities, and oil pipelines because the Iraqi military was using them to support their troops. However, destroying these vital facilities put the civilian population at serious risk. Water became contaminated, and civilians died from waterborne diseases; hospitals no longer had electricity to run operating rooms, dialysis machines, and other medical equipment; a lack of heating oil in the winter and air conditioning in the summer led to civilian deaths, especially among vulnerable populations like the elderly, the sick, and children.

3. *No Means* **Mala in se** *and Weapons of Mass Destruction:* Certain techniques and weapons are considered by their very nature or design to be *mala in se* (evil in themselves). For example, genocide, ethnic cleansing, and mass rape campaigns are patently unjust and can never be justified. While not all just war theorists reject the use of WMDs (such as nuclear, biological, and chemical weapons), they tend to harbor deep suspicions regarding the legitimate or justified use of WMDs precisely because such weapons fail to distinguish between soldiers and civilians. The morality of WMDs and other ordnance that exact heavy civilian casualties (such as land-mines and cluster bombs) will be addressed in detail in the next chapter.

- Critique: Prohibiting the use of certain weapons can seriously hamper a military's effectiveness and could conceivably prolong a war and lead to higher casualties. Forbidding an army to use such weapons to fight an enemy that has no qualms about using landmines or chemical weapons is akin to "fighting with one hand tied behind your back." Furthermore, some argue that the possession of such powerful and heinous weapons serves as a deterrent to some enemies (Why provoke an enemy that has a nuclear arsenal?) or can hasten the end of war because a vulnerable enemy will seek peace rather than risk annihilation. Others claim that a nation could possess WMDs as a deterrent while secretly remaining committed to never using them.

4. **Surrender and Prisoners of War:** While enemy soldiers are legitimate targets when they pose a threat, their status as combatants changes the moment they are captured or surrender. Michael Walzer succinctly summarized the position of prisoners of war (POWs):

> A soldier who surrenders enters into an agreement with his captors: he will stop fighting if they will accord him what the legal handbooks call "benevolent quarantine." . . . Prisoners of war have a right to escape—but if they kill a guard in order to escape, the killing is not an act of war; it is murder. For they committed themselves to stop fighting, gave up their right to kill when they surrendered.[29]

- Critique: What about situations where one cannot guarantee that prisoners will be held? The basic moral principle behind the war conventions is "do unto others as you would have them do unto you." Thus armies treat POWs humanely in the hope or expectation that their own soldiers, if captured, will also be treated humanely. But oftentimes the battlefront is chaotic, and the safe and secure capture of POWs cannot be guaranteed. An enemy soldier captured today could be liberated tomorrow and face you again the day after that. Or your army might be forced into a quick retreat and if you left the POWs behind, you would only be strengthening your enemy's force. In such circumstances, is it legitimate to execute prisoners? Is the idea that POWs have rights too idealistic?

5. *Micro-proportionality:* The use of military force must be proportionate to the objective. In other words, militaries must exercise restraint in their use of firepower. They can legitimately use only the amount of force necessary to achieve their objective. This principle is under constant review and reinterpretation due to advances in technology and the ever increasing potency of modern weaponry. This principle forbids all WMDs because they are by their very design disproportionate.

   - Critique: Some critics claim that the frighteningly destructive capacity of contemporary weapons and the mere existence of WMDs render all wars potentially disproportionate. The idea that combatants will show restraint and not use everything at their disposal, especially when they are vulnerable, is (some argue) naïve. We will address micro-proportionality in the following chapter.

CONCLUSION

At first blush the JWT looks deontological (rule-, law-, or duty-based). It is a collection of rules or norms that can be applied to a particular conflict. In fact, many people use the JWT deontologically. They take the principles and apply them to a particular case; if a war meets all six *ad bellum* principles it must be just. But some of the criteria (last resort, probability of success, and macro-proportionality) seem more consequentialist. They focus on outcomes and objectives. The JWT is best understood, however, as teleological theory tempered by realism. It defines peace as the desired end or goal *(telos)* of war and considers the intentions of those involved. It also takes circumstances or context into account. The greatest strength of the JWT is that it provides a vocabulary or set of key points to frame our conversation and ethical evaluation of warfare. Like the natural law tradition from which it emerged, the JWT does not yield definitive moral judgments that are beyond reproach. Instead, it offers a way to think and talk about war. It gives us a framework around which we can conduct our debate about war.

Often people challenge the JWT for being too theoretical. "This is great to sit around and philosophize about, but has the JWT ever actually had an impact?" they ask. This is a good and fair question. The short answer is, "Yes, it has." Concerning the *jus ad bellum* criteria, political leaders often use the language of the JWT to justify the use of military force. While they may abuse the theory and bend it to their own political objectives, nevertheless they feel compelled to employ the JWT criteria in making their case, which is a way of beginning the conversation. When a president declares that a war is just, this is not the end of the conversation, but the beginning of the debate. It is a proposition, a claim that must be tested. The effects of *jus in bello* criteria are also preeminently practical. They are apparent when soldiers and field commanders show restraint in the use of firepower, or when bomber pilots fly at low altitudes to ensure civilian targets are not hit (thereby placing themselves in greater danger from antiaircraft artillery). World War II was a watershed in the history of war. The carpet bombings of London and Dresden coupled with the nuclear attacks on Hiroshima and Nagasaki laid bare the awesome destructiveness of modern weaponry. Since that war, the analysis of proportionate use of force and discrimination have come to the forefront, which is why the JWT is studied, taught, and debated in military academies and military headquarters around the world.

Finally, one of the most remarkable features of the JWT has been its flexibility and longevity. It has been adapted and changed throughout the centuries in response to the changing technologies and methodologies of combat. Every new type of war or technological development forces a reevaluation of the JWT. While study of the ethics of war may seem abstract and theoretical in the safe haven of the classroom, it is not so. When we are asked as taxpayers and voters, not only as soldiers, to support a proposed or ongoing military venture, we must have a moral compass to guide us in the emotional and political "fog of war," which is often clouded by emotions such as fear, patriotism, and nationalism, as well as by political ideologies and economic interests.

WHERE DO YOU FALL?

Our exploration of Christian approaches to war and peace is presented as a continuum ranging from pacifism (the most "dovish") to holy war (the most "hawkish"). Return now to page 18 where the various approaches are displayed as an array. Based on your deeper understanding of the just war theory, where would you now place yourself on the continuum and why? In other words, how has encountering the ideas, arguments, or perspectives presented in this chapter caused you to reevaluate your own ethic of war and peace?

DISCUSSION QUESTIONS

1. What do you most respect about the JWT and why?

2. What do you least respect about the JWT and why?

3. In this chapter we outlined the *jus ad bellum* and *jus in bello* criteria and explored some of the critiques levied against each. Evaluate each criterion and critique. Do you think the criterion or critiques are valid or not, and why?

4. How might a pacifist respond to the JWT?

5. How might a political realist respond to the JWT?

6. How might a holy warrior respond to the JWT?

7. Are there any circumstances (or can you think of examples) when adhering to the JWT would require just as much sacrifice or moral commitment as pacifism?

8. Is it hypocritical for the Catholic Church to uphold both pacifism and the JWT as morally legitimate? Why or why not?

ENDNOTES

1 It should be noted that the Catholic Church has never formally declared just war theory to be official doctrine, although JWT is recognized as legitimate and has enjoyed a place of prominence for centuries. For examples, see *Catechism of the Catholic Church*, no. 2309 and nos. 2263–2267; Pontifical Council for Justice and Peace, *Compendium of the Social Doctrine of the Church* (U.S. Conference of Catholic Bishops Publishing, 2005), no. 500; U.S. Conference of Catholic Bishops, *The Challenge of Peace*, nos. 80–109, and *The Harvest of Justice Is Sown in Peace*, nos. 12–15.

2 John Howard Yoder, *When War is Unjust: Being Honest in Just-War Thinking* (Minneapolis, MN: Augsburg, 1984), 17.

3 Cicero, *De Republica* 3, trans. C. W. Keyes in the Loeb Classical Library (Cambridge: Harvard University Press, 1988), available in Arthur F. Holmes, ed., *War and Christian Ethics: Classic and Contemporary Readings on the Morality of War* (Grand Rapids, MI: Baker, 2005), 25.

4 Cicero, *De Officiis* I:11–12, trans. W. Miller in The Loeb Classical Library (Cambridge: Harvard University Press, 1913), available in Holmes, ed. *War and Christian Ethics*, 29–30.

5 Augustine, *City of God*, book 19, chap. 13, trans. Henry Bettenson (Harmondsworth, Eng.: Penguin, 1972, 1976), 870.

6 Augustine, *City of God*, book 19, chap. 12, ibid., 866.

7 "In fact one who owes a duty of obedience to the giver of the command does not himself 'kill'—he is an instrument, a sword in its user's hand" (Augustine, *City of God*, book 1, chap. 21, ibid.).

8 Augustine, *Against Faustus the Manichean*, book 22, chap. 70, trans. R. Stothert, *The Nicene and Post-Nicene Fathers*, vol. 4 (Peabody, MA: Hendrickson, 1994), 299, available in Robin Gill, A *Textbook of Christian Ethics* (Edinburgh: T & T Clark, 1995), 269–71.

9 Augustine, *Against Faustus the Manichean*, book 22, chap. 74, in Stothert, *The Nicene and Post-Nicene Fathers*, vol. 4, 69–76, available in Gill, *A Textbook of Christian Ethics*, 273.

10 Augustine, *City of God*, book 4, chap. 15, trans. Henry Bettenson (Harmondsworth, Eng.: Penguin, 1972, 1976), 154.

11 Augustine, *City of God*, book 19, chap. 7, ibid., 862.

12 See Thomas Aquinas, *Summa Theologica* II–II, question 64, article 7, available in Gregory Reichberg, Henrik Syse, and Endre Begby, eds. *The Ethics of War: Classical and Contemporary Readings* (Malden, MA: Blackwell, 2006), 191.

13 Thomas Aquinas, *Summa Theologica* II–II, question 40, article 1, trans. Blackfriars (English Dominicans), *Summa Theologica*, vol. 35

(New York: McGraw Hill, and London: Eyre & Spottiswoode, 1972), 81-83, edited by author; also available in Gill, *A Textbook of Christian Ethics*, 280–82.

14 See Aquinas, *Summa Theologica* II–II, question 42, article 2, ibid., 185–86.

15 Aquinas, *Summa Theologica* II–II, question 64, article 7, ibid., 190.

16 John Howard Yoder, *When War Is Unjust: Being Honest in Just-War Thinking* (Minneapolis, MN: Augsburg, 1984), 34.

17 Francisco Suárez, *The Three Theological Virtues: Charity* (disputation 13), trans. G. L. Williams, A. Brown, and J. Waldron, *Selections from Three Works of Francisco Suárez, SJ* (Oxford: Claredon Press, 1944); also available in Holmes, *War and Christian Ethics*, 201.

18 Hugo Grotius, *On the Law of War and Peace*, Prolegomena, 28, available in Reichberg, Syse, and Begby, *The Ethics of War*, 390, as emended from trans. Francis Kelsey, *The Classics of International Law*, no. 3, vol. 2 (Oxford: Clarendon Press, 1925).

19 Pope Paul VI's Address to United Nations General Assembly, October 4, 1965, available online at *www.christusrex.org/www1/pope/UN-1965.html*.

20 Pope Paul VI, 1972 World Day for Peace address, available at the Vatican Web page, *http://www.vatican.va/holy_father/paul_vi/messages/peace/index.htm*; and *The Development of Peoples* (*Populorum progressio*,1967, Vatican II), no. 87.

21 John Paul II, "Peace: A Gift of God Entrusted to Us!" 1982 World Day for Peace message, available from the Vatican Web page at *http://www.vatican.va/holy_father/john_paul_ii/messages/peace/index.htm*; and see *The Church in the Modern World*, 79.

22 John Paul II, 1982 World Day for Peace message.

23 On the tenth anniversary of *The Challenge of Peace*, the bishops issued an updated statement, *The Harvest of Justice Is Sown in Peace* (1993). It is similar to *The Challenge of Peace* except in its analysis of "current" affairs: it takes a more open stance on wars waged for humanitarian causes. This represents a shift away from the strong presumption against war found in *The Challenge of Peace*.

24 *Origins* 20 (February 21, 1991): 625.

25 See *Just War, Lasting Peace: What Christian Traditions Can Teach Us*, John Kleiderer, Paula Minaert, and Mark Mossa, eds. (Maryknoll, NY: Orbis Books, 2006).

26 Quoted in David Smock, *Religious Perspectives on War: Christian, Muslim and Jewish Attitudes Toward Force after the Gulf War* (Washington, DC: U.S. Institute for Peace Press, 1992), 37.

27 Brian Orend, "War," in *The Stanford Encyclopedia of Philosophy* (Winter 2005 Edition), ed. Edward N. Zalta; available online at *http://plato.stanford.edu/archives/win2005/entries/war/*. See also his *The Morality of War* (Petersborough, Ontario: Broadview, 2007), 105–139.

28 See Michael Walzer, *Just and Unjust Wars* (New York: Basic Books, 1977), 34–51.

29 Ibid., 46.

CHAPTER 5

Challenges to and Adaptations of the Just War Theory

For centuries, the just war theory (JWT) has been the "gold standard" for morally evaluating warfare. It has proved remarkably effective in adapting to the changing nature of warfare and in providing moral categories and a useful moral vocabulary for talking about the ethics of warfare. But it is not above criticism. Occupying the middle position between the two extremes in our continuum of approaches, the JWT is subject to many of the critiques levied against the more "hawkish" positions (political realism and holy war), as well as the more "dovish" types of pacifism. Political realists say the JWT's idea that there can be restraint in war is naïve, while pacifists call it a moral cover story that cloaks violence and selfishness in an aura of virtue that allows people to kill while claiming to serve the greater good. This chapter will explore three of the principal challenges to the JWT, as well as two adaptations of it.

The JWT is not a complete ethical theory for dealing with war. As a teleological theory, it simply provides a way for thinking and talking about the morality and immorality of using deadly force. It does not yield definitive answers to real-life problems. In other words, it doesn't tell us what to do in a particular situation. Instead, it simply helps us to think and talk about warfare so we can discern what ought to be done when conflicts arise.

Just because the JWT does not yield definitive answers does not mean it is useless. Rarely is there unanimity of belief, especially when it comes to moral and ethical questions. Instead, the JWT promotes consensus about what ought to be done and helps to clarify moral quandaries for many people. The JWT is constantly evolving, changing, and adapting to new circumstances, new technologies, and new types of warfare. Most challenges to the JWT represent places where it has not yet "caught up with the times"; they are not its death knell.

THREE PRINCIPAL CHALLENGES TO THE JUST WAR THEORY

CHALLENGE 1: PREEMPTIVE AND PREVENTATIVE STRIKES

The idea that nations have the right to self-defense (and self-preservation) is a long-standing principle of international relations. But do states have to wait until their enemy has attacked in order to defend themselves? Not according to those who subscribe to a strategy sometimes called "anticipatory self-defense." Two types of war waged in anticipation of an attack are *preemptive* and *preventative* wars.[1]

Preemptive wars are waged in the face of an imminent act of aggression (typically measured in days, weeks, or possibly months). Preventative wars are waged to eliminate or mitigate potential or hypothetical threats in the more distant future (for example, destroying nuclear reactors in another country that could be used to create nuclear weapons).

The idea that states have the right to strike first when their enemy poses an imminent threat is fairly logical and enjoys a long history (including Cicero, Thucydides, and Aquinas). In general, this argument claims that if a neighboring state has made viable threats and begins to amass troops on the border, the threatened state can *in anticipation of an imminent invasion* strike out against their enemy to prevent the invasion. The challenge is determining (1) what constitutes a legitimate threat that warrants preemptive military action, and (2) what constitutes imminent?

On an interpersonal level, Hugo Grotius (1583–1645) argues that it is justified to use violence to prevent "a wrong not yet committed," "against a threatened wrong," or "against an anticipated injury,"[2] but only when the danger is immediate and a nonlethal solution is not possible.[3] Grotius further stipulates that fear cannot be the motivating force behind striking first in the name of self-defense. "The danger, again, must be immediate and imminent in point of time, that if the assailant seizes weapons in such a way that his intent to kill is manifest the crime can be forestalled. . . . But those who accept fear of any sort as justifying anticipatory slayings are themselves greatly deceived and deceive others."[4] In other words, if a person is threatening to do you physical harm, you don't have to wait until they hurt you first before you defend yourself, but your decision to "hit him before he hits me" must be based on rational reflection and hard evidence (such as the attacker's behavior, his threats), not on personal feelings of fear or hatred for the attacker.

Grotius applies this same rationale to international relations. Again he rejects fear as a legitimate motivating principle for the use of deadly force. "Fear with respect to a neighboring power is not a sufficient cause [for going to war]. For in order that a self-defense may be lawful it must be necessary; and it is not necessary unless we are certain, not only regarding the power of our neighbor, but also regarding his intention."[5] He further dismisses the idea that one can "take up arms in order to weaken a growing power which, if it becomes too great, may be a source of danger,"[6] or to gain a military advantage.[7] Finally, he admonishes using deadly force as an imagined safeguard in a world that is by nature unpredictable and never entirely secure:

[The idea that t]he possibility of being attacked confers the right to attack is abhorrent to every principle of equity. Human life exists under such conditions that complete security is never guaranteed to us. For protection against uncertain fears we must rely on Divine Providence [God], and on a wariness free from reproach, not on force.[8]

Grotius accepts the legitimacy of preemptive military strikes, but only under restrictive conditions. The threat must be imminent, the malicious or aggressive intent must be certain, and fear cannot be the motivating force.[9]

While preemptive wars enjoy traditional standing in international law, *preventative* wars have long been considered nothing more than wars of aggression. Recently, however, the idea of preventative war has enjoyed a resurgence in popularity. In his 2002 commencement speech at the U.S. Military Academy at West Point, President Bush outlined what has come to be known as "The Bush Doctrine." It includes the claim that terrorism poses a new kind of threat to U.S. security, one which requires the United States to act preventatively. "The war on terror will not be won on the defensive. We must take the battle to the enemy, disrupt his plans, and confront the worst threats before they emerge."[10] He clarified this point a few months later in his 2003 State of the Union address:

Some have said we must not act until the threat is imminent. Since when have terrorists and tyrants announced their intentions, politely putting us on notice before they strike? If this threat is permitted to fully and suddenly emerge, all actions, all words and all recriminations would come too late.[11]

This doctrine became the cornerstone of the United States' "war on terrorism" and was clearly articulated in the 2002 *National Security Strategy of the United States of America*:

We will disrupt and destroy terrorist organizations by: defending the United States, the American people, and our interests at home and abroad by identifying and destroying the threat before it reaches our borders. While the United States will constantly strive to enlist the support of the international community, we will not hesitate to act alone, if necessary, to exercise our right of self-defense by acting preemptively against such terrorists, to prevent them from doing harm against our people and our country. . . . Given the goals of rogue states and terrorists, the United States can no longer solely rely on a reactive posture as we have in the past. The inability to deter a potential attacker, the immediacy of today's threats, and the magnitude of potential harm that could be caused by our adversaries' choice of weapons, do not permit that option. We cannot let our enemies strike first. . . . For centuries, international law recognized that nations need not suffer an attack before they can lawfully take action to defend themselves against forces that present an imminent danger of attack. Legal scholars and international jurists often conditioned the legitimacy of preemption on the existence of an imminent threat—most often a visible mobilization of armies, navies, and air forces preparing to attack. We must adapt the concept of imminent threat to the capabilities and objectives of today's adversaries. . . . The United States has long maintained the option of preemptive actions to counter a sufficient threat to our national security. The greater the threat, the greater is the risk of inaction—and the more compelling the case for taking anticipatory action to defend ourselves, even if uncertainty remains as to the time and place of the enemy's attack. To forestall or prevent such hostile acts by our adversaries, the United States will, if necessary, act preemptively.[12]

While President Bush and the *National Security Strategy of the United States* use the language of preemptive strikes, what they are arguing for, in fact, is *preventative* military action, because the threats they single out are not imminent, but proximate and potential.

Michael Walzer makes a similar case for overriding the normal restraints of the JWT. His "supreme emergency" exception contends that nations are justified in overriding the restraints of the JWT when they face a threat that is both imminent and of an "unusual and horrifying nature."[13] He defines supreme emergency as "when our deepest values and our collective survival are in immediate danger."[14] Walzer recognizes that allowing for exemptions to the JWT is a slippery slope.

By admitting that these traditional rules of war may at times be ignored, the theory becomes vulnerable to loose interpretation. All one has to do to ignore these traditional restraints is cry out, "This is a case of supreme emergency!" which makes the theory meaningless. Thus Walzer vehemently argues that the case for supreme emergency must be conservatively interpreted. Both conditions of supreme emergency must be met: the threat must be both imminent and particularly horrid or devastating. Walzer cautions:

> War is not always a struggle over ultimate values, where the victory of one side would be a human disaster for the other. It is necessary to be skeptical about such matters, to cultivate a wary disbelief of wartime rhetoric, and then to search for some touchstone against which arguments about extremity might be judged.[15]

Not every war is a case of supreme emergency, even when facing defeat. The danger must be so severe that it threatens the very existence of a people, such as an enemy threatening human rights violations or even genocide. Walzer developed the supreme emergency exception to cover instances like the spread of Nazism, which he considers to be a case of an unusually horrifying threat and which serves as the measure of what constitutes a supreme emergency.

The JWT has traditionally allowed for preemptive military strikes by stressing the immediacy of the threat. It has routinely condemned preventative military strikes, however, since its main objective is to restrain military action to curtail the feverish rush to war and allow for peaceful conflict resolution. Preventative war runs contrary to this basic thrust of the JWT; it is nothing more than hawkish political realism dressed in the cloak of self-defense. While Walzer's case for supreme emergency has merit, especially in the wake of Nazism as a genocidal campaign for world domination, his fervent demand that supreme emergency be strictly interpreted is often glossed over. True extreme emergency is extraordinary, rare, and only to be engaged with fear and trepidation.

PRESIDENT BUSH'S 2002 COMMENCEMENT ADDRESS AT THE U.S. MILITARY ACADEMY AT WEST POINT

In his 2002 commencement address at West Point, President Bush argued that al-Qaeda and similar organizations pose the type of threat that meets what Walzer describes as a supreme emergency exception.

> In defending the peace, we face a threat with no precedent. Enemies in the past needed great armies and great industrial capabilities to endanger the American people and our nation. The attacks of September the 11th required a few hundred thousand dollars in the hands of a few dozen evil and deluded men. All of the chaos and suffering they caused came at much less than the cost of a single tank. The dangers have not passed. This government and the American people are on watch, we are ready, because we know the terrorists have more money and more men and more plans.
>
> The gravest danger to freedom lies at the perilous crossroads of radicalism and technology. When the spread of chemical and biological and nuclear weapons, along with ballistic missile technology — when that occurs, even weak states and small groups could attain a catastrophic power to strike great nations. Our enemies have declared this very intention, and have been caught seeking these terrible weapons. They want the capability to blackmail us, or to harm us, or to harm our friends — and we will oppose them with all our power.
>
> For much of the last century, America's defense relied on the Cold War doctrines of deterrence and containment. In some cases, those strategies still apply. But new threats also require new thinking. Deterrence — the promise of massive retaliation against nations — means nothing against shadowy terrorist networks with no nation or citizens to defend. Containment is not possible when unbalanced dictators with weapons of mass destruction can deliver those weapons on missiles or secretly provide them to terrorist allies.

President Bush's 2002 Commencement Address *(continued)*

> We cannot defend America and our friends by hoping for the best. We cannot put our faith in the word of tyrants, who solemnly sign nonproliferation treaties, and then systemically break them. If we wait for threats to fully materialize, we will have waited too long.
>
> Homeland defense and missile defense are part of stronger security, and they're essential priorities for America. Yet the war on terror will not be won on the defensive. We must take the battle to the enemy, disrupt his plans, and confront the worst threats before they emerge. In the world we have entered, the only path to safety is the path of action. And this nation will act.
>
> Our security will require the best intelligence, to reveal threats hidden in caves and growing in laboratories. Our security will require modernizing domestic agencies such as the FBI, so they're prepared to act, and act quickly, against danger. Our security will require transforming the military you will lead—a military that must be ready to strike at a moment's notice in any dark corner of the world. And our security will require all Americans to be forward-looking and resolute, to be ready for preemptive action when necessary to defend our liberty and to defend our lives.[16]

CHALLENGE 2: GUERRILLA WARFARE AND TERRORISM

Like terrorism, *guerrilla warfare* poses serious challenges to the JWT. Also like terrorism, guerrilla warfare is a way of fighting—a methodology—and not an ideology. Typically fought by irregulars (nonprofessional soldiers) against professionally trained, organized, larger, and better-equipped armies, guerrilla war is asymmetrical and unconventional. The guerrillas dress like civilians, hide among civilians (often drawing support from them), fight in small, mobile groups, and attack the larger professional army sporadically and secretively through ambushes, raids, sniper fire, roadside bombs, and similar tactics. The logic of guerrilla warfare is that direct face-to-face combat with the more powerful enemy is suicidal. By using guerrilla warfare, smaller, less powerful forces can combat a militarily superior enemy, especially if that enemy is unfamiliar with the terrain.

Two examples of guerrilla warfare provide an ironic contrast. The colonial patriots in the American Revolution were criticized by the British for refusing to fight face-to-face. The British were a professional and well-armed force, while the patriots were primarily poorly armed farmers. Recognizing that face-to-face combat would be catastrophic, the colonials used guerrilla tactics to "pick away at" the British. In the Vietnam War, the United States was the professional, better armed force and faced the Vietcong, who used guerrilla warfare and snipers to wreak havoc on the large, powerful, but slow U.S. military.

Guerrilla warfare is particularly effective when the guerrillas are able to enlist sympathy and support from the local civilian population, which may provide food, help in hiding, tactical information, and other assistance. While guerrilla warfare is often derided as unethical and cowardly by superior military forces, guerrilla warriors are often hailed as freedom fighters and defenders of the weak by occupied peoples.

Guerrilla war challenges the JWT, which generally assumes that warfare will be between two opposing armies lined up against each other, wearing identifiable uniforms, and having a clear chain of command. In conventional war, traditional JWT concerns like legitimate authority, combatants or noncombatants, rules of surrender, and proportionality are easily identifiable. When a conventional army faces guerrilla forces, however, these traditional JWT concerns are muddied. Guerrilla warriors are effective precisely because they dress like civilians and hide among them. They themselves do not target civilians; instead they coax the conventional army to do so. Seeing themselves as fighting a "war for the people," guerrilla warriors place the civilian population they claim to be fighting for at risk. For once guerrillas attack the

IEDs (improvised explosive devices) proved deadly to U.S. troops in Iraq. These homemade bombs were often placed on the roadside and detonated as military vehicles passed by. They effectively altered and slowed troop movements. The damage done to this truck was from an IED outside of Baghdad.

conventional army, the army starts to see all civilians as potential threats. It is a short step from, "My enemy is hiding among the civilians and dresses and looks like any ordinary citizen" to "The civilians are my enemy." By goading traditional armies to thwart the noncombatant immunity principle, guerrilla warriors hope to turn the hearts and minds of the people against the professional army. Thus the primary objective of guerrilla war is not military, but political.

Walzer strongly condemns guerrilla warfare as unethical:

> Guerrillas don't subvert the war convention by themselves attacking the civilians. . . . Instead, they invite enemies to do it. . . . They seek to place the onus of indiscriminate warfare on the opposing side. . . . They attack stealthily, deviously, without warning, and in disguise. They violate the implicit trust upon which the war convention rests: soldiers must feel safe among civilians if civilians are ever to be safe from soldiers.[17]

For Walzer, guerrillas don't enjoy any of the rights or protections afforded to soldiers precisely because they thwart the war conventions. In using the civilian population as a cover and for support, guerrillas are responsible for any "collateral damage," since it was their activity that put the civilian population at risk. Guerrilla warriors turn the people they claim to be fighting for into legitimate targets. Nevertheless, guerrilla warfare (and terrorism) have proven to be remarkably effective and will remain a viable method of combat for militarily weaker forces.

Like guerrilla warfare, *terrorism* is a type of asymmetrical warfare that seeks political ends. While Carl von Clausewitz claimed that all warfare is nothing more than politics pursued through different means, terrorism takes this sentiment to the extreme. Unfortunately the terms *terrorist* and *terrorism* are frequently used imprecisely, often referring to any violent act or form of coercion. Not all acts of violence or coercion are terrorism. The U.S. Department of Defense defines terrorism as the "calculated use of unlawful violence to inculcate fear; intended to coerce or intimidate governments or societies in pursuit of goals that are generally political, religious, or ideological."[18] Fear is the immediate objective of terrorism, while the long-term objectives are political.

The key difference between guerrilla warfare and terrorism lies in the willingness to target civilians. Whereas guerrilla warriors see themselves as fighting in "the people's name" and often draw support from the civilian population, terrorists intentionally target civilians "in order to cause a psychological reaction (fear, shock, panic) that is out of proportion to the magnitude of the attack in order to perpetuate political or other goals."[19] Like guerrilla warfare, it is an effective means of combat for a militarily weaker force, but, unlike guerrilla warfare, its success is not dependent on garnering sympathy and support from the majority of the civilian population. In fact, terrorists tend to operate in areas where they have little support from the local community. Terrorists pick random targets such as buses, shopping centers, and restaurants to create a sense of fear in the general populations

"UNDERSTANDING GUERRILLA WARFARE" BY MAJOR JOHNIE GOMBO, U.S. MARINE CORPS

If placed on a continuum depicting the forms of warfare based on the extent of combat and the selection of targets, guerrilla warfare would be located between terrorism and conventional warfare. Terrorism involves a limited amount of combat against any target, military or civilian. Conventional warfare involves extended combat, and limits the warfare to military targets. Guerrilla warfare, being located in between, involves combat which is mostly quick skirmishes, but may include extended battles, and is limited to military targets.

The guerrillas' philosophy is that they represent the people. For a viable guerrilla movement to continue, the support of the masses is necessary. Therefore, the guerrillas attempt to win the support of the masses by attacking an oppressive government or occupying force. In addition, the guerrillas treat the masses with respect and dignity, and capitalize on the oppressive behavior of the enemy. Many feel guerrilla warfare is the result of the masses being forced to produce goods and services without an adequate amount of compensation. It is one of the guerrillas' philosophies to take advantage of the masses' discontent with the current government's or occupying forces' policies. This philosophy is very political in nature, and is part of the guerrillas' indoctrination.

The guerrillas have an intense political indoctrination process, such that, the guerrillas are not only fighting for military goals, but also for political goals. This adds to the intensity and dedication of the guerrillas. Part of normal guerrilla training is to be continually indoctrinated in the political goals of the guerrilla warfare movement. These goals normally revolve around the desire to free the country and people from the oppression of the enemy. The guerrillas want to fight for the motherland, and against the cruelties, avarice, and maltreatment that the enemy has inflicted upon the masses.[20]

or symbolic targets such as government offices, houses of worship, and historical sites.

Marianne Cusimano Love, political science professor at The Catholic University of America and a terrorism expert, argues that because "terrorism is inherently a political act" and "a battle of ideas more than a battle of competing militaries,"[21] ultimately terrorists are not defeated on the battlefield, but in the war for hearts and minds, in the battle of ideas. Terrorists, like guerrilla warriors, want to provoke overreaction by their enemies. The JWT is relevant to fighting an enemy that engages in terrorism precisely because it acts as a restraining force. It helps prevent conventional armies from "taking the bait" from terrorists. It helps to prevent overreaction to the provocation.

Commenting on the U.S. "war on terror," Love observes:

> It is essential to realize that we are not forced to choose between upholding ethical norms [like the JWT] or pragmatically advancing U.S. power [political realism]. Ethics versus power politics is a false choice. . . . . Ethics and the just war tradition are power politics' assets. . . . . Any U.S. violations of ethical standards are broadcast immediately and globally, undermining international support and creating a greater sympathy for terrorist causes. Because of disproportionate U.S. power in the world, U.S. behavior is held to a higher standard than the behavior of its adversaries, who are perceived as having fewer choices in combating such a powerful foe.[22]

In support of her position—that a war against terrorist organizations like al-Qaeda will not be won on the battlefield but in the struggle to win the hearts and minds of people from whom they recruit—she points to the 9/11 Commission that urged the United States to "engage the struggle of ideas."[23] Combating terrorism exclusively or even primarily through military means is ineffective and counterproductive. Prisons like Abu Ghraib and Guantanamo Bay, coupled with destruction of vital infrastructure and civilian casualties, serve to concretize the image of the United States as an aggressive hegemon bent on world domination. As

EXCERPT FROM
THE 9/11 COMMISSION REPORT

We [the United States] should offer an example of moral leadership in the world committed to treat people humanely, abide by the rule of law, and be generous and caring to our neighbors. . . . If the United States does not act aggressively to define itself in the Islamic world, the extremists will gladly do the job for us.[24]

Love points out, the United States spent nearly $500 billion on the military in 2006, but the State Department's budget for public diplomacy worldwide was $685 million in 2004, with only a fraction spent in the Muslim world.[25] Love's point is the United States is losing the war on terror precisely because it views it primarily as a military operation and not as a public relations campaign.

An interesting parallel can be made with the Cold War. In July 1947, George Kennan argued in *Foreign Affairs* that the United States would win the Cold War with the Soviet Union through a policy of containment, which he understood to be a political policy and not a military strategy.[26] This policy did not actively pursue the defeat of the Soviet Union. Instead it played a waiting game under the rationale that communism would ultimately implode because it contained "the seeds of its own decay." As a false philosophy left to its own devices, communism would disillusion people with its inability to deliver what it promised. In the face of such an enemy, the argument went, all the United States had to do was "measure up to its own best traditions and prove itself worthy of preservation as a great nation,"[27] while also resisting any spread of communism. Similarly, Love argues that ideas are stronger than guns and that in the war on terrorism, which is really a war against Islamic radicalism, the United States needs to engage "the most powerful tools at its disposal: ideas, moral persuasion, [and] moderated responses that protect innocents."[28]

Others also warn against characterizing the dispute against terrorist organizations as a war. General Wesley Clark (former supreme commander of NATO) and Kal Raustiala (law professor and director of the UCLA Burkle Center for International Relations), in their article "Why Terrorists Aren't Soldiers," argue, "Treating terrorists as combatants [instead of as criminals] is a mistake for two reasons. First, it dignifies criminality by affording terrorist killers the status of soldiers."[29] It ignores that soldiers are professionally trained and held accountable to JWT principles like noncombatant immunity, which terrorists wantonly violate. Treating terrorists as soldiers gives them undeserved status and infers legitimacy not only to their cause but to their means. Second, by labeling terrorists as combatants and not as criminals, it potentially opens the door to justifying military control over the civilian population, because a war against an enemy that hides among civilians turns civil society into a battleground. Terrorists, they argue, are best categorized as criminals and not combatants or soldiers. As such, they ought to be prosecuted via the criminal justice system, not military courts.

Terrorists are not soldiers precisely because they do not accept any of the responsibilities that come with being soldiers, such as wearing a uniform and adhering to principles such as noncombatant immunity and micro-proportionality. Thus, terrorism poses challenges to the JWT only if one sees terrorism as falling under the category of war. Although it shares some commonality with war (the use of armed force for political purposes), it is best characterized as criminal activity. Organizations like al-Qaeda are not nation-states, nor are they seeking to become one (although they may have desires to influence nation-states). They are a subnational ideological or religiously driven organization that intentionally targets civilians; as such, what they are doing is murder, which is a crime. Of course, organizations like al-Qaeda do not see themselves as targeting civilians. The terrorist attacks of 9/11 were aimed at the Pentagon (the seat of U.S. military power),

"THE WAR ON TERROR"

The phrase "war on terror" has become popular since the September 11, 2001 terrorist attacks in the United States, but this phrase is misleading. There is no war on terror in the manner that the United States once waged a war against Germany, Italy, and Japan. Terrorism is a tactic, a way of fighting, not a nation-state, ideology, or even a political or religious movement. To say we are fighting a war on terror is confusing. It is a form of hyperbole that says, "We are engaged in a concerted effort to diminish this type of violence." The idea that we will know a world in which terrorism is no longer used is unrealistic. The best a war on terror (like a "war on drugs") can hope to accomplish is to minimize the impact of terrorism.

the White House (a symbol of U.S. political power), and the World Trade Center (a symbol of Western global capitalism and economic power), all of which in the ideology of al-Qaeda are legitimate targets in their war against Western political, economic, social, religious, and cultural hegemony.

CHALLENGE 3: WEAPONS OF MASS DESTRUCTION

Weapons of mass destruction (WMDs), such as nuclear, biological, and chemical weapons, present two of the most damning criticisms levied against the JWT. The first challenge is not about the weapons per se, but about how they represent the latest version of a tactic or mind-set called *total war*. Total war refers to a war without limits in which traditional ethical restraints (such as noncombatant immunity, fair treatment of prisoners of war, and proportionality) are no longer seen as applicable. Total war is a mind-set that calls for the utter destruction of one's enemy. The war ends when the enemy is utterly defeated. This mind-set is not new. In many ways, it is a secular version of holy war. As Mumtaz Ahmad (associate professor in political science at Hampton University and a former fellow of the Brookings Institution) notes, "If you feel you are fighting for a just cause or for the sake of God and develop a highly exaggerated sense of moral self-righteousness, then you tend to fight to the finish."[30] There is a fine line between the less stringent interpretations of the JWT and the more hawkish approaches such as holy war (or political realism); the latter's "fighting for God's cause" (or for the homeland) becomes the former's "fighting for a just cause." In both cases, the claim to be fighting for some superior value serves to rationalize behavior that is typically off limits. While there is nothing novel about total war, what is new is the capacity to wage it. WMDs enable modern militaries to wage total war and achieve its objective with alarming efficiency. Whereas in centuries past the complete destruction of an enemy often required a concerted effort over an extended period, modern technology has made this achievable with relative ease.

The second challenge that WMDs present is more obvious and concerns the nature of these weapons. Nuclear, chemical, and biological weapons, by their very design, violate the *jus in bello* principles of discrimination and proportionality. A nuclear, chemical, or biological weapon cannot distinguish between civilians and combatants, and these weapons tend to kill in massive numbers. For the sake of simplicity, we will focus primarily on nuclear weapons, although many of the challenges to the JWT arise from biological and chemical weapons as well.

The U.S. nuclear attacks on Hiroshima and Nagasaki, Japan, at the close of World War II, made the threat of nuclear war a reality. More than 220,000 men, women, and children were killed in those attacks, with tens of thousands dying later from radiation poisoning and other illnesses in what Pope Paul VI called "butchery of untold magnitude."[31] WMDs are not just "big bombs." They are *qualitatively different* from any other type of weapon that has ever existed. They efficiently kill in never before seen numbers, pose a real threat to all life on the planet (planetary genocide), and lack the ability to distinguish between civilians and soldiers. Thus, many have questioned whether the mere existence of such weapons renders the idea of just war irrelevant. In a world where every war has the potential of becoming indiscriminate and disproportionate, all wars become unjust.

Nuclear weapons have changed how war is evaluated.

In recognition of this new age of warfare, the bishops at the Second Vatican Council called for "an evaluation of war with an entirely new attitude" (*The Church in the Modern World*, no. 80). The U.S. Catholic bishops, writing in the context of the Cold War, answered that call with their 1983 pastoral letter, *The Challenge of Peace*. They openly questioned the value of the U.S. nuclear stockpiles and whether pursuing the development of nuclear weapons and the maintaining of a nuclear arsenal are moral. In other words, they quickly moved past the question, "Is it ever justified to use nuclear weapons?" (to which they unequivocally say "No" since such weapons are indiscriminate and disproportionate) to the question, "Is it justified to even possess nuclear weapons?"

In asking this question, the bishops disputed the logic of the political realists. The prevailing realist position of the day argued in favor of nuclear stockpiles under the rubric of deterrence, or what had alternatively been called "the balance of power," "the balance of terror," or MAD (Mutually Assured Destruction). The logic of deterrence is that no one would ever attack or even threaten a state that had nuclear stockpiles because the potential for reprisal was suicidal. In this argument, nuclear weapons are used as leverage in geopolitical negotiations. The balance of power argument (MAD) related to the two superpowers of the Cold War — the United States and Soviet Union. Each possessed enough nuclear weapons to destroy the other several times over, and these weapons systems could be configured so that as soon as either side launched an attack, the other could either manually or automatically launch an equally genocidal attack. The net result in such a scenario would be the annihilation of both the U.S. and Soviet populations (at best) or planetary annihilation (at worst). This MAD scenario was supposedly a strong enough disincentive to render the actual use of nuclear weapons a moot point. No one would "push the button" because to do so would be the same as launching an attack on themselves. In other words, peace was assured because no would be stupid enough ever to start a nuclear war since it would end in planetary annihilation. While some counter by arguing the strategy was successful (no global nuclear genocide occurred), living in fear hardly constitutes living in peace except under a minimalist understanding of peace. Also as the Cuban missile crisis of October 1962 illustrates, the fact that global nuclear genocide did not occur was in part due to luck.

Recognizing that using nuclear weapons is unjustified according to the JWT, one of the key ethical questions to emerge from this scenario was, "Is it moral to possess nuclear weapons if a state never plans on using them?" In other words, "Is it ethical for a state to maintain nuclear stockpiles (to derive the benefits of deterrence) by vowing to itself never to actually use them?" In this case, a state would not publicly disclose its commitment never to use its nuclear weapons. This is similar to the argument that it is morally acceptable to own a handgun, so long as one never loads or uses it. It is a strategy of bluffing. Morally the question is, "Is it ethical to threaten to do what one does not intend to ever actually do?" Returning to the handgun analogy, imagine robbing a store with an unloaded gun. Obviously you do not intend on killing anyone, but the store clerk doesn't know the gun is unloaded, so as far as the victim is concerned it makes little difference. The clerk assumes you are willing and able to kill. While only threatening to use nuclear weapons is certainly better than (or not as bad as) actually using them, Paul Ramsey, Michael Walzer, and a host of other ethicists agree, "Whatever is wrong to do is wrong to threaten,"[32] because for the threat to be credible it must be possible. States must possess the weaponry and trained personnel to use it. This brings us to the very edge of the slippery slope. One cannot be poised on the brink of nuclear annihilation and claim to be taking the moral high ground, precisely because it is so easy to fall.

The Catholic Church offers another critique of the possession of nuclear weapons, this one linking it to economics and poverty. The billions of dollars spent on developing and maintaining nuclear stockpiles can be seen as "an act of aggression against the poor,"[33] argue the bishops. Here we see the application of the ancient biblical principle of the preferential option for the poor (discussed in chapter 1): social, political, and economic decisions ought to be weighed against what they do to, with, and for the poor and vulnerable. While many are quick to dismiss this criticism as naïve or far afield, it does cut to the core of Christian ethics. It is a question about priorities. Christians who look to the life, teaching, and example of Jesus for inspiration ask, "Where lies the greater duty, national self-defense or care for the poor?" How or where a nation spends its money reflects its priorities and its ethical commitments.

Finally, we must address the possibility of limited nuclear war. A limited nuclear war uses nuclear material on a much smaller scale or in an area that does not affect civilians. Here our analysis of WMDs explicitly includes chemical and biological weapons, which are typically designed to work on a smaller scale. While the technology for limited nuclear weapons remains in development and is untested in combat, biological and chemical weapons have been used for decades. The limited use of WMDs poses serious challenges to the JWT because such weapons can easily become stepping stones to total war. They up the ante and move a war to the next level. In other words, if one nation is willing to use this class of weaponry, then why can't its enemy? With nuclear weapons, it is just a matter of degree before one reaches bombs the size of those used on Hiroshima and Nagasaki or larger.

TWO ADAPTATIONS OF THE JUST WAR THEORY

Having explored three challenges to the JWT, we now turn our attention to how it is being developed and adapted to our contemporary context. We do this by looking at *jus post bellum* ethics and the Just Peacemaking Perspective.

JUS POST BELLUM: POSTWAR JUSTICE

In recent years, a small but growing chorus of just war theorists have been calling for the development of postwar criteria to complement the *jus ad bellum* and *jus in bello* categories. *Jus post bellum* ethics is seen as the natural extension of the JWT, which addresses reasons for going to war and behavior in war, but seems to assume that moral responsibilities dissipate with the smoke of the battlefield. *Post bellum* ethics is beginning to emerge because the destructive nature of modern weaponry now extends the pernicious effects of war well beyond the formal battle. This new class of weapons, which I call Weapons of Long-Term Destruction (WLTDs), includes WMDs as well as other ordnance that continue to claim lives long after the formal war has ended. WLTDs have long-range effects beyond initial human casualties and continue to cause damage and claim victims for generations after the armed conflict has ended. The JWT needs to adapt to this new reality. In addition to the long-term destruction wreaked by nuclear, biological, and chemical weapons, other developments" in warfare make the need for *jus post bellum* criteria paramount. We will briefly explore three examples: landmines, cluster bombs, and depleted uranium shells.

LANDMINES AND CLUSTER BOMBS

Antipersonnel landmines are designed to maim rather than kill an enemy soldier. Placed on the ground, they detonate when someone steps on or near them, sending shrapnel into the immediate area, often amputating the leg of any adult in the area, but not immediately killing them. The logic is that an injured soldier consumes more resources on the battlefield than a dead

BOMBS THAT KEEP ON KILLING

Unexploded ordnance, such as landmines and cluster bombs, claim up to twenty thousand victims a year (1,500 per month or forty each day). Most of them are civilians and the majority of them are children. In 1991, the International Campaign to Ban Landmines, a group of grassroots organizations under the leadership of Jodi Williams (discussed later in this chapter) was formed to get nations to adopt and ratify the Mine Ban Treaty. The ICBL was awarded the 1997 Nobel Peace Prize for their efforts, which have resulted in 156 signatories to the Mine Ban Treaty. Forty countries have not signed, including China, Egypt, Finland, India, Israel, Pakistan, Russia, and the United States. For more on landmines, the ICBL, and the treaty, visit *http://www.icbl.org/*.

one. Retreating armies often sow landmines in order to halt the progress of their pursuers, but they do not carefully map where the mines have been placed. Landmines are also used to create buffer zones and secure borders.

Antipersonnel landmines are small, light, easy to use, and cheap. They have been described as "the perfect soldier, ever vigilant." However, they cannot distinguish between soldiers and civilians, and they remain active until triggered, often decades after the fighting has ended. While "smart mines" (which self-destruct or self-deactivate after a set period or can be controlled by satellite) are available, most landmines are "dumb"; they remain active until detonated.

Landmines seriously hamper postwar reconstruction efforts by rendering swaths of land unusable, slowing relief efforts, delaying the return of war refugees, and killing livestock on which the rural poor depend. Children are particularly vulnerable to landmines in postwar regions because in rural and agrarian communities, it is often children who have chores (fetching water, tending flocks, and farming) that take them into mine-seeded fields and woods. Since children are shorter than adults, a landmine that amputates an adult's leg at the knee can damage vital internal organs in a child and often prove fatal. Landmines effectively continue the war until every mine has either claimed a victim or been removed.

Cluster bombs are dropped on the battlefield from the air or launched from ground rockets from a distance of up to twenty miles away. These bombs contain hundreds of smaller bomblets (approximately one by three inches) which are released over the target and blanket a two hundred-yard area. One M26 rocket, for example, contains 640 bomblets. Twelve M26 rockets can be launched in sixty seconds. The bomblets explode on impact or just above the ground, creating an eight-yard kill zone. They can penetrate four inches of steel, thereby disarming tanks and other vehicles, and killing any person in the area. This remarkably effective weapon raises moral problems because approximately 5 percent of the bomblets do not detonate on impact. These "duds" often remain armed and detonate long after the formal battle has ended. A thirty-year study by Humanitarian International revealed that cluster bombs have claimed more than one hundred thousand lives with 98 percent of the victims being civilians, most of them children. In a massive blunder during the wars in Iraq and Afghanistan, the United States used yellow bomblets that were the same color as food packages that were also being air-dropped. Children went out to collect what they thought was food aid only to detonate unexploded bomblets. [34]

DEPLETED URANIUM SHELLS

Despite its innocuous name, depleted uranium (DU) has a radioactive half-life of 4.5 billion years and maintains 60 percent of natural uranium's radioactivity. It is highly valued by militaries because its high density enables it to penetrate most kinds of armor. This enables militaries to fire shells from greater and safer distances. DU is cheaper, more readily available, and more effective than its closest alternative, tungsten. As a by-product of nuclear weapons manufacturing and nuclear energy, this low-level radioactive waste is abundant, making it "better than free," because any DU used for military ordnance does not have to be stored in toxic waste dumps. DU ordnance has been used in Afghanistan, Bosnia, Iraq, Kosovo, Kuwait, Serbia, and Somalia. According to the Pentagon, more than 320 tons of DU (944,000 rounds) were used in the 1991 Gulf War. Exact figures on the number of DU shells used in the 2003 U.S.-Iraq conflict are unavailable.

The long-term effects of DU raise serious moral questions. When a 120-mm DU shell strikes metal, the DU vaporizes and then settles as dust, contaminating an area up to fifty meters. This dust can be inhaled, ingested, or enter the human body through open wounds. DU is even more deadly once it enters the food chain, where it gathers strength as it moves up and onto the kitchen table. While U.S. Army studies conclude that DU poses no significant health risks, the United Kingdom's Atomic Energy Authority estimates that a half million people in Kuwait and Iraq could die due to the use of DU in the first Gulf War alone. The health risks associated with DU include chromosomal damage, stillborn births, birth defects, renal collapse, infertility, leukemia, and a host of other cancers. Following the 1991 Gulf War, for example, cancer rates in Iraq increased seven to ten times and birth deformities increased four- to sixfold. In the Basra area of Iraq, where DU shells were heavily used, stillborn births and congenital birth defects rose by 250 percent between 1989 and 1999. Ironically (or perhaps hypocritically), the United States invaded Iraq in 2003 for violating U.N. sanctions and because of a perceived threat of WMDs and then used weapons defined by the United Nations as WMDs in the invasion.[35]

JUS POST BELLUM CRITERIA
As the example of WLTDs illustrates, the effects of contemporary warfare endure for years, decades, and possibly centuries. One serious flaw in the JWT is the assumption that ethical responsibilities end with the formal battle. In an effort to correct this lacuna, Tobias Winright (the author of our foreword) and I have identified four *post bellum* criteria:[36]

1. ***Just Cause:*** Centuries ago Augustine noted that the *telos* of a just war is not simply victory on the battlefield, but the *tranquillitas ordinis,* "the tranquility that comes from order," or what we have been calling, "a just and lasting peace." The classical just war tradition identifies self-defense, defense of human rights (for example, humanitarian intervention), restitution (that is, regaining what was wrongfully taken), redress (that is, taking possession of what is wrongfully withheld), and legitimate punishment as the only "just causes" for going to war. It follows that the conclusion of any just war must be the accomplishment of the objectives that served as the grounds for just cause in the *ad bellum* phase.

   Satisfying the just cause demands is different from returning to the *status quo ante bellum.* As Walzer notes, the status quo before the war is precisely what led to war in the first place. The goal of a just war must be to establish social, political, and economic conditions that are substantially more stable, more just, and less prone to chaos than what existed prior to the fighting. The *post bellum* just cause principle has three primary objectives: it holds parties accountable to their declared mission (that is, what they claimed as the just cause in the *ad bellum* period), it restrains parties from seeking additional gains once the battle has ended (such as the seizure of land or capital or regime change), and it restrains postwar responses by the victors.

2. ***Reconciliation:*** If the primary objective of a just war is a just and lasting peace, then there can be no peace without reconciliation. The goal of reconciliation is to transform a relationship of animosity, fear, and hatred into one of tolerance, if not respect; to turn enemies into friends; and to bring emotional healing to the victims of war. A parallel between the sacrament of reconciliation in the Catholic Church and *post bellum* reconciliation is instructive here.

   The Catholic sacrament of reconciliation (sometimes called confession or penance) is a ritual through which an individual's sins are forgiven by God. The Church teaches that this sacrament was instituted by Christ and requires certain actions of the penitent: to sincerely feel contrite (sorry) for having done wrong; to confess (admit) his or her guilt to a priest, who acts not as a judge but as an instrument or vehicle through which God's forgiveness is given; and to make some kind of satisfaction or penance, typically some act that seeks to repair the damage done to the offended.[37] After confessing his or her sins, the individual is absolved (forgiven), which the act of penance then perfects or completes.

The sacrament of reconciliation is not cheap grace, a facile way to do whatever you want and then simply expect God to forgive because you confess. Rather, it recognizes that humans always fall short of God's expectations and that sin damages not only the individual but the entire community. Reconciliation is a way to repair damaged relationships (to reconcile people to one another and to God) and to return the individual to the community in good standing.

The postwar reconciliation phase contains these same basic elements of reconciliation: sincere admission of wrong-doing, satisfaction (penance), absolution, and the return of the offending party to full communion. The goal of reconciliation, whether sacramental or *jus post bellum*, is justice tempered by mercy. Some object to making reconciliation an aim of the *post bellum* period, arguing that it trivializes the brutality of war by reducing the crimes of war to an area of disputation and fails to recognize war as a violent crime. I would argue that such detractors operate out of an impoverished understanding of reconciliation, seeing it primarily as a "forgive-and-forget" approach, whereas a richer understanding of reconciliation requires acknowledgment of guilt and reparation (penance) before absolution is given.

While reconciliation might seem a lofty ideal, the relationships between the Allied Forces of World War II and Germany, Italy, and Japan reveal that adversarial relationships can be reconciled in a relatively short time. The success of truth and reconciliation commissions, such as those used in

South Africa and Guatemala, provide further evidence of the power of admission of guilt, apology, and forgiveness. Practically speaking, the reconciliatory aims can be promoted by addressing four key areas: ceasefire agreements; restrained postwar celebrations that are joyful for the end of a war but do not denigrate the former enemy; public and transparent postwar settlement processes (best carried out by a third party that is independent of the victors), and apologies.

3. *Punishment:* While reconciliation aims to rebuild relationships, the punishment phase's primary objectives are justice, accountability, and restitution. The legitimacy of punishment depends on several factors: publicity and transparency (punishments ought to be meted out through public forums to which many, if not all, have access); proportionality and discrimination (appropriate punitive measures ought not be excessively debilitating and must make distinctions based on level of command and culpability); and competent authority (punishments ought to be assigned by an authority that is recognized as legitimate by all sides). In all likelihood, the legitimacy of the punishment phase depends on an independent authority to avoid even the appearance of victors acting as judge, jury, and executioner of the vanquished (also known as victor's justice).

The punishment phase consists of two principal parts: compensation (restitution) and war crimes trials. In both cases, due care must be taken to ensure that the principal architects of the aggression are punished and that the civilian population is not unduly burdened. One of the more difficult questions faced is whether to grant immunity to tyrants. While justice demands that tyrants be held accountable, frequently tyrants are willing to step down and end their reigns of terror only if guaranteed they will not be prosecuted or punished. Refusing to "make a deal with the devil" can prolong their stay in power and lead to more bloodshed. The issue becomes a question of principle versus practicality.

4. ***Restoration:*** The goal of a just war is not simply the cessation of violence, but political, economic, social, and ecological conditions that allow citizens to flourish. In other words, a just war should seek to create an environment that permits citizens to pursue a life that is meaningful and dignified. Some of the practical concerns addressed under this phase include:

- Security and Policing: Safety is one of the principal concerns once war has ended. Having had their military and police forces decimated or dismantled, defeated nations are vulnerable to invasion from hostile neighbors, civil war, or anarchy. To emerge from the chaos of war, some type of security is needed. This typically comes from other nations who act as peacekeepers by securing borders and by training new military and police personnel. The victor in the war should not presume to be the one best suited for this job. Also, there are significant differences between policing (with the aim of serving and protecting the populace and deterring crime) and military aims (which tend to be more aggressive in their use of force). The practical challenges in this phase include recruiting and training new police officers (especially if the previous police force had been complicit in abuses of power by the previous regime); training military personnel to make the shift from military operations to policing; gaining the trust of the local population; and removing weapons from civilians.

- Political Reform: Returning a nation to the *status quo ante bellum* (the prewar political situation) is not desirable because those were the conditions that led to war in the first place. While the terms *nation building* and *regime change* often connote restructuring the political infrastructure of a defeated nation in ways that are advantageous to the victor (puppet regimes), political reform is really a recognition that a functional government is necessary for securing the common good and providing a host of public services needed for a return to normalcy (such as education, health care, social services, roads, electricity, water). The degree of political reform needed is relative to the depravity of the previous regime and the resources available within the nation. Finally, nations do not surrender their right to political autonomy (national sovereignty) upon defeat, nor is the victor granted *carte blanche*.[38]

- Economic Recovery: War is destructive and expensive. It often interrupts normal commerce, manufacturing, and transportation by coopting them as part of the war effort. Wars also tend to destroy the infrastructure necessary for a robust economy (such as roads, bridges, rail lines, ports, electrical grids). The faster a postwar economy is refashioned into a peacetime economy and the sooner citizens are able to return to meaningful and well-paying jobs, the sooner the nation can transition from war to peace and order. If war has been waged for decades, a nation may have a workforce with no employable skills other than soldiering and thus need job training. Economic recovery programs (such as loans, aid packages, incentives for industry, trade agreements) are essential to rebuilding a postwar economy.

- Social Rehabilitation: War destroys not only infrastructure but lives as well. Wars tend to cause massive migration (refugees and internally displaced people) and to handicap people physically and emotionally. *Jus post bellum* requires attention to how people transition to times of peace, including attending to people who have been victimized by war and soldiers who may suffer from post-traumatic stress disorder.

- Ecological Cleanup: As noted earlier, WLTDs extend the pernicious effects of war for years into the future. They render swaths of land unusable, which hampers the return of refugees and agriculture. Those that resort to WLTDs need to be held accountable for cleanup efforts and costs so that postwar reconstruction is possible. Requiring militaries to include cleanup costs in their cost-benefit analysis would render many WLTDs prohibitively expensive and thus have the added benefit of retarding their use.

A just war can be fought or ended unjustly, and an unjust war can be fought or ended justly. Obviously, if a war is unjust (*ad bellum* or *in bello*), then the obligations *post bellum* are all the greater. The addition of *jus post bellum* analysis enriches the JWT by emphasizing that ethical and moral responsibility for war do not end when combat ends.

THE JUST PEACEMAKING PERSPECTIVE

In recent years, an alternative to both the JWT and pacifism has emerged. The Just Peacemaking Perspective (JPP) falls between these two traditional Christian approaches to war and peace and therefore adds a new point on our continuum of approaches (see chart on page 18).

Like the JWT, the JPP takes human sinfulness seriously. It holds that a world without war is idealistic, yet it does not succumb to a fatalism that holds war and violence are inevitable. Unlike the JWT, which only applies once war has been declared, the JPP takes a proactive approach to conflict resolution by advocating that serious steps be taken to prevent disputes from degrading into armed conflict. The JPP focuses on what causes conflict and therefore sees peacemaking as the ever vigilant effort to establish justice. It is not naïvely optimistic. It does not labor under a utopian vision of a world without violence, but instead identifies steps that may diminish the number of wars. In this sense, it is less a theory than a commitment to concrete actions that foster peace founded in justice.

The JPP's principle that peace is much more than the absence of violence operates out of the conviction that peace is founded in rightly ordered relationships based in fairness, justice, respect, and honesty. Thus the JWT, which focuses only on the period immediately prior to conflict and then behavior in battle, is ill-equipped to seek its supposed primary end: the *tranquillitas ordinis* (a just peace). The JPP directs attention to what leads up to armed conflict and seeks to mitigate the circumstances that cause parties to see armed conflict as inevitable. Thus, like pacifists, those who hold to the JPP contend that peace is achievable but takes a

"If you want peace, work for justice."

—Pope Paul VI[39]

concerted effort, and that nonviolent conflict resolution is both normative for Christians and largely unexplored and underdeveloped in international affairs. The JPP also serves as a corrective to forms of pacifism that are passive.

The JPP is similar to the contemporary JWT (as opposed to the classical JWT). Both seek a just peace as their primary objective; both are concerned that the JWT has become a way to rationalize the use of deadly force; and both take "conservative" approaches to war, namely that going to war is justified only in extreme situations that require rigorous justification—so rigorous and rare that all wars ought to be assumed to be unjust and unwarranted until definitively proven otherwise.

The JPP emerged in 1990 on the eve of the U.S. bombings of Iraq during the first Gulf War. Christian ethicists were frustrated that the Christian tradition offered only two courses of action: wage war against Iraq for invading Kuwait (the just war tradition) or continue to use sanctions and other nonviolent approaches to pressure Iraq to abandon its aggression (the pacifist approach). Both options were seen as wanting. Out of this frustration a third alternative emerged, one that critiqued both just war theorists and pacifists. Under the leadership of Glen Stassen, a professor of Christian ethics from Fuller Theological Seminary, a group of twenty-three scholars identified "seven steps of just peacemaking." These steps draw heavily from a biblical understanding of justice, from the teachings of Jesus (especially the Sermon on the Mount in Matthew 5–7 and Luke 6:12–20), and from a sense that "an ethic of peace and war that still operates with only pacifism and just war theory is outdated."[40] As evidence of the timeliness and practicality of the JPP, many mainstream Christian churches have adopted positions similar to it including the U.S. Conference of

Catholic Bishops, the Presbyterian Church (U.S.A.), United Methodist Church, and United Church of Christ. Later the theory was refined into "ten practices for abolishing war" organized under three basic imperatives: peacemaking initiatives, justice, and love and community.[41] A description of each follows.

PEACEMAKING INITIATIVES

1. *Support direct nonviolent action:* Nonviolent direct action includes many strategies: acts of civil disobedience, boycotts, strikes, protests, publication of facts surrounding instances of injustice, sanctuary movements that house and protect victims of injustice, accompaniment projects in which third-party observers or monitors place themselves in potential conflict zones to call attention to a situation and dissuade the use of deadly force (see "Accompaniment NGOs" below), and any efforts that seek to call attention to injustices and remedy them without resorting to violence. Mohandas Gandhi, Martin Luther King Jr., and Dorothy Day demonstrated the effectiveness of such efforts (see chapter 2).

ACCOMPANIMENT NGOS

Several international nongovernmental organizations that sponsor accompaniment projects in the name of peace. The description of the following representative groups is adapted with few changes from their Web pages.

Witness for Peace *(http://www.witnessforpeace.org/)*

Witness for Peace (WFP) is a politically independent, nationwide grassroots organization of people committed to nonviolence and led by faith and conscience. WFP's mission is to support peace, justice, and sustainable economies in the Americas by changing U.S. policies and corporate practices that contribute to poverty and oppression in Latin America and the Caribbean.

Accompaniment NGOs *(continued)*

Christian Peacemaker Teams *(http://www.cpt.org/)*

Christian Peacemaker Teams (CPT) arose from a call in 1984 for Christians to devote the same discipline and self-sacrifice to nonviolent peacemaking that armies devote to war. Enlisting the whole church in an organized, nonviolent alternative to war, today CPT places violence-reduction teams in crisis situations and militarized areas around the world at the invitation of local peace and human rights workers. CPT embraces the vision of unarmed intervention waged by committed peacemakers ready to risk injury and death in bold attempts to transform lethal conflict through the nonviolent power of God's truth and love.

2. *Take independent initiatives to reduce the threat of war:* An independent initiative is a unilateral effort to reduce the escalation toward conflict. War typically arises out of a series of encounters that increase tensions between parties. Independent initiatives are when one side takes a step back from conflict (such as pulling troops away from the conflict zone or halting production of weaponry) in the hopes of decreasing the sense of distrust, hatred, and fear that their adversary harbors against them. Typically such efforts are most effective when they are visible and verifiable, when they occur independently of the slow process of negotiations, when they are publicly announced in advance and carried out when promised, when they decrease the threat to the other side, when they are part of a series of efforts (not just one token gesture), and when the reason for doing so is declared, thereby encouraging the other side to reciprocate.

3. *Use cooperative conflict resolution:* Cooperative conflict resolution aims at getting adversarial parties to agree to work together toward a peaceful resolution. It begins with getting them to see they have a shared problem and a mutual interest in resolving it peacefully. It requires effort from both parties: to listen to each other and try to understand the opposing

perspective, even if they disagree with it; to acknowledge how their own contributions have led to the conflict; to negotiate in good faith; to view the other side as a partner in solving a common problem (not as an adversary they must defeat or take advantage of); to commit to justice and peace as essential to establishing long-term solutions; and to take risks in the name of peace. Practically speaking, this means identifying persons and groups on all sides of the conflict that are willing to dialogue and then getting them to interact with one another (for example, peace talks).

4. *Acknowledge responsibility for conflict and injustice and seek repentance and forgiveness:* Like the *jus post bellum* category of the JWT, the JPP draws heavily on the Christian concept of reconciliation and conversion. This implies a "change of heart," a transformation from an old to a new way of living. As such, acknowledgment of wrongdoing (confession) is essential to seeking peace. The flip side to confession is forgiveness, a willingness to move beyond wrongs of the past in the hope of a better future. This step calls on leaders to make public statements acknowledging wrongdoing by themselves or those under their command and sincere gestures of repentance. For example, in the last decade Japanese officials have issued statements of remorse and apologies for the suffering and damage done to the Chinese people before and during World War II, as an attempt to better relations between the two nations.

JUSTICE

5. *Advance democracy, human rights, and religious liberty:* One of the more curious and promising observations of the last fifty years has been that the more liberalized a nation's political and economic system is, the less likely that nation is to seek war as a means of conflict resolution. Democracies rarely fight with each other. Instead they tend to employ negotiation and other peaceful means to resolve their conflicts. Likewise, countries with functioning open markets are less likely to wage war against each other. The typical explanation for this

phenomenon is that in politically and economically open societies, where the human rights of the citizens are respected and there is a functioning free press, leaders are held accountable to the people. Since most people find war extremely distasteful, leaders (out of self-interest) tend to seek peaceful ends to conflicts. Thus advancing participatory forms of governance, human rights, an active civil society, and open markets can be an effective peacemaking tool.

6. ***Foster justice and sustainable economic development:*** Poverty is a leading cause of war. "Sustainable development" refers to the process of economic and social progress from poverty to self-sufficiency that is often achieved through economic and political reform programs (such as economic aid packages and low-interest loans that have social, political, and economic benchmarks) as long as they (1) do not wantonly destroy the environment, (2) are under the direction of the local community, and (3) look to long-term economic self-sustainability. This is not a band-aid approach to poverty. It refers to development programs that address the root causes of poverty and social instability, such as food and water shortages, lack of education, human rights issues, and health care. Deprivation often sows seeds of resentment and hostility. Those with "nothing to lose" may see armed conflict as the only way to address the injustice of poverty, while in communities where there is infrastructure (jobs, farms, schools, hospitals, and so on) and the prospect of a better tomorrow, people are less likely to resort to violence precisely because they have something to lose. A key insight of the JPP is that one of the best ways to seek peace is to eliminate both the proximate and distant causes of war, and that the distant causes of war are often rooted in social injustice. In recent years, several U.N. organizations that seek to alleviate global poverty (such as the World Bank, International Monetary Fund, and Human Development Programme) have been making steps toward addressing the connection between poverty, political reform (democracy), sustainable development, and war.

LOVE AND COMMUNITY

7. ***Work with emerging cooperative forces in the international system:*** For many, the world of international relations is akin to Hobbes' man in the state of nature. These political realists claim that while there are rules (laws) and rulers that govern life within a society or nation, the relationship between states is one in which might makes right. Globalization challenges this outdated assumption. The international system (that is, the rules and practices that govern relationships and exchanges between states) now includes many nonstate actors: global corporations and conglomerates (Viacom, Matsushita Corporation, Sony, PepsiCo, Walt Disney); global trade bodies and agreements (World Trade Organization); global terrorist networks and organized crime syndicates (al-Qaeda); cartels; and global nongovernmental organizations, non profit groups, and religious entities (see "Global NGOs" below). In this new global political arena, the older model whereby states viewed themselves as competing with each other (militarily and economically) is giving way to a more cooperative model. Military prowess is now largely eclipsed by economic might, and former competitors now represent potential markets. Nations are learning that a cooperative model for global relations, as opposed to a competitive one, is far more beneficial to national interests and international peace.

GLOBAL NGOS

A host of global nongovernmental organizations work for peace and sustainable development. While we have not yet reached the level of complete global integration, we have an emerging global civil society that is fostered by global NGOs. The following descriptions of each group come from their Web pages.

Global NGOs *(continued)*

International Red Cross and Red Crescent Movement
(http://www.redcross.int/)

The world's oldest NGO, the International Red Cross and Red Crescent Movement is devoted to alleviating human suffering, especially in times of armed conflict and violence. The mission of the IRCRCM is to prevent and alleviate human suffering wherever it may be found; to protect life and health and ensure respect for the human being, in particular in times of armed conflict and other emergencies; to work for the prevention of disease and for the promotion of health and social welfare; to encourage voluntary service and a constant readiness to give help by the members of the movement and a universal sense of solidarity toward all those in need of its protection and assistance. In pursuing its mission, the IRCRCM is guided by its fundamental principles: humanity, impartiality, neutrality, independence, voluntary service, unity, universality.

Amnesty International *(http://www.amnesty.org/)*

Amnesty International (AI) is a worldwide movement of people who campaign for internationally recognized human rights. AI's vision is of a world in which every person enjoys all the human rights enshrined in the Universal Declaration of Human Rights and other international human rights standards. AI is independent of any government, political ideology, economic interest, or religion. It does not support or oppose any government or political system, nor does it support or oppose the views of the victims whose rights it seeks to protect. It is concerned solely with the impartial protection of human rights.

Greenpeace *(http://www.greenpeace.org/international/)*

Greenpeace is an independent global campaigning organization that acts to change attitudes and behavior, to protect and conserve the environment, and to promote peace by catalyzing an energy revolution, defending the world's oceans, protecting the world's ancient forests, working for disarmament and peace, creating a toxic-free future, and campaigning for sustainable agriculture.

Global NGOs *(continued)*

Doctors without Borders/ Médecins Sans Frontières
(http://www.doctorswithoutborders.org/)

Doctors Without Borders/Médecins Sans Frontières (MSF) is an independent international medical humanitarian organization that delivers emergency aid to people affected by armed conflict, epidemics, natural or man-made disasters, or exclusion from health care in more than seventy countries. Each year, MSF doctors, nurses, logisticians, water and sanitation experts, administrators, and other medical and nonmedical professionals depart on more than 4,700 aid assignments. They work alongside more than 25,800 locally hired staff to provide medical care.

In emergencies and their aftermath, MSF provides essential health care, rehabilitates and runs hospitals and clinics, performs surgery, battles epidemics, carries out vaccination campaigns, operates feeding centers for malnourished children, and offers mental health care. When needed, MSF also constructs wells and dispenses clean drinking water, and provides shelter materials like blankets and plastic sheeting. Through longer-term programs, MSF treats patients with infectious diseases such as tuberculosis, sleeping sickness, and HIV/AIDS, and provides medical and psychological care to marginalized groups such as street children.

Catholic Relief Services *(http://crs.org/)*

CRS is the official international relief and development agency of the U.S. Catholic community. CRS serves the poor in nearly one hundred countries overseas through programs in emergency relief, HIV and AIDS, health, agriculture, education, microfinance and peacebuilding. The mission of CRS is to assist impoverished and disadvantaged people overseas, working in the spirit of Catholic social teaching to promote the sanctity of human life and the dignity of the human person. Although its mission is rooted in the Catholic faith, its operations serve people based solely on need, regardless of their race, religion, or ethnicity. Within the United States, CRS engages Catholics to live their faith in solidarity with the poor and suffering of the world.

Global NGOs *(continued)*

American Friends Service Committee
(http://www.afsc.org/)

The American Friends Service Committee carries out service, development, social justice, and peace programs throughout the world. Founded by Quakers in 1917 to provide conscientious objectors with an opportunity to aid civilian war victims, AFSC's work attracts the support and partnership of people of many races, religions, and cultures.

AFSC's work is based on the Quaker belief in the worth of every person and faith in the power of love to overcome violence and injustice. The organization's mission and achievements won world-wide recognition in 1947 when it accepted the Nobel Peace Prize with the British Friends Service Council on behalf of all Quakers.

American World Jewish Services *(http://www.ajws.org/)*

American Jewish World Service (AJWS) is an international development organization motivated by Judaism's imperative to pursue justice. AJWS is dedicated to alleviating poverty, hunger, and disease among the people of the developing world regardless of race, religion, or nationality. Through grants to grassroots organizations, volunteer service, advocacy, and education, AJWS fosters civil society, sustainable development, and human rights for all people, while promoting the values and responsibilities of global citizenship within the Jewish community.

8. *Strengthen the United Nations and international efforts for cooperation and human rights:* For the same reasons outlined previously (global economic integration, widespread recognition of human rights, and global communications), the United Nations is upheld by many just peace advocates as the best mechanism for resolving interstate conflicts and especially for advocating a just peace. The United Nations is not a global government. It does not have authority over other states. It functions as a common-ground meeting place where many of the aims and means of the JPP are actively sought

(such as sustainable development, third-party negotiations, nonviolent conflict resolution, economic sanctions that do not harm citizens, and advocacy for human rights). While not perfect, the United Nations represents one of the most mature global or international institutions for advocating just peace.

9. *Reduce offensive weapons and weapons trade:* Some of the JPP practices are more theoretical (commitment to cooperative conflict resolution and work with emerging cooperative forces in the international system), while others are much more practical in their focus. The commitment to reducing nuclear weapons proliferation (through treaty agreements and monitoring programs) and efforts at nuclear disarmament (whereby nations reduce their nuclear stockpiles), as well as efforts to curtail the weapons trade in general, is one of the most pragmatic practices of the JPP. Positive steps away from WLTDs have been made in recent decades. For example, 189 nations have signed the Nuclear Nonproliferation Treaty (1968), agreeing not to transfer nuclear weapons material or knowledge to other states and commit to nuclear disarmament; 177 states have signed the Comprehensive Nuclear Test Ban Treaty (1996), which prohibits the development of new types of nuclear weaponry; and 153 nations have signed the Mine Ban Treaty (discussed earlier in this chapter). Under the leadership of Soviet prime minister Mikhail Gorbachev and U.S. presidents Ronald Reagan and George H. Bush, the nuclear stockpile of the United States and USSR/Russia decreased from 47,000 to 15,500 warheads. Despite these signs of hope, the list of nuclear states continues to grow. While the Cold War has ended, the threat of nuclear weapons remains a frightful reality, with new actors and scenarios including the potential of terrorist organizations with nuclear capabilities.

10. *Encourage grassroots peacemaking groups and voluntary associations:* With the spread of democracy, participatory forms of governance, a growing global civil society, and the advent of advanced communication tools such as e-mail and the Internet, the power of the individual is unprecedented.

The JPP realizes that while peace is nearly universally desired, concerted efforts at peacemaking are typically carried out by a minority of "peaceniks." If the JPP is ever to gain traction in the hearts and minds of the majority, which can then pressure political, military, and economic leaders to actively seek peace, then grassroots peacemaking efforts (local peace groups) are essential. Peacemaking must no longer be the pet project of the leftist extreme; it has to become mainstream. Thus grassroots and voluntary organizations must be encouraged, and they need to learn how to make their message appear not as unrealistic idealism, but as a necessary and realistic alternative to current global affairs.

GRASSROOTS PEACE GROUPS

Many grassroots organizations are devoted to peace and justice, such as Amnesty International and American Friends Service Committee (see "Global NGOs"). Other grassroots peacemaking groups are listed below. The description of each group is adapted with few changes from its Web page.

Catholic Peace Fellowship
(http://www.catholicpeacefellowship.org/index.asp)
The purpose of the Catholic Peace Fellowship is to support Catholic conscientious objectors through education, counseling, and advocacy. Guided by a personalist philosophy, the CPF seeks to resist war by helping those who choose not to participate in it, one person at a time.

Pax Christi *(http://www.paxchristi.net/)*
Pax Christi International is a nonprofit, nongovernmental Catholic peace movement working on a global scale on a wide variety of issues in the fields of human rights, security and disarmament, economic justice, and ecology.

Grassroots Peace Groups *(continued)*

Veterans for Peace *(http://www.veteransforpeace.org/)*
A nonprofit educational and humanitarian organization of U.S. veterans dedicated to increasing public awareness of the costs of war, ending the arms race and war, seeking justice for vets and war victims, and restraining government from intervening in the internal affairs of other nations. Members draw on their personal experiences and perspectives gained as veterans to raise public awareness of the true costs and consequences of militarism and war — and to seek peaceful, effective alternatives.

The lists of NGOs devoted to peace and justice (along with the Web addresses) have been provided in this chapter for two reasons. First, they illustrate that the JPP is not just a theory. It has real-world implications. This leads to the second reason for the list. As an ethics professor, I frequently hear my students protest: "But what can I do? I'm only one person!" *New York Times* columnist and best-selling author Thomas Friedman coined the phrase "the super-empowered individual" to describe how well-networked individuals (like former vice president Al Gore, his holiness the Dalai Lama, or even Osama Bin-Laden) can effect global change through new communications technology. In an era of global integration and super-empowered individuals, it will take the efforts of thousands of grassroots organizations like those listed above and tens of thousands of individuals — like my students — to bring about a global just peace.

With awareness and knowledge comes responsibility. As someone reading this book, likely a college student, you are one of the most educated and therefore most powerful people on the planet. And so the protest, "What can I do?" becomes the question, "What will you do?" As anthropologist Margaret Mead once said, "Never doubt the power of a small group of committed individuals to change the world. It is the only thing that ever has."

SUPER-POWERED INDIVIDUALS

A super-powered individual is a person or small group that is able to have a wide-reaching effect on political policies or human behavior, typically through the use of technology (Internet) and social networking.

While the examples of Al Gore's work on the environment, the Dalai Lama's advocacy for the people of Tibet, and Osama Bin-Laden's ability to inspire thousands worldwide in his war against the United States and Western imperialism are well known, examples of super-powered individuals who are less well known include Jodi Williams (born 1951), who shared the 1997 Nobel Peace Prize with the International Campaign to Ban Landmines (an organization she helped found). Her work began humbly with coordinating the efforts of several NGOs that worked with victims of landmines and ultimately led to a mine ban treaty, which 156 nations have signed. Regarding her work, she said:

> When we launched the International Campaign to Ban Land-mines (ICBL), we had no idea what we might be able to ultimately accomplish. We knew we would be able to do something that would help mine victims around the world, but beyond that we were not sure where our work would lead us. But we started the Campaign because it was the right thing to do. It was a way to help victims of war and also begin to get people everywhere to think about the impact of weapons — sometimes long after the wars are over.[42]

Jason Russell, Bobby Bailey, and Laren Poole went on a trip to Africa in the spring of 2003. Film students from Southern California, they stumbled upon tens of thousands of children in Northern Uganda who would commute from their rural villages to sleep in large groups in the cities out of fear of being abducted as child soldiers for the rebel Lord's Resistance Army. Shocked by what they saw, they did what they knew best, they made a

Super-Powered Individuals *(continued)*

documentary to educate others about these invisible children. *Invisible Children* began as a rough-cut documentary and has grown into a grassroots movement of tens of thousands. They seek to "transform apathy into activism," and their efforts include: teams of college-aged activists roaming the United States, educating others about the children of Northern Uganda; a microenterprise program selling bracelets, with proceeds going toward education of Ugandan children; mass civil demonstrations and advocacy that have contributed to having the U.S. State Department dedicate a senior-level representative on this issue, which in turn resulted in peace talks between the LRA and the Ugandan government. (Visit *http://www.invisiblechildren.com/home.php* to learn more.)

DEFENDING THE JUST WAR THEORY

These challenges to the JWT are sound, but not damning. The JWT, properly understood, is not a complete moral theory that answers all questions about the ethics of war *ad bellum, in bello,* and *post bellum.* It is a teleological theory with a just peace as its *telos*—its goal or object. Thus the JWT should be viewed as a tool that shapes our conversation about the ethics of war and peace. In its defense, I offer three closing arguments.

First, the JWT has stood the test of time. It has proven to be remarkably adaptive and relevant to the shifting social, political, and historical contexts of the ages. Starting in the ancient world of empire, through the Middle Ages, through two world wars, into the postmodern nuclear era, and now into the period of global terrorism, the JWT has matched the shifts in technology, the nature of warfare, and the geopolitical landscape. Throughout the centuries, it has provided a way to talk about war by providing moral and legal criteria for ethically evaluating the use of force. It will remain a relevant and useful tool for as long as war remains.

Second, it has helped curtail the slide into total war. By upholding *ad bellum* and *in bello* rules, regulations, norms, and expectations, the JWT acts as a moral "speed bump" in the descent into anarchy that often accompanies war. In response to those who claim the JWT is too theoretical or abstract and that it doesn't help prevent war, I answer: even if acts of aggression, violations of human rights, and war crimes are judged after the fact, the mere existence of such rules sets up a level of expectation and, when coupled with effective prosecution of crimes, can serve as a deterrent against the excessive use of force and aggression. Furthermore, the JWT is taught in military academies around the world. Military personnel exercise the *in bello* principles of discrimination and proportionality on a daily basis, while political leaders are forced to justify their saber rattling according to the *ad bellum* criteria.

Finally, my perspective as a Christian professor of ethics particularly shapes my appreciation of the JWT as a third way,"avoiding the extremes of pacifism and political realism. To the pacifists, I yield the moral high ground. Their position is principled and fits better into the Christian tradition, especially the example of Jesus. Pacifists rightly appeal to the real hope and divine promise of the fulfillment of the Reign of God. They do not, however, adequately consider human sinfulness, as Augustine and Niebuhr have illustrated. The JWT is not a secular philosophical ethic that has crept into the Christian tradition. It is based on a theological understanding of human nature. We are sinful, selfish, greedy, and violent. The greatest evidence of this claim is the cross itself. If humankind were not so enslaved to sin and violence, then why was it necessary for Jesus Christ to die on the cross? Standing in the shadow of the cross, we realize the depravity of human sinfulness and the necessity of moral restraint.

Political realism is too pessimistic. It rightly cautions us to take human sinfulness seriously, but it does not fully account for the human capacity to act reasonably and altruistically. Not every conflict must devolve into total war. Humans do seek peace, abhor violence, and can reconcile with one another. From a Christian perspective, political realism represents a denial of Christ's promise that the Reign of God is growing secretly, imperceptibly in our midst. The JWT, when interpreted conservatively (in a manner similar to the contemporary JWT or the JPP) affirms the Christian eschatological hope in the coming Reign of God without glossing over the reality of sin.

The JWT is an incomplete and an interim ethic. It is incomplete because it does not yield concrete answers to the problems of war and peace, and it is an interim ethic, from a Christian perspective, because it applies only in the era between Christ's resurrection and second coming. When the Reign of God is definitively established on earth, swords will be beaten into plowshares and spears into pruning hooks (Isa 2:4; Mic 4:3); but until that time, sin, greed, and violence will hold sway and must be resisted.

WHERE DO YOU FALL?

Our exploration of Christian approaches to war and peace has been presented as a continuum ranging from pacifism (the most "dovish") to holy war (the most "hawkish"). Return now to page 18 where the various approaches are displayed as an array. Based on your deeper understanding of pacifism and political realism, holy war, the just war theory, and challenges to the just war theory, where would you now place yourself on the continuum and why? In other words, how has encountering the ideas, arguments, or perspectives presented in this book caused you to reevaluate your own ethic of war and peace?

DISCUSSION QUESTIONS

1. Is the war on terrorism a case of supreme emergency?

2. Evaluate the rationales behind preemptive war and preventative war. Do you think either is a valid argument? What are the implications of these two doctrines?

3. Critique Maryann Cusimano Love's argument that combating terrorism is best understood as a war for the hearts and minds of people (a political operation) and not as a military operation.

4. The discussion of WMDs focused primarily on nuclear weapons. Adapt the principles and arguments used in that analysis to chemical and biological weapons.

5. What do you think of the Catholic position that the development and maintenance of nuclear stockpiles is a form of theft from the poor?

6. Critique the *jus post bellum* criteria. What are the strengths and weaknesses of Allman and Winright's criteria (identify at least two of each)?

7. Critique the Just Peacemaking Perspective. What are its strengths (identify at least two)? What are its weaknesses (identify at least two)?

8. At the end of the section, "Two Adaptations of the JWT," the author addresses you, the reader. What is your response to his challenge or invitation to work for a global just peace that he brings up at the end of the section, "Challenges to the JWT"? Are you already doing something as part of the global effort for a just peace? If yes, what and why? If no, why not?

9. The author ends the chapter with three arguments in defense of the JWT. What is his position? What are its strengths and weaknesses?

ENDNOTES

1 The terms *preemptive war* and *preventative war* are often used interchangeably, which can be confusing.

2 Hugo Grotius, *De Jure Belli Ac Pacis* (*On the Right of War and Peace*), in *Classics of International Law*, no. 3, trans. James Dame Maguire (Washington, DC: Carnegie Institute, 1913), book 2, chap.1, sec. 2, para. 1.

3 Ibid., chap. 1, sec. 4, para. 2.

4 Ibid., chap. 1, sec. 5, para. 1.

5 Ibid., chap. 22, sec. 5, para. 1.

6 Ibid., chap. 1, sec. 1, para. 7.

7 Ibid., chap. 22, sec. 6.

8 Ibid., chap. 1, sec. 17.

9 Grotius also declares that seeking "complete security" cannot serve as justification for striking out at every potential enemy, since absolute safety is impossible in this world. All of us must live with some degree of vulnerability.

10 George W. Bush's 2002 West Point commencement speech is available online at *http://www.whitehouse.gov/news/releases/2002/06/20020601-3.html*.

11 George W. Bush, "State of the Union," January 28, 2003, available online at *http://www.whitehouse.gov/news/releases/2003/01/20030128-19.html*.

12 National Security Council, "Strengthen Alliances to Defeat Global Terrorism and Work to Prevent Attacks against Us and Our Friends," Chapter 3 in The National Security Strategy of the United States of America (2002), available online at *http://www.whitehouse.gov/nsc/nss3.html*.

13 Michael Walzer, *Just and Unjust Wars: A Moral Argument with Historical Illustrations* (New York: Basic Books, 2000), 253.

14 Michael Walzer, *Arguing About War* (New Haven, CT: Yale University Press, 2004), 33.

15 Walzer, *Just and Unjust Wars*, 253.

16 George W. Bush's 2002 West Point commencement speech.

17 Walzer, *Just and Unjust Wars*, 180–82.

18 *Department of Defense Dictionary of Military and Associated Terms* (Washington, DC: United States Department of Defense, April 2001), 428.

19 Maryann Cusimano Love, "Effective Ways to Fight Terrorism While Retaining Our Values," in *Just War, Lasting Peace: What Christian Traditions Can Teach Us*, eds. John Kleiderer, Paula Minaert, and Mark Mossa (Maryknoll, NY: Orbis Books, 2006), 61.

20 Available at *http://www.globalsecurity.org/military/library/report/1990/GJ.htm*.

21 Love, 62.

22 Love, 64.

23 *The 9/11 Commission Report: Final Report of the National Commission on Terrorist Attacks upon the United States* (New York: W. W. Norton, 2004), 375.

24 *The 9/11 Commission Report*, 375–77.

25 Love, 65.

26 Mr. X [George Kennan], "The Sources of Soviet Conduct," *Foreign Affairs* 25.4 (1947), 566–82.

27 Nicholas Thompson, "A War Best Served Cold," *New York Times*, July 31, 2007, A19.

28 Love, 63.

29 Wesley Clark and Kal Raustiala, "Why Terrorists Aren't Soldiers," *New York Times*, July 8, 2007, A19.

30 Mumtaz Ahmad, quoted in "The Utility of the Just War Criteria," in David R. Smock, *Religious Perspectives on War: Christian, Muslim, and Jewish Attitudes toward Force after the Gulf War*, (Washington, DC: United States Institute of Peace Press, 1992), 13.

31 Paul VI, "World Day of Peace Message," 1976, available online at *http:/www.vatican.va/holy_father/paul_vi/messages/index.htm*.

32 Paul Ramsey, "A Political Ethics Context for Strategic Thinking," in *Strategic Thinking and Its Moral Implications*, ed. Morton Kaplan (Chicago: University of Chicago Center for Policy Study, 1973), 134–35. Compare Walzer, *Just and Unjust Wars*, 272.

33 The *Challenge of Peace*, no. 128.

34 Roger Hodge, "Weekly Review," *Harpers* (November 6, 2001), available online at *http://harpers.org/archive/2001/11/WeeklyReview 2001-11-06#20030929233915-9880061469*; Richard Norton-Taylor and Owen Bowcott, "British Use of Cluster Bombs Condemned," *The Guardian* (April 4, 2003), available online at *http://www.guardian. co.uk/politics/2003/apr/04/uk.iraq1*; "The Cluster Bomb Controversy," BBC News (April 3, 2003), available online at: *http://news.bbc.co.uk/ go/pr/fr/-/2/hi/uk_news/2912617.stm*.

35 Mark Allman, "Postwar Justice," *America* 193.11 (October 17, 2005), 9–13.

36 Mark Allman and Tobias Winright, "*Jus Post Bellum*: Extending the Just War Theory," in William J. Collinge, ed., *Faith in Public Life*, College Theology Society Annual, vol. 53 (Maryknoll, NY: Orbis, 2008), 241–66; and *After the Smoke Clears: Just War Theory and Postwar Justice* (Maryknoll, NY: Orbis, forthcoming 2009).

37 *Catechism of the Catholic Church*, nos. 1440–1470.

38 Brian Orend has done considerable work on *jus post bellum* ethics, especially in the area of regime change. He argues, "coercive postwar regime change is permissible provided: 1) the war itself was just and conducted properly; 2) the target regime was illegitimate, thus forfeiting its state rights; 3) the goal of the reconstruction is a minimally just regime; and 4) respect for *jus in bello* and human rights is integral to the transformation" (Orend, *The Morality of War* [Peterborough, Ontario: Broadview Press, 2006], 203).

39 Pope Paul VI, 1972 World Day for Peace address, available at the Vatican Web page, *http://www.vatican.va/holy_father/paul_vi/ messages/peace/index.htm.*

40 Glen Stassen, *Just Peacemaking: Ten Practices for Abolishing War* (Cleveland, OH: Pilgrim Press, 1998), 1. It is worth noting that Stassen and the other scholars on this project did not choose the subtitle of the book. They do not think these steps will abolish war, rather they hope to reduce the instances of war.

41 See Stassen, *Just Peacemaking.*

42 "ICBL — Frequently Asked Questions," available online at *http:// www.icbl.org/cgi-bin/faq/landmines/index.cgi?subject=996244752#0 996244892.*

CHAPTER 6

Conclusion

We end where we began. War is about killing. Those of us who study war and debate the moral and ethical quandaries that it poses from the safety of the classroom must never lose sight of this fact. When a nation goes to war it engages in state-sanctioned killing; it intentionally and violently kills and turns ordinary citizens into killers. Even if the cause is just, no war is victim free and no war can ever be considered perfectly just in the sense that it is waged only for right reasons, with pure intent, and using honorable means. The fog of war renders perfect moral clarity impossible.

In our discussion of the ethics of war, we must always be mindful of this moral ambiguity, especially when evaluating the choices and behavior of soldiers in the midst of battle. They do not always (if ever) enjoy the leisure of reflection. They often must act in an instant based on emotion and imperfect information. In short, soldiers in battle must rely on instinct, character, and preparation, which is why academic exercises that force us to wrestle with these issues are so important. Professional soldiers have devoted significant time to training and study. They have worked to form their character and hone their instincts so that faced with split-second decisions, they can rely on what they have learned.

We study war in times of peace to practice the critical thinking and rational argumentation the ethical realities of war demand. We hope that in times of war, we will know the right thing to do because we've already thought about it. To use the language of virtue theory, we will have developed the proper character and nurtured the relevant virtues that allow us to make informed ethical decisions quickly. Just as soldiers in the heat of battle do not have the luxury of deliberation, so too when nations are faced with an imminent threat, they must rely on instinct, and instinct can be trained. We revisit battles and wartime decisions after the fact to learn from the good, the bad, and the morally ambiguous, so that if faced with similar situations in the future, we can draw from experience and will know what to do.

I am a theologian, not a soldier. I chose to devote my life to theology out of my commitment to the life and teaching of Jesus Christ. I chose to focus on ethics because, while I enjoy the intellectual rigor of theological debate, I wanted my work to make a difference in the lives of real people, especially those who suffer. My hope is that in studying, teaching, and writing on the ethics of war and peace, I might contribute in a small way to how others think about the ugly reality called *war*, a reality we will face time and again throughout our lives.

I first became convinced of the importance of this work during Gulf War I (1991). While the evening news showed video of bombs being dropped on bridges and homes, with the silhouettes of human beings running for cover, some Americans cheered from their living rooms as if the home team had just scored a touchdown. My commitment to this work was reaffirmed in the second Gulf War (2003–), when once again America went to war with few questions asked. Instead, fueled by a mixture of fear and anger at the events of September 11, the saber rattling began and those of us who questioned the war were either dismissed as naïve or had our patriotism challanged.

I am an American and I am a Christian. In the language of Saint Augustine, I have dual citizenship: I belong to "the City of Man" and "the City of God." For American Christians, these two commitments are often seen as one and the same. We sing "God Bless America" and place the American flag in our churches, treating religious and national symbols as if they were identical. Or we compartmentalize our lives. We affirm our religious values on Sunday but fail to bring those commitments of faith to the public square, often rationalizing this moral schizophrenia under a distorted commitment to the separation of church and state. The early Christians understood that patriotism all too easily could devolve into idolatry, wherein love of country becomes the worship of a false god.

American Christians have a heavy burden to bear. As citizens of the most powerful nation on earth (economically, militarily, politically, and culturally), we have a unique responsibility to the rest of the world. Let me be clear, I am not hinting at some kind of "Global Manifest Destiny," "American Exceptionalism," or the idea that America is "the city built on the hill," a "light for all the world." No, these ideas from our heritage have justified brutal slaughter of Native Americans and violence against the world's poor. Here I am simply referring to the responsibility that comes with power. In popular culture, it is sometimes called the Spider-Man principle, the name inspired by a scene in the film *Spider-Man* when Peter Parker's (Spider-Man's) uncle declares just before he dies, "With great power comes great responsibility."[1] As a Christian, I prefer the earlier version of this moral maxim: "From everyone to whom much has been given, much will be required" (Luke 12:48, NRSV). As an American Christian, I must be vigilant in keeping my priorities and commitments straight: I am a disciple of Christ first and a citizen of the United States second. Whenever the values of these two identities conflict, I must always choose the former.

In focusing on Christian ethics and morals, I am not suggesting that Christians have a monopoly on addressing questions of war, peace, and social responsibility. Other faith traditions and those who profess no faith at all also have moral and ethical commitments on these issues. In the appendix, we examine the rich traditions of Judaism and Islam regarding free will, responsibility for others, social justice, and ethics of war and peace—traditions that include teachings on pacifism, holy war, and just war. Likewise, Hinduism, Buddhism, and nearly every other religious tradition has its own social ethic and something to say about war and peace in particular. War, peace, and justice are not only Christian or even religious concerns, they are human concerns. This book primarily focuses on the Christian theologies of war and peace, however, and I humbly leave to others the task of extrapolating and adapting what we have explored here to other religious and nonreligious ethical systems.

This examination of Christian attitudes and approaches toward war and peace is designed to help us map the sometimes conflicting duties to God and country, especially difficult in times of war. I framed the Christian approaches to war and peace using three schools of thought: pacifism, just war, and holy war. We began with simple definitions of each. Pacifism I initially defined as a commitment to peace grounded in justice and a refusal to resort to violence as a means of settling disputes, but later expanded to include seven types of pacifism. Holy war I introduced as any war waged either because God commands it (or at least because people believe that God has commanded it) or for other religious reasons (such as to defend or spread one's faith), then later identified ten types of holy war. Finally, I presented just war, first as a religious or philosophical theory that contends war, although regrettable, is sometimes warranted, but only if certain criteria are met (*jus ad bellum*, *jus in bello*, and *jus post bellum*). I went on to identify two interpretations of the just war theory: the classical just war tradition (which tends to adhere to a looser interpretation of the *ad bellum* criteria, especially just cause) and the contemporary just war tradition (which holds to a strict interpretation of the just war criteria, especially last resort, and operates out of a strong presumption against the use of force).

The danger in presenting these three schools of thought in this manner is that people sometimes see them as "camps," with high walls separating pacifism from just war from holy war. In presenting them along a continuum of approaches, as our chart does on page 18, I've tried to stress that this is more of a sliding scale. For example, the differences between strategic pacifism, just peacemaking, and contemporary just war theory are difficult to discern. Furthermore, one need not be a just war theorist to find its categories, language, and questions useful. John Howard Yoder, a pacifist, found the just war theory helpful in thinking and talking about war, even though he rejected war. Likewise pacifists can glean insights from the perspectives of Christian or political realists and vice versa. The just peacemaking perspective, with its commitment to eliminating the conditions that lead to war, is typically a position that everyone can endorse. Finally, some of the approaches we've encountered don't fit nicely within the scale at all. For example, the distinction between a politically engaged pacifism and separatist pacifism applies to all forms of pacifism; similarly, Christian realism applies to everything from strategic pacifism to holy war, while political realism, as a thoroughly secular philosophy, stands outside the Christian tradition completely, even though many Christians adhere to it.

Throughout this book you have been asked to identify where you fall on this continuum. Look back to the introduction—where did you place yourself on the continuum when you had only a basic understanding of the three schools of thought? How has your approach to war and peace changed (if at all) through the course of learning more about pacifism, holy war, and just war? How have the ideas, writers, and arguments you've encountered caused you to change your position, or how have they reaffirmed your position?

When I teach my war and peace course my students almost always ask me, "Where do you fall? What are you?" I don't like to reveal my own commitments until the end of the course, because

I want my students (and you the reader) to come to your own decision. Nevertheless, a careful reader can probably discern my own commitments and prejudices.

I am a contemporary just war theorist with a strong affinity for just peacemaking. This is not a decision I have reached easily. As I stated in chapter 5, to the pacifists I yield the moral high ground. Christian pacifism is rooted in Scripture and tradition, the cornerstones of the Christian faith. Yet I also find credible Christian realism's challenge to pacifism, even if the realists' dismissal of pacifism as naïve and their critique of pacifists as overly confident in the goodness of human nature are overly facile. The Augustinian heritage of Christian realism, which takes human sinfulness seriously, is both theologically well grounded (in both Scripture and tradition) and experientially verifiable. The reality of human sinfulness is all too apparent. We live in a world in which evil is real, and it is not a lack of faith to say that sometimes force, while regrettable and even sinful, is the lesser of two evils (such as in cases of humanitarian intervention). This being said, the just war theory is a slippery slope. Allowing the use of force even under strict conditions opens the door to loose interpretation. In the emotional buildup to war, gaining an objective perspective is nearly impossible; everything looks like a "supreme emergency" that warrants the use of force.

In class, I compare the JWT in the Christian church to having a handgun in one's home. Like all analogies, it has its limits, but I think it's a helpful exercise for explaining my reluctant contemporary just war position. If I keep a gun in my home, I do so with the knowledge that this is extremely dangerous and, statistically speaking, there is a strong chance that it could be used against a member of my own family. But it also could be used to protect my family in the event of a dangerous situation, such as facing a violent criminal. If I am willing to keep a gun in my home, then it is incumbent upon me to safeguard it by keeping it unloaded and in a locked and secure place, putting a trigger lock on it, storing the keys to these locks in separate locations, keeping the ammunition in a separate place, and making sure everyone in my home is trained in firearm safety. But even all of these precautions don't guarantee that the gun won't be misused.

The JWT is like keeping a gun in the church (theologically, not literally). It justifies the use of deadly force (in rare instances), which is at best problematic for Christians. This means that if one wants to be a Christian just war theorist, then one must also take steps to establish sufficient safeguards to ensure this deadly ethic will not be misused. For those who support the JWT, this analogy is challenging. Am I a hypocrite because I don't keep a gun in my home (precisely because doing so is dangerous and because I find it un-Christian) yet believe in and defend the legitimacy of the JWT? How can I support the "gun in the church" when I reject a gun in my home? In response to the charge of hypocrisy, I appeal to an argument Augustine made centuries ago, namely that the ethics that govern personal life are different than the ethics that govern larger entities such as the church or the state. Government and church have unique responsibilities for the common good, responsibilities which differ from those of the individual. To exercise these responsibilities, government and church also need recourse to certain actions that are not available to individuals.

Jesus Christ was a pacifist, and Christians ought to actively pursue building the Reign of God by pursuing justice. But we are also called to love our neighbor as ourselves, and love is more than simply feelings: it expresses itself in action, as the cross so aptly illustrates. We live in a world in which tyrants, demagogues, and hate-based ideologues fuel unspeakable atrocities. It is ethically irresponsible, I believe, to stand by while others are brutally assaulted and slaughtered. As the book of Leviticus reminds us, "you shall not . . . stand by idly when your neighbor's life is at stake. . . . You shall love your neighbor as yourself" (19:16,18). Sin is not limited to what I do, but includes what I fail to do. This ancient distinction between sins of commission and sins of omission is beautifully captured in the *Confiteor*, a prayer often said at the beginning of the Catholic celebration of Eucharist. "I confess to almighty God, and you my brothers and sisters, that I have sinned through my own fault, in my thoughts, in my words, in what I have done and what I have failed to do." We are responsible for one another and to God, for what we do and for what we fail to do. In particular, we will be judged (as Matt 25:31–46 reminds us) by what we have done to the least of God's children.

In a world in which sin is real, we cannot expect to live the Kingdom of God ethic perfectly. This is not a lack of faith in the power of the cross; it is affirmation of our need for Christ. War, which is always about killing, highlights this reality. My hope is that in reading this book and discussing it with others, you have wrestled with this paradox and formed a coherent and defendable position. All of us, whether we believe in God or not, long for a world at peace. As a Christian, I have reason to hope that what the prophets revealed will someday become reality:

> They shall beat their swords into plowshares
> and their spears into pruning hooks;
> One nation shall not raise the sword against another,
> nor shall they train for war again.
>
> (Isa 2:4 and Mic 4:3)

ENDNOTE

1 This line originally appeared in the Marvel comic *Amazing Fantasy* 15 (August 1962), by Stan Lee and illustrated by Steve Ditko, in which Spider-Man debuted.

Jewish and Muslim Perspectives on War and Peace

This book has focused almost exclusively on a continuum of approaches to war and peace within the Christian tradition. It would be impossible to devote a similar amount of attention to pacifism, just war, and holy war in both Judaism and Islam in a single volume, but it would also be irresponsible to ignore these other traditions, for two principal reasons. First, Judaism, Christianity, and Islam share a common heritage. All three are "children of Abraham" (that is, all three trace their religious lineage back to a common patriarch, Abraham). Secondly, all contemporary wars have global ramifications, including religious and cultural dimensions. It is impossible to talk about war as if religion and culture didn't matter. Recent conflicts in the Middle East highlight this point. Some have characterized these conflicts (especially U.S. and European involvement in Iraq) as a "clash of civilizations" between the Western secularized or Christian culture and Arab or Muslim culture.[1] Meanwhile, decades of fighting between Israeli and Palestinian forces continues to destabilize the region, a conflict portrayed as a Jewish-Muslim hostility. Thus, any serious study of the Christian traditions on war and peace must engage in comparative religious studies.

JUDAISM

A BRIEF INTRODUCTION

Judaism is one of the smallest religions in the world (less than 1 percent of the world's population is Jewish), but its historical significance is hard to overemphasize. Both Christianity and Islam, the two largest religions in the world, share scriptural traditions, historical foundations, and a number of ethical commitments with their Jewish predecessors. Many Christians have a distorted view of Judaism. They tend to reduce Judaism to biblical Judaism. Their primary information about Judaism comes from the Christian Scriptures; for this reason, many assume contemporary Judaism is similar to the Judaism that Jesus practiced. But Judaism, like any centuries-old religion, has adapted and changed over the years. The Judaism of Jesus' time and place (first-century CE Palestine) is different from the Judaism of Europe in the Middle Ages, which is different from the Judaism practiced in twenty-first-century America.

Jewish beliefs and practices are not monolithic. No central authority decides matters of doctrine or ethics (such as a pope or Vatican in the Roman Catholic Church). Judaism is an intellectually vibrant tradition that thrives on debate and argument. The primary source of authority for Jewish belief and practice is the Hebrew Bible, called the *tanakh* (commonly referred to by Christians as the Old Testament). The Hebrew Bible consists of three main parts:

- Torah (or Pentateuch in Greek): The first five books of both Hebrew and Christian Scriptures includes Genesis (from creation through three generations of Abraham's family, the earliest Israelites), Exodus (the liberation of the Israelites from slavery in Egypt and their journey to Mount Sinai), and Leviticus, Numbers, and Deuteronomy (regulations received at Mount Sinai and progress to the edge of the land promised to Abraham). Torah ("instruction" or "law") refers to these five books, or to the covenant stipulations received at Mount Sinai (including the Ten Commandments), or, more generally, to God's cumulative instruction to the Israelites embedded in these stories, experiences, directions, and their interpretation.

- Nevi'im (The Prophets): The Jewish Bible groups together a theological account of the Israelite kingdoms (Joshua through 2 Kings) and proclamations of the prophets who critiqued the religious, social, political, and economic institutions and practices of the community (for example, Isaiah, Jeremiah, Ezekiel, Hosea, Micah, Amos). The primary role of a prophet was not to predict the future, but to remind the Israelites—especially their political, religious, and judicial leaders—of God's priorities and to call them back to right relations with God and one another. The prophets tended to emphasize the importance of social justice, and, in particular, they stressed the obligation to care for the poor and weak as more important than questions of ritual, purity, or worship. These first two sections (Torah and Prophets) were already the normative Scriptures in Jesus' time.

- Ketuvim (The Writings): Grouped at the end of the Hebrew Bible are books of many types, long honored but accepted as Scripture late in the first century CE: hymns (Psalms), wisdom literature (Proverbs), five books read at festivals (Ruth, Esther, and others), and later theological "histories" (Chronicles, Ezra, Nehemiah).

Another authoritative source for Judaism is the Talmud, a collection of teachings and interpretations of the Torah by wise and respected rabbis through the centuries. While it does not enjoy the same authority as Scripture, it is highly esteemed.

Covenant and Torah are two central tenets of Jewish theology. The covenant refers to the special relationship between God and the Jewish people. It was first established with Abraham and Sarah (Genesis 15–21) and reaffirmed during the Exodus when God intervened to liberate the Israelites from slavery in Egypt. It is best summed up in God's promise, "You will be my people and I will be your God" (Ezek 36:28; Jer 11:4; 24:7; 30:22, 31:1; Lev 26:12). The covenant is often described like a marriage, wherein God is the husband and the Jewish people (collectively) are God's spouse. Sometimes Jews are referred to as "God's chosen people," which is not meant to imply the exclusion of anyone else, but rather to capture the notion that God and the Jewish people enjoy a special relationship: "if you hearken to my voice and keep my covenant, you shall be my special possession, dearer to me than all other people" (Exod 19:5).

Closely related to the idea of covenant is the Jewish notion of Torah (more familiar to Christians from the Greek New Testament as *law*). While for many the word *law* connotes restrictions and limitations that come with penalties, in Judaism the Torah gives life. In other words, the *law* (Torah) is not a limitation; it outlines the practices, customs, and obligations of living the covenant. Using the marriage analogy, think about what you must do to keep a marriage (or any loving relationship) alive and healthy. Both parties must be faithful, honest, committed to spending time together, and so on. The Torah functions in a similar fashion. The laws are the rules for keeping the relationship (the covenant) alive.

JUDAISM AND PACIFISM

As we saw in Chapter 3 on holy war, the Hebrew Bible contains quite a bit of divine violence: God expels Adam and Eve from the Garden of Eden with a sword-wielding angel; God floods the entire earth and drowns every living creature except those saved in Noah's ark; God intercedes on behalf of the Israelites in Egypt by sending ten plagues and drowning the Egyptian army; God provides the land and security for their settlement by slaughtering several local peoples. These are but a few examples.

Historically, however, until 1948 Jews had not had control of a fully independent state and its armies since the Babylonian conquests of Jerusalem about 600 BCE. Two unsuccessful attempts

MAJOR DIVISIONS IN JUDAISM

Judaism has four major sects (divisions):

- Orthodox: the most traditional sect, keeping kosher dietary regulations and following an almost literal interpretation of religious law;
- Conservative: less strict in their interpretation of religious law than the Orthodox;
- Reform: more liberal than the Conservatives in their interpretation of the law;
- Reconstructionist: also more liberal in their interpretation of the law, but often maintaining traditional customs.

to revolt against Roman rule (66–70 and 132–135 CE) deflated Jewish hope for military victory. Moving beyond the biblical era, centuries of Jewish experience as victims of violence have colored Judaism's stance on war and pacifism. Self-defense in the Jewish tradition is often not merely a discussion of individual self-defense or even defense of a large group of people, but rather it is about the survival of the Jewish people as a whole. In this context, Judaism has defended the notion of a just war, the right to national self-defense, and the legitimate use of force to protect the weak and vulnerable. Because recent history includes an attempt to kill all Jews in Europe, and nuclear weapons coupled with hostilities in the Middle East make the obliteration of the modern state of Israel a real threat, contemporary Judaism stresses the right to self-defense. As Michael Broyde, director of the law and religion program at Emory University School of Law, concludes:

It is clear that the Jewish tradition does not favor pacifism as a value superior to all other values or incorporate it as a basic moral doctrine within Judaism. . . . But it is crucial to emphasize that the Jewish tradition does not reject pacifism as a practical response to immorality or evil. Rather, tactical pacifism has a place as the clearly superior alternative to cooperating with evil [but] . . . what is obvious to all students of Jewish law and ethics [is]: *Theological pacifism has no place in the Jewish tradition.*"[2]

This should not suggest that Judaism fails to esteem peace.[3] As a religion that affirms the sanctity of life, Judaism always sees violence as regrettable, something that ought to be restrained and used only as a last resort in the name of self-defense. As Broyde asserts: "There is one element of pacifism that is clearly found in the Jewish tradition: the minimization of violence. In nearly all situations where Jewish law allows violence to prevent an evil from occurring, it mandates that the minimal amount of violence be used to accomplish one's goal."[4] Thus Jewish pacifism is closer to the contemporary JWT in that it seeks a just peace and is governed by micro- and macro-proportionality. Indeed the word *shalom*, often translated as "peace," refers not simply to the absence of war and conflict, but to wholeness, integrity, righteousness, and justice. Furthermore, *shalom* is not simply a peace that one waits patiently for God to deliver. It is inherent upon all Jews to pursue *tikkun olam*, "to repair or heal the world," by actively working for social justice. Judaism does not have a pacifist tradition as robust as Christian pacifism. It does not demand absolute or even principled pacifism, but it certainly is a peace-loving and peace-seeking tradition. The traditional Jewish approach to questions of war and peace is closer to strategic pacifism or just war.

JUDAISM AND JUST WAR

The just war tradition is principally a Christian tradition in the sense that it was primarily developed by Christian theologians and later evolved as a Western political theory in the Christian cultures of Europe and North America. This is not to suggest, however, that ideas about rules of war and just and unjust wars are the exclusive possession of Christian and Western thinkers. In fact, Judaism and Islam both have just war traditions.

The Jewish just war tradition is less developed and less systematic than the Christian version primarily because Jews, unlike Christians, have not "enjoyed" much political or military power. Much of the tradition is based on Deuteronomy 20 and the Talmud. The elements of the Jewish just war theory may be described as follows:

Just Cause: In the Jewish tradition there are three types of war: wars commanded by God, or holy wars (*milhemet mitzvah*, or *herem*), obligatory wars, or defensive wars (*milhemet hovah*), and permitted wars, wars of choice, or optional wars (*milhemet reshut*).[5] As was discussed in chapter 3, Jewish holy wars (*herem*) are an historical oddity, namely the conflicts described in accounts of the Exodus and settlement, and they offer little help in understanding the Jewish just war tradition. Judaism does not permit wars waged for the expansion of the faith. Religious belief cannot be imposed by force because faith requires assent of the will. The war against the Canaanites was not waged because they were idolaters per se, but because they threatened the right worship of God. Religious conversion cannot serve as a justification for waging war; only when the Jewish people and their right to freely worship God are threatened can resort to force be justified.

Defensive wars are seen as obligatory because they are justified only when there is no other option (that is, as a last resort). They include wars to defend Israel and all Jews from acts of aggression (self-defense) and defense of the weak and vulnerable from unjust attack, which is similar to Augustine's justification of war as an act of charity (neighbor-love). Remember that Jesus' greatest commandment, "You shall love the Lord your God with all your heart, with all your soul, with all your mind, and with all your strength," which he coupled with, "You shall love your neighbor as yourself" (Mark 12:30–31), was nothing more than a combination of two commandments from the Hebrew Bible (Deut 6:4–5 and Lev 19:18). Defensive wars are not merely permissible in Judaism, they are mandatory. Failing to come to the aid of a person in need is seen as contributing to their victimization. You shall not "stand by idly when your neighbor's life is at stake" (Lev 19:16) is a principle that can be expanded to include whole nations. One is held morally responsible not only for what one has done but also for what one has failed to do.

Optional wars include wars waged to expand the borders of Israel (to increase territory), to weaken the threat of enemies (pre-emptive and preventative wars), and for the sake of glory, all of which require greater justification. These kinds of optional wars are found throughout the tradition, and it should be noted that the validity of optional wars is debated.

Legitimate Authority: Political authority has a long and troubled history in Judaism. Moses is depicted as the religious, military, and political leader of the Israelites during the Exodus. When the task of adjudicating disputes between the people became too time-consuming, he appointed a panel of judges. Later, during accounts of the settlement period, the people implored the prophet Samuel to give them a king, like other nations. Initially Samuel refused because God should be their king, but ultimately God relented because of their persistence. God granted them a king, with the warning that their king will "take your sons" and use them for his armies and "to make his implements of war" (1 Samuel 8).

In the postbiblical period, the authority to wage war was considered self-evident in obligatory wars, but only the king could declare a *milhemet mitsvah*. The traditional biblical exemptions from military service (such as having crops still in the field, being engaged but not yet married, or possessing a timid disposition [Deut 20:5–9]) were suspended in times of national self-defense. For optional wars, the traditional exemptions remained in place. Optional wars, however, required the consent of the Sanhedrin, a body of Jewish elders responsible for religious, moral, social, and political affairs. All of this suggests that within the tradition there is an expectation that the decision to wage war rests with some type of political authority (king or elders).[6]

For most of their history, Jews have been political outsiders, a religious minority within a larger empire, often seeing themselves as a people in exile or a people apart from mainstream society. In such an environment, Jews were able to watch political developments from a detached position. Wars between Christian nations or wars between Christians and Muslims were not a Jewish concern, although Jews may have been victims of wars such as the Crusades. In the early modern period, however, with the rise of nationalism, people began to identify themselves not just in terms of religious or ethnic identity but as members of the same nation. Jews came to see themselves not as a people set apart, but as full citizens of the countries in which they lived. In the aftermath of World War I, especially, Jews came to interpret the requirement to defend the nation-state in wars of self-defense as obligatory as well. It was one of the duties of citizenship. World War II, for obvious reasons, was interpreted as both a war of national defense and a defense of the faith.

Right Intention: In a manner similar to Augustine, Judaism holds that peace is the primary aim, or goal, of war. This is not peace at any cost or peace as the absence of war. It is a just peace *(mishpat shalom)* that brings order, harmony, and justice to human relations and right worship of God. Isaiah described this perfect, just, and holy peace as a time when there will be no more war under a future king in Jerusalem, later adapted to messianic hope (Isa 2:4 and Mic 4:3). Maimonides (1194–1270), a medieval Spanish rabbi who fled Spain during the Inquisition, warned "that even the most naturally upright of men is enveloped in violence and anger when setting off to battle against an enemy,"[7] which suggests that one must fight with pure intentions, by not rejoicing in the defeat of one's enemy, but in the defeat of evil. Again, as in the Christian tradition, a just war is not simply one that has just cause; rather, the motivation (interior disposition) must also be rightly ordered since war involves killing, which under normal circumstances would be a sin. It is the intention that makes this normally abhorrent act tolerable.

Last Resort and Macro-proportionality: Again, like Augustine, the Jewish tradition sees war as a regrettable state of affairs, a sign of human sinfulness that taints everyone involved. For example, King David fought just wars but was forbidden by God to build

THOU SHALL NOT KILL?

Many mistakenly believe that the commandment in Exodus 20:13 is, "Thou shalt not kill," whereas "Thou shalt not murder" is a better translation. The difference between killing and murder has to do with legality and premeditation. Murder refers to an illegal (or unauthorized) and premeditated taking of a person's life. Killing also involves the taking of life, but includes accidental deaths, killing in self-defense, and other "justified" killings.

the temple because "you are a warrior, you have spilt blood" (1 Chron 28:3).

The book of Deuteronomy gives both descriptions and prescriptions for Israelite warfare for entering Canaan, from the vantage point of editors writing perhaps five hundred years later. When the Israelites wanted to pass through the land of the Ammonites, God said, "When you approach the frontier of the Ammonites, do not harass them or engage them in battle, for I will not give the land of the Ammonites to you," thus showing that peace is preferable to war (Deut 2:19, NRSV). Moses promises the Ammonite king that the Israelites will only pass through their land and will pay for any food and water they consume (Deut 2:26–30; see also Judg 11:12–28). The Ammonite king, however, confronts the Israelites, who retaliate. "At that time we captured all his towns, and in each town we utterly destroyed men, women, and children. We left not a single survivor. Only the livestock we kept as spoil for ourselves, as well as the plunder of the towns" (Deut 2:34–35, NRSV). The Israelite victory is interpreted as won by the hand of God, since "the LORD our God gave him over to us; and we struck him down, along with his offspring and all his people" (Deut 2:33, NRSV). The Israelite rules of war are more explicitly detailed in Deuteronomy 20:10–15, where it offers the general rule, "When you draw near to a town to fight against it, offer it terms of peace" (20:10, NRSV) — which sounds reasonable—but the passage goes on to declare:

> If it accepts your terms of peace . . . then all the people in it shall serve you at forced labor. If it does not submit to you peacefully, but makes war against you, then you shall besiege it; . . . you shall put all its males to the sword. You may, however, take as your booty the women, the children, livestock, and everything else in the town, all its spoils. (Deut 20:11–14, NRSV)

These biblical examples of last resort hardly compare to the contemporary understanding of last resort because they are described from the theological certainty of God's victory. The requirement of offering terms of peaceful surrender does not require negotiation or any kind of compromise with one's enemy. This is closer to what we today would term "unconditional surrender," which most just war theorists deride as immoral and ineffective. Seeking peace first has been interpreted, by some rabbis, as applying only in optional wars, not defensive wars. There is further debate as to when "last resort" applies. Must one wait until attacked before a war becomes obligatory? What if a former enemy is amassing troops at the border? Can a preemptive strike be considered obligatory, or is it merely optional? If only optional, is it still justified?

Concerning behavior in war *(jus in bello)*, compassion is the overriding concern. The Jewish just war tradition offers three *jus in bello* criteria: the need to distinguish between combatants and noncombatants (discrimination), a strong concern for the environmental impact of war *(jus post bellum)*, and a restrained use of force (micro-proportionality).

Deuteronomy 20 distinguishes between combatants and noncombatants. After an offer of peace has been rejected, all of the men (presumably because they are soldiers) are to be "put to the sword," while the women and children are to be spared. This example is considered disproportionate by today's standard since it involves the slaughter of all men, including wounded soldiers and prisoners of war.

The Talmud tempers the severity of these commands in several ways. First, the opportunity to flee before a battle must be afforded to civilians and soldiers not wishing to fight. According to Maimonides, when Joshua entered Israel, he sent three letters to the Canaanites. The first was an invitation to flee before the impending invasion, the second offered terms of peace, and the third was a warning to prepare to fight. Maimonides codified this example and declared that when a city is under siege, the invading army must surround only three sides of the city, leaving the fourth as an avenue of escape (although obviously it should be monitored to prevent the enemy from using this as an avenue for reinforcement). The practice of leaving an escape route is not only a principle of compassion but also serves to discriminate between civilians and soldiers. After three warnings and an opportunity to escape, anyone left behind is considered a combatant. This principle applies only to optional wars, not obligatory ones. The Talmud also explicitly forbids waging optional wars when the casualty rate would most likely exceed a sixth of the population (Shevuot 35b). This not only limits civilian causalities, it also prohibits futile wars, which later the just war tradition addresses under the probability of success principle.[8]

Judaism's just war tradition is by far the most ecologically sensitive among the three Abrahamic religions. Deuteronomy 20:19–20 explicitly forbids the wanton destruction of orchards. Fruit trees typically take years, if not decades, to reach maturity; cutting them down condemns future generations to starvation, making this a disproportionate and indiscriminate response. This passage has been expanded over the centuries to include prohibitions of damaging other basic resources: destroying life-sustaining infrastructure; salting fields; poisoning wells; destroying food warehouses; using chemical, biological, and nuclear weapons; destroying electrical grids and water treatment facilities; and so on.

Concerning the proportionate use of force (micro-proportionality), the Jewish just war tradition distinguishes between legitimate and illegitimate targets. If a target is illegitimate, than any use of force is condemned, whereas if it is legitimate, any use of force is permitted, so long as it doesn't cause long-term environmental destruction.

Judaism, like Christianity, contains pacifism, just war, and holy war strains. While this exploration has focused primarily on biblical arguments, it is worth noting again that contemporary Judaism is not the same as Israelite religion or the Judaism of Jesus' time. The establishment of the modern state of Israel in 1948 and the following decades of violence, including numerous clashes with Egypt, Syria, and Lebanon (most notably the War of Israeli Independence and the Six-Day War), and the seemingly never-ending Israeli-Palestinian conflict (which includes combating organizations linked to terrorism such as the Palestinian Liberation Organization, Hamas, and Hezbollah) have forced modern Judaism to develop its own theologies of war and peace. Thus, while I have argued that holy war tradition in Judaism is restrained to biblical accounts of the Exodus and settlement, it should be noted that the concept of holy war has never completely disappeared from the tradition. As Rueven Firestone notes:

> "Holy war," sanctioned or even commanded by God, is a common and recurring theme in the Hebrew Bible. Rabbinic Judaism largely avoided discussion of holy war for the simple reason that it became dangerous and self-destructive. . . . The rabbis therefore built a fence around the notion through two basic strategies: to define and categorize biblical wars so that they became virtually unthinkable in their contemporary world and to construct a divine contract between God, the Jews, and the world of the Gentiles that would establish an equilibrium preserving the Jews from overwhelming Gentile wrath by preventing Jewish actions that could result in war. The notion of divinely commanded war, however, was never expunged from the repertoire of Jewish ideas. Remaining latent, it was able to be revived when the historical context seemed to require it. Such a revival occurred with the rise of Zionism and particularly after the 1967 and 1973 wars.[9]

Similarly, the Jewish JWT has adapted and changed over the centuries, most recently in conjunction with laws concerning when war is acceptable for the state of Israel *(jus ad bellum)* and protocols for the Israeli Defense Forces *(jus in bello)*.[10]

ISLAM

A BRIEF INTRODUCTION

Islam is the second largest and fastest growing religion in the world. Muslims (as the practitioners are called) see themselves as members of one religious community (the *umma*), which includes three main groups. Sunni Muslims are the largest group (about 85 percent of the Muslim population). Sunni Islam emphasizes adherence to basic Muslim doctrines (as opposed to strict uniformity of belief in all things) and allows for cultural adaptation. It stresses logical persuasion in resolving religious debates. Shiite Muslims, the next largest group (about 10 percent), stress the importance of the imam (local religious leader) as the proper authority for interpreting the Qur'an (the principal holy book of Islam). Sufi Muslims are the smallest group and represent the mystical branch of the faith, emphasizing a personal relationship with God through deep prayer and asceticism. As Rueven Firestone observes:

> Islam, as all religious civilizations, represents a complex system of values and ritual, theology and folklore, law and faith. Like all religions, it contains within it both the deep and the simple, the sublime and the cruel, the exalted and the ignoble. Like Judaism and Christianity, Islam is multifaceted, offering a variety of responses to the questions and perplexities of the human condition. It cannot fairly be forced into a single wrapping. Just as Judaism and Christianity rarely have a single view on issues of religious import, whether it be in the areas of theology, ritual, or epistemology, as well as the more commonly known issues of law and interpretation, so, too, Islam offers a range of views. Not only are there differences among Shi'ites, Sunnis, and Sufis, of which some educated Westerners may be generally familiar, within each of these and other Muslim groups may be found an abundance of subgroups expressing different views and trends. As Aziz al Azmeh [prominent Islamic scholar and author of

Islams and Modernity (London: Verso, 1993)] articulates it, there are many "Islams."[11]

Muslims consider their faith to be the perfection of the other great monotheistic religions (Judaism and Christianity), and as such they share a common heritage with Jews and Christians. For Muslims, these other Abrahamic traditions also are "People of the Book," because all three have received revelations from the one true God. For Muslims, Muhammad (about 570–632 CE), the "seal of the prophets," is the last prophet or great messenger of God. He received a series of revelations in the sixth century (starting in 610) that were written down and became the Qur'an. Muhammad began preaching this message of strict monotheism in Mecca, a city of remarkable religious pluralism. He was persecuted for his beliefs, his strict moral code, and for denouncing other religions as false. In 622, he and his followers left Mecca for Medina (the emigration known as *Hijra*), a neighboring city where he enjoyed a considerable following and was able to establish the first Muslim community. In 630, Muhammad and his followers captured the city of Mecca without taking a single life. They then enjoyed religious, political, and economic dominance of the region. One of the most remarkable accomplishments in the Prophet's life was the ability to engender loyalty based on religious association over and against tribal loyalties. In the pre-Islamic era, the Arabian Peninsula was an amalgamation of tribal groups. According to Firestone, these pre-Islamic tribal wars were fought primarily for financial gain (to seize land, livestock, or goods) or for honor (to revenge a wrong or insult). In this era, social identity was based on tribal membership, and honor defending the tribe was highly esteemed. Muhammad was able to cause a social identity shift among the believers whereby they primarily viewed themselves as belonging to the *umma* (the Muslim community, which included people from multiple tribes) over and above their tribal identity.[12]

During the great Islamic Conquest (633–651), Islam expanded rapidly throughout the Middle East and North Africa. Ultimately Islam spread to Europe, reaching Spain in the early eighth century and Austria in the seventeenth century; this threatened the hegemony of Christianity in Europe. With the fall of the Turkish-based Ottoman Empire (1299–1923 CE), Islam's influence declined. Currently Islam is experiencing another period of rapid growth throughout the entire world, based on conversion rather than conquest.

The Qur'an for Muslims is the definitive word of God. It allows no alteration and is considered authoritative only when in the original Arabic (while translations are permitted, they are not considered the word of God). The Qur'an is the perfect and complete revelation of God's will. Many Christians assume that the Qur'an for Muslims is like the Bible for Christians. A better analogy is the Qur'an for Muslims is like Jesus Christ is to Christians: God's perfect and complete revelation. The Qur'an contains numerous types of instruction: praises of God; stories about prophets; discussions of the afterlife; rules concerning marriage, divorce, and the care of orphans; treatises on the importance of family and community; ritual practices, dietary laws, and a host of other topics. The passages concerning war and peace represent only a fraction of the larger work, which is important to keep in mind in this exploration of Muslim ethics of war and peace. One problem Islam continually struggles with is how to interpret and apply the centuries-old doctrines of the Qur'an to contemporary problems. To aid in the interpretation and understanding of the Qur'an, Muslims look to the Hadith (a collection of sermons, sayings, and biographical accounts of Muhammad) and the Shari'a (social, political, economic, legal, and moral codes based on the Qur'an and Hadith and compiled by Muslim scholars over the centuries). Islam is a religion founded on debate, rational argument, and interpretation of divine and respected sources. As such, it does not easily yield definitive universal statements. Outside of a few core beliefs ("There is one God Allah and Muhammad is his prophet"), it is hard to say, "All Muslims believe . . ." Ethical teachings in Islam are left to the persuasiveness of the argument and the authority of the teacher.

JIHAD: JUST WAR, HOLY WAR, OR FORM OF PACIFISM?

The word *islam* actually means "peace" or "submission." While this seems odd to many non-Muslims, since the two terms are not normally considered synonymous, it reflects a core belief in Islam. Personal peace can only be achieved by surrendering oneself to the will of God, and peace among all peoples will happen only when the entire world accepts the authority of God and Islam. Islam, like Christianity, is predominantly exclusive and has a history of being aggressive in seeking coverts. It holds it is the perfect religion and that its mission is to convert the entire world.

Any discussion of Muslim ideas about war and peace immediately turns to the word *jihad*, but other words are also used in the Qur'an, such as *qital* (fighting) and *harb* (wars for purely secular, that is, nonreligious reasons). Many non-Muslims assume *jihad* means "holy war," which reduces this complex and foundational idea of Islam to its most violent dimension. Better translations of the term are "struggle," "to exert oneself," or "concerted effort toward a noble end." In this vein, the term *jihad* is most often used in ways that have nothing to do with war, such as "jihad of the heart" (the struggle against sin), "jihad of the tongue" (struggling to speak well of others and avoid slander and gossip), or as Muhammad said, "The best jihad is [speaking] a word of justice to a tyrannical leader."[13]

Islam distinguishes between two types of jihad: *al-jihad al-akbar*, "the greater struggle," and *al-jihad al-asghar*, "the lesser struggle." The greater jihad is internal. It is the concerted effort to submit or conform one's will and desires to the will of God. It is the constant struggle to put God and God's law above and before all selfishness. It is the struggle against sin, which is constant and lifelong. The lesser jihad refers to times when Muslims must resort to force to defend or spread the faith. It is a subsection of or a footnote to the greater jihad and requires significant justification.

While many Muslims rightly decry that *jihad* is routinely misunderstood by most non-Muslims and falsely translated to mean "holy war," there is hardly uniformity of belief among

Muslims themselves regarding how to interpret and understand jihad. The principal debate is over whether to take it literally or metaphorically. This debate is fueled by seemingly contradictory passages in the Qur'an itself and the fact that the Prophet's own stance on the use of force changed over his lifetime. In the Qur'an, one finds what are called "peace" and "sword passages." The peace passages were revealed to the Prophet during his time in Mecca (610–622), when Islam was a minority religion, and in the early Medina years, before Muslims gained political dominance in the region.

For example, peace passages in the Qur'an for dealing with non-Muslims counsel[14]:

> Therefore follow what has been revealed to you from your Lord. There is no god but Him. Avoid the pagans. Had Allah pleased, they would not have worshipped idols. We have not made you their keeper, you are not their guardian. (6:106)

> Proclaim what you are bidden [required to do] and avoid the idolaters. We will Ourself sustain you against those that mock you and serve other gods beside Allah. They shall before long know the truth. (15:94)

> Call men to the path of your Lord with wisdom and kindly exhortation. Reason with them in the most courteous manner. . . . Be patient, then: Allah will grant you patience. Do not grieve for the unbelievers, nor distress yourself at their intrigues. (16:125–127)

> Be courteous when you argue with People of the Book, except with those among them who do evil. Say: "We believe in that which is revealed to us and which was revealed to you. Our God and your God is one. To Him we surrender ourselves." (29:46)

> Those who dispute Our revelations shall know that they have no escape. . . . Let evil be rewarded with evil. But he that forgives and seeks reconcilement shall be rewarded by Allah. . . . To endure with fortitude and to forgive is a duty incumbent on all. (42:35–43)

These passages clearly show an attitude of tolerance toward nonbelievers and encourage walking away from arguments about religion. Other passages suggest that this strategy is only temporary, however:

> Many of the People of the Book wish, through envy, to lead you back to unbelief, now that you have embraced the faith and the truth has been made plain to them. Forgive them and bear with them until Allah makes known His will. He has power over all things. (2:109)

> But because they [the Jews] broke their covenant, We laid on them Our curse and hardened their hearts. They have perverted the words of the Scriptures and forgotten much of what they were enjoined. You will find them deceitful, except for a few of them. But pardon them and bear with them. Allah loves the righteous.

> With those that say they were Christians We made a covenant also, but they too have forgotten much of what they were enjoined. Therefore We stirred among them enmity and hatred, which shall endure till the Day of Resurrection, when Allah will declare to them all that they have done.

> People of the Book! Our apostle has come to reveal to you much of what you have hidden from the Scriptures, and to forgive you much. A light has come to you from Allah and a glorious Book, with which He will guide to the paths of peace those that seek to please Him; He will lead them by His will from darkness to light; He will guide them to a straight path. (5:13–16)

In other words, tolerance may only be an interim ethic, observed "until God gives his command."

With the great migration to Medina in 622, the political outsider status of Muhammad and the Muslim community changed, and so did the content of the revelation. Muhammad authorized raids against pilgrims traveling to and from the pagan shrines in Mecca, raids justified as redressing wrongs committed against Muslims from when they lived in Mecca and as a way of disrupting worship of false gods. Violence becomes more prominent in the Qur'an passages from this era, as the sword passages reveal:

Fight for the sake of Allah those that fight against you, but do not attack them first. Allah does not love the aggressors.

Kill them wherever you find them. Drive them out of the place from which they drove you. Idolatry is worse than carnage. But do not fight them within the precincts of the Holy Mosque unless they attack you there; if they attack you put them to the sword. Thus shall the unbelievers be rewarded; but if they mend their ways, know that Allah is forgiving and merciful.

Fight against them until idolatry is no more and Allah's religion reigns supreme. But if they mend their ways, fight none except the evil-doers. . . . If anyone attacks you, attack him as he attacked you. (2:190–194)

Fighting is obligatory for you, as much as you dislike it. But you may hate a thing although it is good for you, and love a thing although it is bad for you. Allah knows, but you do not.

They ask you about the sacred month. Say: "To fight in this month is a grave offense; but to debar others from the path of Allah, to deny Him, and to expel His worshippers from the Holy Mosque, is far more grave in His sights. Idolatry is worse than carnage."

They will not cease to fight against you until they force you to renounce your faith—if they are able. But whoever of you recants and dies an unbeliever . . . shall be the tenants of Hell. (2:216–218; see also 8:38–39)

If you fear treachery from any of your allies, you may retaliate by breaking off your treaty with them. Allah does not love the treacherous.

Let the unbelievers not think that they will escape Us. They have not the power to do so. Muster against them all the men and cavalry at your disposal, so that you may strike terror into the enemies of Allah and the faithful.

If they incline to peace, make peace with them, and put your trust in Allah.

Prophet, rouse the faithful to arms. If there are twenty steadfast men among you, they shall vanquish two hundred; and if there are a hundred, they shall rout a thousand unbelievers, for they are devoid of understanding. (8:59–66)

Proclaim a woeful punishment to the unbelievers, except those idolaters who have honored their treaties with you and aided none against you. With these keep faith, until the treaties have run their term. Allah loves the righteous.

When the sacred months are over slay the idolaters wherever you find them. If they repent and take to prayer and pay the alms-tax, let them go their way. Allah is forgiving and merciful.

If an idolater seeks asylum with you, give him protection so that he may hear the word of Allah; and then convey him to safety. For idolaters are ignorant men. (9:4–7)

Allah has been with you on many a battlefield. (9:25)

Believers, why is it that when it is said to you: "March in the cause of Allah," you linger slothfully in the land? Are you content with this life in preference to the life to come? Few indeed are the blessings of this life, compared to those of the life to come.

If you do not fight He will punish you sternly and replace you by other men. . . . Whether unarmed or well-equipped, march on and fight for the cause of Allah, with your wealth and your persons. This will be best for you, if you but knew it. (9:38–45)

Prophet, make war on the unbelievers and the hypocrites and deal rigorously with them. Hell shall be their home: an evil fate. (9:73)

Believers, make war on the infidels who dwell around you. Deal courteously with them. Know that Allah is with the righteous. (9:123)

When you meet the unbelievers in the battlefield strike off their heads and, when you have laid them low, bind your captives firmly. Then grant them their freedom or take ransom from them, until War shall lay down her armor.

Thus shall you do. Had Allah willed, he could Himself have punished them; but He has ordained it thus that He might test you. (47:4–5)

These passages are quoted at length because often Qur'anic passages on war and peace are taken out of context to amplify the violence. For example, the passage "kill them wherever you find them" (2:190) makes it clear that it is referring to defensive wars and not wars against all non-Muslims. These passages also contain several limits, which parallel Christian just war criteria: do not attack first (no aggression), do not fight on holy ground, and stop once those you are fighting repent (no vengeance). The passages from Surahs 8 and 9 were written at a time when the Muslim community had made treaties with their Jewish, Christian, and pagan neighbors. The pagan tribes violated the agreements, which the Qur'an then takes as justification for retaliation as a form of self-defense. It also clearly states that Muslims must honor the agreements with those who have kept the treaties. Again it's not a command to kill all non-Muslims, only those who threaten the Muslim community. Thus we can conclude that while the use of force to defend the faith in self-defense, and to defend the weak is acceptable, nonetheless, nonviolent conflict resolution, tolerance, and forgiveness are preferred. This leads Sohail Hashmi to summarize the tradition:

> The Prophet's rejection of armed struggle during the Meccan period was more than mere prudence based on the Muslims' military weakness. It was, rather, derived from the Qur'an's still unfolding conception that the use of force should be avoided unless it is, in just war parlance, a "last resort." . . . Active nonviolent resistance and open defiance of pagan persecution is the proper Muslim response, according to these verses, and was, in fact, the Prophet's own practice during this period. . . . Clearly, jihad in this extended period of the Prophet's life meant nonviolent resistance.[15]

The Qur'an explicitly commands beleivers to seek peace. These passages, indeed the entire Qur'an, include repeated reminders of

Allah's forgiving and merciful nature, which Muslims are exhorted to emulate. One passage that is often overlooked when discussing the Qur'an on war and peace emphasizes these qualities:

> It may well be that Allah will put good will between you and those with whom you have hitherto been at odds. Allah is mighty. He is forgiving and merciful.
>
> Allah does not forbid you to be kind and equitable to those who have neither made war on your religion nor driven you from your homes [that is, making friends with non-Muslims is acceptable]. Allah loves the equitable. But he forbids you to make friends with those who have fought against you on account of your religion and driven you from your homes or abetted others so to do. Those that make friends with them are wrongdoers. (60:7–8)

War in the Qur'an is often interpreted as a concession, a necessary evil, similar to Augustine's idea that violence is normally to be rejected, but is on occasion necessary. Those who refuse to fight are branded as cowards (4:75, 95), apostates (3:167–168), and hypocrites (63:1–3 and 9:73–74). Those who fight are promised financial reward (booty) and eternal life in the event they die fighting for Allah (4:72–74; 9:38–39, 71–72; and 47:6–8).

Firestone rejects the traditional evolutionary interpretation of the Qur'an. This theory claims that the peace passages from the Mecca era are supplanted by the sword verse of the Medina era. He suggests that the great lengths to which the Qur'an goes to justify the use of force and the condemnation of those who fail to fight as both cowards and faithless suggest there was considerable resistance within the *umma* to the Prophet's resorting to violence because the social identity shift was not complete. "In the pre-Islamic period, kinship required that one go off to battle to protect the viability or honor of one's kinship group. In the new and evolving system, which becomes that of classical Islam, religious responsibility required that one go off to battle to protect the viability or honor of the new community of believers by fighting in the path of God."[16]

Muhammad may have had a difficult time convincing Muslims that "the cause of God" (a phrase that occurs seventy times in the Qur'an) was worth fighting and dying for; in other words, he did not fully replace tribal identity and loyalty with religious identity and ideological commitment. The old kinship-based identity seems to have lingered and thus required strong exhortations to justify fighting in the cause of God.[17] The exhortations to fight for the cause of Allah appeal to duty, honor, the promise of reward, and fear of punishment.

One must avoid proof texting the Qur'an by looking only at the peace or sword verses. Indeed, the Qur'an is a mixture of both. Firestone's theory that the sheer volume of sword verses indicates there must have been resistance to using force within the *umma* seems plausible. Taken together, he says, these verses

> reveal how the transition from pre-Islamic to Islamic systems of personal and community identity, social structure, governance, and conduct toward outsiders was a painful process. Pre-Islamic fighting was non-ideological and was conducted either for material gain or to retaliate or exact revenge on unrelated or distant kinship groups. . . . Fighting in the fully developed Islamic system, on the other hand, became a highly ideological issue. . . . Motivation to engage in war moved from economic incentive and kinship commitment to the ideological responsibility of religious commitment, and it created the awkward situation in which new Muslims were commanded to fight against members of their own intimate kinship groups because of their new religious affiliation. Religious affiliations replaced kinship affection as the religious community replaced the tribe, but the transition was difficult.[18]

Contemporary Islam has seen a resurgence in jihadist thinking. While the idea of jihad as struggle (internal and external) has always been central to Islam, the more militant understanding has been amplified by political extremists. Contemporary jihadism is a relatively recent phenomenon stemming from a lack of effective political and religious leadership in the postcolonial era. It is not accidental that jihadist groups recruit from nations with failed or repressive governments. Social, political, and economic conditions are significant factors in the popularity of extremist groups. As Evan Goldstein observes:

> The clash of ideas within Islam about the meaning of jihad stems in large part from the militants' claims that Muslims live in a state of emergency [similar to Walzer's concept of supreme emergency] brought about by illegitimate and corrupt governments, the presence of a Jewish state on Muslim land [Israel], and more generally, the pervasiveness of Western culture in the Muslim world.[19]

Whereas once the jihad tradition closely paralleled the JWT, with strict prohibitions on the use of force all under the careful watch of Muslim scholars and jurists (Shari'a), today with a much more widely literate Muslim population and advances in communications, these groups are able to more readily disseminate their beliefs and tap into the despair and resentment of poor and politically disenfranchised Muslims to promote their agenda.

Unfortunately many non-Muslims have a skewed view of Islam. We often hear phrases like "Muslim terrorists" or "militant Muslims" or "Islamic jihadists," phrases that give the impression that Islam is a violent religion. While these groups do exist and possess a power disproportionate to their size, they represent a small minority of the Muslim population, one which many Muslims reject as outside the faith by their very actions. Perhaps the best way to communicate how outside the norm these groups are is by analogy. The Ku Klux Klan (KKK) claims to be a Christian organization. They espouse a racist doctrine of white supremacy and have engaged in acts of terror against persons of color and non-Protestants, all based on a perverted interpretation of Scripture. The vast majority of Christians recognize that the KKK is not a Christian organization. So-called Muslim terrorist groups, like al-Qaeda, Islamic Jihad, Hamas, and Hezbollah, are as Muslim as the KKK is Christian. Nevertheless, Islam does seem to be at a crucial stage in its history. Judaism claimed holy war early in it history and ultimately abandoned it. Christianity went through its crusade and holy war periods and has since rejected these. Islam, the youngest of the three Abrahamic faiths, is now wrestling with its own stance toward holy war, as well as whether Islam is compatible with Western secularized culture and democracy. Many Muslim scholars (such as Khaled Abou el-Fadl, Omid Safi, and Amina Wadud) are working hard to distance mainstream Islam from Muslim extremists. They argue that terrorist organizations that justify the use of violence under the banner of jihad represent a perversion or anachronism of the religion. Despite their claims to be devout Muslims, these extremists by their actions are so far beyond the pale they can be described as political warriors using the veil of religiosity as a moral cover to justify their politically motivated violence.

There is a popular saying that Muslim extremists have "hijacked Islam." Speaking in the wake of the September 11, 2001 terrorist attacks, Yusuf Islam, the former pop singer Cat Stevens and a convert to Islam, decried not only the violence done on that day, but the ongoing violence done to Islam itself. "Today, I am aghast at the horror of recent events and feel it a duty to speak out. Not only did terrorists hijack planes and destroy life, they also hijacked the beautiful religion of Islam."[20] John Kelsay criticizes such interpretations as too simplistic, arguing, "It is not sufficient to say that [the 9/11 terrorists] hijacked Islam or that they exist outside an Islamic framework. It is more complex than that." These groups, argues Kelsay, draw on the Qur'an and Islamic tradition.[21] What seems clear from this discussion is that like the just war theory within the Christian tradition, jihad is open to multiple interpretations.

CHRISTIAN HOLY WAR AND MUSLIM JIHAD: A COMPARISON

While the Christian holy war and Muslim jihad traditions are long and complex, they share some similarities. Both religions claim to seek peace, yet both have a tradition in which total war is justified because it is either fought at God's command or to defend or spread the faith. While Judaism also shares this belief, such actions are reported only in the biblical stories from the Exodus to early monarchy; once the land had been delivered into the hands of the Israelites, the holy war tradition ended. Both Christianity and Islam today have largely rejected the idea of holy war as inconsistent with (if not hypocritical to) the mainstream tradition. While some jihadists use the Qur'an to justify their violence, they are largely rejected by mainstream Muslims.

An interesting and telling comparison can be made between historical Christian holy war and contemporary Muslim jihad. In 1095, in a speech at the Council at Clermont, Pope Urban II issued the call for the first crusade. In 1998, the World Islamic Front (in which Osama Bin-Laden and Ayman al Zawahiri are principal signatories) issued a *fatwa* (teaching) calling for a jihad (armed struggle) against the United States and Israel.[22] In placing these two calls for holy war side by side here, one immediately sees a remarkable similarity in how each makes its case (see "Christian Holy War and Muslim Jihad Side by Side"). Even though these statements come from two different religious traditions, two different cultures, and are separated by nine hundred years, they make similar claims for their holy war:

1. It will bring peace to their native land, which is being torn apart by internal strife.

2. It will bring economic rewards to those who fight.

3. It will merit forgiveness of all the sins of those who die fighting, and God will reward them with eternal life.

4. It is willed by God and is therefore a religious obligation.

Jihad enjoys a long, complex, and honorable place in Islam. It has also been used to justify horrific acts of violence. The debate around jihad rests on whether it is best understood as a kind of just war theory or a form of holy war.

CHRISTIAN HOLY WAR AND MUSLIM JIHAD SIDE BY SIDE

Speech at Clermont in 1095: Pope Urban II (Robert the Monk version)

This account of Urban II's speech was written about twenty-five years after Urban's visit to France and does not claim to give more than a general idea of the pope's arguments for the first crusade.

In the year of our Lord's Incarnation one thousand and ninety-five, a great council was celebrated within the bounds of Gaul, in Auvergne, in the city which is called Clermont. Over this Pope Urban II presided, with the Roman bishops and cardinals. This council was a famous one on account of the concourse of both French and German bishops, and of princes as well. Having arranged the matters relating to the Church, the lord pope went forth into a certain spacious plain, for no building was large enough to hold all the people. The pope then, with sweet and persuasive eloquence, addressed those present in words something like the following, saying:

Jihad against Jews and Crusaders: World Islamic Front Statement (February 23, 1998)

Shaykh Usamah Bin-Muhammad Bin-Ladin

Ayman al-Zawahiri, amir of the Jihad Group in Egypt

Abu-Yasir Rifa'i Ahmad Taha, Egyptian Islamic Group

Shaykh Mir Hamzah, secretary of the Jamiat-ul-Ulema-e-Pakistan

Fazlur Rahman, amir of the Jihad Movement in Bangladesh

Praise be to Allah, who revealed the Book, controls the clouds, defeats factionalism, and says in His Book: "But when the forbidden months are past, then fight and slay the pagans wherever ye find them, seize them, beleaguer them, and lie in wait for them in every stratagem (of war)"; and peace be upon our Prophet, Muhammad Bin-'Abdallah, who said: I have been sent with the sword between my hands to ensure that no one but Allah is worshipped, Allah who put my

Speech at Clermont (cont.)	*Jihad against Jews (cont.)*

"Oh, race of Franks, race from across the mountains, race beloved and chosen by God, — as is clear from many of your works, — set apart from all other nations by the situation of your country as well as by your Catholic faith and the honor which you render to the holy Church: to you our discourse is addressed, and for you our exhortations are intended. We wish you to know what a grievous cause has led us to your country, for it is the imminent peril threatening you and all the faithful which has brought us hither.

"From the confines of Jerusalem and from the city of Constantinople a grievous report has gone forth and has repeatedly been brought to our ears; namely, that a race from the kingdom of the Persians, an accursed race, a race wholly alienated from God, 'a generation that set not their heart aright and whose spirit was not steadfast with God,' violently invaded the lands of those Christians and has depopulated them by pillage and fire. They have led away a part of the captives into their own country,

livelihood under the shadow of my spear and who inflicts humiliation and scorn on those who disobey my orders.

The Arabian Peninsula has never — since Allah made it flat, created its desert, and encircled it with seas — been stormed by any forces like the crusader armies spreading in it like locusts, eating its riches and wiping out its plantations. All this is happening at a time in which nations are attacking Muslims like people fighting over a plate of food. In the light of the grave situation and the lack of support, we and you are obliged to discuss current events, and we should all agree on how to settle the matter.

No one argues today about three facts that are known to everyone; we will list them, in order to remind everyone:

First, for over seven years the United States has been occupying the lands of Islam in the holiest of places, the Arabian Peninsula, plundering its riches, dictating to its rulers, humiliating its people, terrorizing its neighbors, and turning its bases in the Peninsula into a spearhead through

Speech at Clermont (cont.)

and a part they have killed by cruel tortures. They have either destroyed the churches of God or appropriated them for the rites of their own religion. They destroy the altars, after having defiled them with their uncleanness. . . . The kingdom of the Greeks is now dismembered by them and has been deprived of territory so vast in extent that it could be traversed in two months' time.

"On whom, therefore, is the labor of avenging these wrongs and of recovering this territory incumbent, if not upon you, you upon whom, above all other nations, God has conferred remarkable glory in arms, great courage, bodily activity, and strength to humble the heads of those who resist you? Let the deeds of your ancestors encourage you and incite your minds to manly achievements: the greatness of King Charlemagne, and of his son Louis, and of your other monarchs, who have destroyed the kingdoms of the Turks and have extended the sway of Church over lands previously possessed by the pagan. Let the holy sepulcher of our Lord

Jihad against Jews (cont.)

which to fight the neighboring Muslim peoples.

If some people have in the past argued about the fact of the occupation, all the people of the Peninsula have now acknowledged it. The best proof of this is the Americans' continuing aggression against the Iraqi people using the Peninsula as a staging post, even though all its rulers are against their territories being used to that end, but they are helpless.

Second, despite the great devastation inflicted on the Iraqi people by the crusader-Zionist alliance, and despite the huge number of those killed, which has exceeded 1 million . . . despite all this, the Americans are once against trying to repeat the horrific massacres, as though they are not content with the protracted blockade imposed after the ferocious war or the fragmentation and devastation.

So here they come to annihilate what is left of this people and to humiliate their Muslim neighbors.

Third, if the Americans' aims behind these wars are religious and economic, the aim is also

Speech at Clermont (cont.)

and Saviour, which is possessed by unclean nations, especially arouse you, and the holy places which are now treated, with ignominy and irreverently polluted with the filth of the unclean. Oh, most valiant soldiers and descendants of invincible ancestors, do not degenerate your progenitors, but recall the valor of your progenitors.

"But if you are hindered by love of children, parents, or of wife, remember what the Lord says in the Gospel, 'He that loveth father or mother more than me is not worthy of me.' 'Every one that hath forsaken houses, or brethren, or sisters, or father, or mother, or wife, or children, or lands, for my name's sake, shall receive an hundredfold, and shall inherit everlasting life.' Let none of your possessions retain you, nor solicitude for your family affairs. For this land which you inhabit, shut in on all sides by the seas and surrounded by the mountain peaks, is too narrow for your large population; nor does it abound in wealth; and it furnishes scarcely food enough for its cultivators. Hence it is that you murder and devour

Jihad against Jews (cont.)

to serve the Jews' petty state and divert attention from its occupation of Jerusalem and murder of Muslims there. The best proof of this is their eagerness to destroy Iraq, the strongest neighboring Arab state, and their endeavor to fragment all the states of the region such as Iraq, Saudi Arabia, Egypt, and Sudan into paper statelets and through their disunion and weakness to guarantee Israel's survival and the continuation of the brutal crusade occupation of the Peninsula.

All these crimes and sins committed by the Americans are a clear declaration of war on Allah, his messenger, and Muslims. And ulema have throughout Islamic history unanimously agreed that the jihad is an individual duty if the enemy destroys the Muslim countries. This was revealed by Imam Bin-Qadamah in "Al-Mughni," Imam al-Kisa'i in "Al-Bada'i," al-Qurtubi in his interpretation, and the shaykh of al-Islam in his books, where he said: "As for the fighting to repulse [an enemy], it is aimed at defending sanctity and religion, and it is a duty as agreed [by the ulema]. Nothing

Speech at Clermont (cont.)

one another, that you wage war, and that very many among you perish in [internecine] strife."

[*Another of those present at the Council of Clermont, Fulcher of Chartres, thus reports this part of Urban's speech: "Let those who have formerly been accustomed to contend wickedly in private warfare against the faithful fight against the infidel, and bring to a victorious end the war which ought already to have been begun. Let those who have hitherto been robbers now become soldiers. Let those who have formerly contended against their brothers and relatives now fight against the barbarians as they ought. Let those who have formerly been mercenaries at low wages now gain eternal rewards. Let those who have been exhausting themselves to the detriment both of body and soul now strive for a twofold reward." See a complete translation of Fulcher's report of Urban's speech in* **Translations and Reprints,** *vol. 1. no. 2.]*

"Let hatred therefore depart from among you, let your quarrels end, let wars cease, and let all dissensions and controversies slumber. Enter upon the road to

Jihad against Jews (cont.)

is more sacred than belief except repulsing an enemy who is attacking religion and life."

On that basis, and in compliance with Allah's order, we issue the following *fatwa* to all Muslims:

The ruling to kill the Americans and their allies—civilians and military—is an individual duty for every Muslim who can do it in any country in which it is possible to do it, in order to liberate the al-Aqsa Mosque [in Jerusalem] and the holy mosque [Mecca] from their grip, and in order for their armies to move out of all the lands of Islam, defeated and unable to threaten any Muslim. This is in accordance with the words of Almighty Allah, "and fight the pagans all together as they fight you all together," and "fight them until there is no more tumult or oppression, and there prevail justice and faith in Allah."

This is in addition to the words of Almighty Allah: "And why should ye not fight in the cause of Allah and of those who, being weak, are ill-treated (and oppressed)? — women and children, whose cry is: 'Our

Speech at Clermont (cont.)

the Holy Sepulcher, wrest that land from the wicked race, and subject it to yourselves. That land which, as the Scripture says, 'floweth with milk and honey' was given by God into the power of the children of Israel. Jerusalem is the center of the earth; the land is fruitful above all others, like another paradise of delights. This spot the Redeemer of mankind has made illustrious by his advent, has beautified by his sojourn, has consecrated by his passion, has redeemed by his death, has glorified by his burial.

"This royal city, however, situated at the center of the earth, is now held captive by the enemies of Christ and is subjected, by those who do not know God, to the worship of the heathen. She seeks, therefore, and desires to be liberated and ceases not to implore you to come to her aid. From you especially she asks succor, because as we have already said, God has conferred upon you above all other nations great glory in arms. Accordingly, undertake this journey eagerly for the remission of your sins, with the assurance of the reward of

Jihad against Jews (cont.)

Lord, rescue us from this town, whose people are oppressors; and raise for us from thee one who will help!'"

We—with Allah's help—call on every Muslim who believes in Allah and wishes to be rewarded to comply with Allah's order to kill the Americans and plunder their money wherever and whenever they find it. We also call on Muslim ulema, leaders, youths, and soldiers to launch the raid on Satan's U.S. troops and the devil's supporters allying with them, and to displace those who are behind them so that they may learn a lesson.

Almighty Allah said: "O ye who believe, give your response to Allah and His Apostle, when He calleth you to that which will give you life. And know that Allah cometh between a man and his heart, and that it is He to whom ye shall all be gathered."

Almighty Allah also says: "O ye who believe, what is the matter with you, that when ye are asked to go forth in the cause of Allah, ye cling so heavily to the earth! Do ye prefer the life of this world to the hereafter?

Speech at Clermont (cont.)

imperishable glory in the kingdom of heaven."

When Pope Urban had ur-
banely said these and very
similar things, he so centered
in one purpose the desires of
all who were present that all
cried out, "It is the will of God!
It is the will of God!" When the
venerable Roman pontiff heard
that, with eyes uplifted to heav-
en, he gave thanks to God and,
commanding silence with his
hand, said:

"Most beloved brethren,
today is manifest in you what
the Lord says in the Gospel,
'Where two or three are gathered together in my name, there
am I in the midst of them'; for
unless God had been present
in your spirits, all of you would
not have uttered the same cry;
since, although the cry issued
from numerous mouths, yet
the origin of the cry was one.
Therefore I say to you that God,
who implanted this in your
breasts, has drawn it forth from
you. Let that then be your war
cry in combats, because it is
given to you by God. When an
armed attack is made upon the
enemy, this one cry be raised

Jihad against Jews (cont.)

But little is the comfort of this
life, as compared with the hereafter. Unless ye go forth, He
will punish you with a grievous
penalty, and put others in your
place; but Him ye would not
harm in the least. For Allah hath
power over all things."

Almighty Allah also says:
"So lose no heart, nor fall into
despair. For ye must gain mastery if ye are true in faith."[23]

Speech at Clermont (cont.)

by all the soldiers of God: 'It is the will of God! It is the will of God!' [*Deus vult! Deus vult!*]

"And we neither command nor advise that the old or those incapable of bearing arms, undertake this journey. Nor ought women to set out at all without their husbands, or brother, or legal guardians. For such are more of a hindrance than aid, more of a burden than an advantage. Let the rich aid the needy and according to their wealth let them take with them experienced soldiers. The priests and other clerks, whether secular or regulars are not to go without the consent of their bishop; for this journey would profit them nothing if they went without permission. Also, it is not fitting that laymen should enter upon the pilgrimage without the blessing of their priests.

"Whoever, therefore, shall determine upon this holy pilgrimage, and shall make his vow to God to that effect, and shall offer himself to him for sacrifice, as a living victim, holy and acceptable to God, shall wear the sign of the cross of the Lord on his forehead or on his breast. When, indeed, he shall return from his journey, having fulfilled his vow, let him place the cross on his back between his shoulders. Thus shall ye, indeed, by this twofold action, fulfill the precept of the Lord, as lie commands in the Gospel, 'he that taketh not his cross, and followeth after me, is not worthy of me.'"[24]

CONCLUSION

Religion and war have always been strange bedfellows. The three Abrahamic faiths have so much in common. All three profess belief in a single God; all three share a common origin and sacred texts; and the ethics of all three are similar. Yet tragically they also share centuries of violence, which might too easily be explained by the old adage, "No one fights like family." But my own experience also teaches that no one loves or forgives like family, either. Hans Küng, a Catholic theologian and advocate for interreligious dialogue, said, "There will be no peace among the nations without peace among the religions. There will be no peace among the religions without dialogue and cooperation among the religions."[25] To which I humbly add, dialogue begins with compassionate understanding.

DISCUSSION QUESTIONS

1. Has this comparison changed how you think about Judaism or Islam with regard to war and peace? If so, how? If not, why not?

2. What was your understanding of jihad prior to reading this chapter? Has your view changed? If so, how? If not, why not?

3. Some organizations like al-Qaeda claim to be fighting a defensive war, that is, Islam is under attack from Western secular culture, as well as economic and military power, and so it must defend itself. What is your opinion of this claim?

4. Do you agree with Hans Küng that "There will be no peace among the nations without peace among the religions"? What can leaders within the three Abrahamic faiths do to promote peace in the world?

ENDNOTES

1 Samuel Huntington, "The Clash of Civilizations?" *Foreign Affairs* 73:3 (Summer 1993): 22–49; and *The Clash of Civilizations and the Remaking of World Order* (New York: Simon & Schuster, 1998).

2 Michael J. Broyde, "Fighting the War and the Peace: Battlefield Ethics, Peace Talks, Treaties, and Pacifism in the Jewish Tradition," in J. Patout Burns, ed., *War and Its Discontents: Pacifism and Quietism in the Abrahamic Traditions* (Washington, DC: Georgetown University Press, 1996), 17–19 (italics in original).

3 For example, see Broyde, "Fighting the War and the Peace," and Everett Gendler, "The Pursuit of Peace: A Singular Command," in Burns, *War and Its Discontents*, 31–46; Yehudah Mirsky, "The Political Morality of Pacifism and Nonviolence: One Jewish View," in Burns, 47–66; Naomi Goodman, "Pacifism and Nonviolence: Another Jewish View," in Burns, 67–73; and Jeremy Milgrom, "'Let your love for me vanquish your hatred for him': Nonviolence and Modern

Judaism," in Daniel Smith-Christopher, ed., *Subverting Hatred: The Challenge of Nonviolence in Religious Traditions* (Maryknoll, NY: Orbis, 1998),115–39.

4 Broyde, "Fighting the War and the Peace," 18.

5 Jewish scholars debate whether the tradition recognizes two or three types of war. The Talmud identifies two types of permitted war: obligatory (which includes wars commanded by God and those of defensive wars) and permitted, or optional wars. Other scholars separate wars commanded by God from defensive wars and thus have three types of war. See Broyde, "Fighting the War and the Peace," 4 (especially notes 21–24); "War" in *The Oxford Dictionary of the Jewish Religion*, ed. R. J. Zwi Werblowsky and Geoffrey Wigoder (New York: Oxford University Press, 1997), 718–19; and "War," in *The Encyclopedia of Judaism*, ed. Geoffrey Wigoder (New York: New York University Press, 1989), 795–96.

6 "War," in *Oxford Dictionary of the Jewish Religion*, 718–719.

7 Commentary on the Torah, verse 14, quoted in Norman Solomon, "Judaism and the Ethics of War," *International Review of the Red Cross* 87.858 (June 2005): 301.

8 See Broyde, "Fighting the War and the Peace," 8–12.

9 Rueven Firestone, "Holy War in Modern Judaism? 'Mitzvah War' and the Problem of the 'Three Vows,'" *Journal of the American Academy of Religion* 74.4 (2006): 954.

10 See Arye Edrei, "Divine Spirit and Physical Power: Rabbi Shlomo Goren and the Military Ethic of the Israeli Defense Forces," *Theoretical Inquiries in Law* 7.257 (December 1, 2005): 257–300.

11 Rueven Firestone, *Jihad: The Origin of Holy War in Islam* (New York: Oxford University Press, 1999), 13–14.

12 See Firestone, *Jihad*, 74, and Qur'an 3:103.

13 Quoted in Firestone, *Jihad*, 17.

14 *The Koran*, N. J. Dawood, trans. (Harmondsworth, Middlesex, England: Penguin Books, 1956, 1986).

15 Sohail Hashmi, "Interpreting the Islamic Ethics of War and Peace," in Jack Miles and Sohail Hashmi, eds., *Islamic Political Ethics: Civil Society, Pluralism, and Conflict* (Princeton, NJ: Princeton University Press, 2002), 201–202.

16 Firestone, *Jihad*, 74.

17 Ibid., 73–79.

18 Ibid., 91.

19 Evan Goldstein, "How Just Is Islam's Just-War Tradition?" *The Chronicle Review* (April 18, 2008): B9.

20 Yusef Islam, "Searchlighting Islam," *Islamic World News* 22 (December 2001), available online at *http://www.islamicbulletin.com/newsletters/issue_22/dec01-worldnews.htm*.

21 Quoted in Goldstein, "How Just Is Islam's Just-War Tradition?" B8.

22 Traditionally the authority to issue a *fatwa* (ruling) is reserved to the Shari'a schools or to scholars of Islamic law. Bin-Laden and the World Islamic Front are not recognized as scholars of Islamic law and therefore do not have the authority to issue *fatwas*.

23 Original in Arabic; this translation is available online at the Federation of American Scientists, *http://www.fas.org/irp/world/para/docs/980223-fatwa.htm*.

24 James Harvey Robinson, ed., *Readings in European History:* vol. 1 (Boston: Ginn & Co., 1904), 312–16, available online at *http://www.fordham.edu/halsall/source/urban2-5vers.html*.

25 Hans Küng, "Global Ethic and Human Responsibility," submitted to the High-level Expert Group Meeting on "Human Rights and Human Responsibilities in the Age of Terrorism," April 1–2, 2005, Santa Clara University; available online at *http://www.scu.edu/ethics/practicing/focusareas/global_ethics/laughlin-lectures/global-ethic-human-responsibility.html*. See also *Küng's Global Responsibility: In Search of a New World Ethic* (London: SCM Press/New York: Continuum, 1991).

CHURCH DOCUMENTS CITED

Below is a list of Catholic Church documents cited in this text. The papal and conciliar documents are listed with the shorter English version first, as that is how the title is cited in this text.

All Vatican documents can be found at the Holy See Web site (*www.vatican.va*).

SELECTED ANTHOLOGIES OF CATHOLIC SOCIAL TEACHING

O'Brien, David J., and Thomas A. Shannon, eds. *Catholic Social Thought: The Documentary Heritage.* Maryknoll, NY: Orbis, 1992, 2003.

Walsh, Michael, and Brian Davies, eds. *Proclaiming Justice and Peace: Papal Documents from* Rerum Novarum *through* Centesimus Annus. Mystic, CT: Twenty-Third Publications, 1991.

PAPAL AND CONCILIAR DOCUMENTS

Apostolate of the Laity—Apostolicam actuositatem (Decree on the Apostolate of the Laity). Second Vatican Council, 18 November 1965.

Capital and Labor—Rerum novarum (Encyclical on Capital and Labor). Pope Leo XIII, 15 May 1891.

Constitution on the Church—Lumen gentium (Dogmatic Constitution on the Church). Second Vatican Council, 21 November 1964.

Divine Revelation—Dei verbum (Dogmatic Constitution on Divine Revelation). Second Vatican Council, 18 November 1965.

In Our Time—Nostra aetate (Declaration on the Relation of the Church to Non-Christian Religions). Second Vatican Council, 28 October 1965.

Nature of Human Liberty—Libertas praestantissimum (Encyclical on the Nature of Human Liberty). Pope Leo XIII, 20 June 1888.

On Human Work—Laborem exercens (Encyclical on Human Work, on the Ninetieth Anniversary of Rerum novarum). Pope John Paul II, 14 September 1981.

On Reconstruction of the Social Order—Quadragesimo anno (Encyclical on Reconstruction of the Social Order, on the Fortieth Anniversary of Rerum novarum). Pope Pius XI, 15 May 1931.

On Religious Freedom—Dignitatis humanae (Declaration on Religious Freedom). Second Vatican Council, 7 December 1965.

On Social Concern—Sollicitudo rei socialis (Encyclical on Social Concern, on the Twentieth Anniversary of Populorum progressio). Pope John Paul II, 30 December 1987.

On the Development of Peoples—Populorum progressio (Encyclical on the Development of Peoples). Pope Paul VI, 26 March 1967.

On the Family—Familiaris consortio (Apostolic Exhortation on the Role of the Christian Family in the Modern World). Pope John Paul II, 22 November 1981.

On the Hundredth Anniversary of Rerum novarum—Centesimus annus (Encyclical on the Hundredth Anniversary of Rerum novarum). Pope John Paul II, 1 May 1991.

On the Religious Situation in Mexico—Firmissimam constantiam (Encyclical on the Religious Situation in Mexico). Pope Pius XI, 28 March 1937.

Peace on Earth—Pacem in terris (Encyclical on Establishing Universal Peace in Truth, Justice, Charity, and Liberty). Pope John XXIII, 11 April 1963.

The Church in the Modern World—Gaudium et spes (Pastoral Constitution on the Church in the Modern World). Second Vatican Council, 7 December 1965.

U.S. CONFERENCE OF CATHOLIC BISHOPS

Economic Justice for All. Pastoral Letter on Catholic Social Teaching and the U.S. Economy, 1986.

The Challenge of Peace: God's Promise and Our Response. Pastoral Letter on War and Peace, 1983.

The Harvest of Justice Is Sown in Peace. Statement commemorating the tenth anniversary of *The Challenge of Peace*, 1993.

OTHER VATICAN DOCUMENTS

Catechism of the Catholic Church. English translation for the United States of America copyright © 1994, 1997, United States Catholic Conference, Inc.

Compendium of the Social Doctrine of the Church. English translation for the United States of America copyright © 2004 United States Conference of Catholic Bishops.

ACKNOWLEDGMENTS

The excerpts from the Catechism are from the English translation of the *Catechism of the Catholic Church* for use in the United States of America. Copyright © 1994 by the United States Catholic Conference, Inc.—Libreria Editrice Vaticana. English translation of the *Catechism of the Catholic Church: Modifications from the Editio Typica* copyright © 1997 by the United States Catholic Conference, Inc.—Libreria Editrice Vaticana. Used with permission.

The excerpts from *The Challenge of Peace* in chapter 4 are from *The Challenge of Peace: God's Promise and Our Response* (Washington, DC: United States Catholic Conference, 1983), numbers 74, 78, 83, 86, 92–93, and 120–121, respectively. Copyright © 1983 by the United States Catholic Conference. Used with permission.

RECOMMENDED READING

GETTING STARTED

For those who are new to the study of war and peace, I suggest beginning with the following shorter articles from reference sources:

Dwyer, Judith. "Peace." In *The New Dictionary of Theology*. Edited by Joseph Komonchak, Mary Collins, and Dermot Lane, 748–53. Collegeville, MN: Liturgical Press, 1987.

———. "War." In *The New Dictionary of Theology*. Edited by Joseph Komonchak, Mary Collins, and Dermot Lane, 1093–95. Collegeville, MN: Liturgical Press, 1987.

Fiala, Andrew. "Pacifism." In *The Stanford Encyclopedia of Philosophy* (summer 2007). Edited by Edward N. Zalta. *http://plato.stanford.edu/archives/sum2007/entries/pacifism/*.

Himes, Kenneth. "War." In *The New Dictionary of Catholic Social Thought*. Edited by Judith Dwyer, 977–82. Collegeville, MN: Liturgical Press, 1994.

Orend, Brian. "War." In *The Stanford Encyclopedia of Philosophy* (winter 2005). Edited by Edward N. Zalta. *http://plato.stanford.edu/archives/win2005/entries/war/*.

Two excellent encyclopedias on war and peace include numerous articles on both theoretical and practical topics:

Palmer-Fernandez, Gabriel and Ian Maclean, eds. *The Encyclopedia of Religion and War.* New York: Routledge, 2004.

Wells, Donald A., ed. *An Encyclopedia of War and Ethics.* Westport, CT: Greenwood Press, 1996.

Two excellent anthologies include foundational writings (ancient to contemporary) on the ethics of war and peace:

Holmes, Arthur F., ed. *War and Christian Ethics: Classic and Contemporary Readings on the Morality of War.* 2nd ed. Grand Rapids, MI: Baker, 2005.

Reichberg, Gregory, Henrik Syse, and Endre Begby. *The Ethics of War: Classic and Contemporary Readings.* Malden, MA: Blackwell, 2006.

Online sources explore both theoretical and practical aspects of war and peace:

British Broadcasting Corporation (BBC), "Religion and Ethics: The Ethics of War." Available at *http://www.bbc.co.uk/religion/ethics/war/*.

Rigstad, Mark. *JustWarTheory.com.* Available at *http://www.justwartheory.com/*.

University of San Diego. "Ethics Updates." Edited by Lawrence M. Hinsman. Available at *http://ethics.sandiego.edu/index.asp*. Under "Applied Ethics," see "War, Peace, and Terrorism."

United States Naval Academy, Stockdale Center for Ethical Leadership. Available at *http://www.usna.edu/Ethics/*.

FURTHER READING

Additional recommended reading in the area of war and peace:

Abou el-Fadl, Khaled. "Terrorism Is at Odds with Islamic Tradition." *Los Angeles Times* (22 August 2001): B13.

Allman, Mark. "Postwar Justice." *America* 193.11 (17 Oct 2005): 9–13.

Allman, Mark, and Tobias Winright. "*Jus Post Bellum*: Extending the Just War Theory." *College Theology Society Annual* 2007, vol. 53 (Maryknoll, NY: Orbis, 2008): 241–64.

———. *After the Smoke Clears: Just War Theory and Postwar Justice.* Maryknoll, NY: Orbis, forthcoming 2009.

Asfaw, Semegnish. "Christian Perspectives on the Responsibility to Protect (R2P)." *Bulletin of the Boston Theological Institute* 7.2 (Spring 2008): 18–19.

Asfaw, Semegnish, Guillermo Kerber, and Peter Weiderud, eds. *The Responsibility to Protect: Ethics and Theological Reflections.* Geneva: World Council of Churches Publications, 2005.

Baxter, Michael J. "Just War and Pacifism: A 'Pacifist' Perspective in Seven Points." *Houston Catholic Worker* 24.3 (May–June 2004). Available online at *http://www.cjd.org/paper/baxpacif. html.*

Burns, J. Patout, ed. *War and Its Discontents: Pacifism and Quietism in the Abrahamic Traditions.* Washington, DC: Georgetown University Press, 1996.

Cahill, Lisa Sowle. *Love Your Enemies: Discipleship, Pacifism, and Just War Theory.* Minneapolis, MN: Fortress Press, 1994.

Clough, David L., and Brian Stiltner. *Faith and Force: A Christian Debate about War.* Washington, DC: Georgetown University Press, 2007.

Cortright, David. *Gandhi and Beyond: Nonviolence for an Age of Terrorism.* Boulder/London: Paradigm, 2006.

Crossan, John Dominic. *God and Empire: Jesus against Rome, Then and Now.* San Francisco: HarperSanFrancisco, 2007.

Elshtain, Jean Bethke. *Just War against Terror: The Burden of American Power in a Violent World.* New York: Basic Books, 2003.

———. *Just War Theory.* New York: New York University Press, 1991.

Fahey, Joseph. *War and the Christian Conscience: Where Do You Stand?* Maryknoll, NY: Orbis, 2005.

Firestone, Reuven. *Jihad: The Origin of Holy War in Islam.* New York: Oxford University Press, 1999.

Hauerwas, Stanley. *The Peaceable Kingdom: A Primer in Christian Ethics*. Notre Dame, IN: University of Notre Dame Press, 1983.

Himes, Kenneth. "Pacifism and the Just War Tradition in Roman Catholic Social Teaching." In *One Hundred Years of Catholic Social Thought: Celebration and Challenge*. Edited by John Coleman, 329–44. Maryknoll, NY: Orbis, 1991.

Ibrahim, Anwar. "Who Hijacked Islam?" *Time* (8 October 2001). Available online at *http://www.time.com/time/world/article/0,8599,178470,00.html*.

Johnson, James Turner. *The Holy War Idea in Western and Islamic Traditions*. University Park, PA: Pennsylvania State University Press, 1997.

———. *Morality and Contemporary Warfare*. New Haven, CT: Yale University Press, 1999.

———. *The Quest for Peace: Three Moral Traditions in Western Cultural History*. Princeton, NJ: Princeton University Press, 1987.

———. "Response to Terrorism: Moral Challenges." William C. Stutt Lecture Series, Annapolis, MD: United States Naval Academy (20 November 2001). Transcript available online at *http://www.usna.edu/ethics/Publications/JohnsonPg1-20_Final.pdf*.

Keen, Sam. *Faces of the Enemy: Reflections of the Hostile Imagination*. San Francisco: Harper & Row, 1986.

Kelsay, John, *Arguing about the Just War in Islam*. Cambridge, MA: Harvard University Press, 2007.

———. *Islam and War*. Louisville, KY: Westminster John Knox Press, 1993.

Kelsay, John and James Turner Johnson, eds. *Cross, Crescent, and Sword: The Justification and Limitation of War in Western and Islamic Traditions*. New York: Greenwood Press, 1990.

———. *Just War and Jihad: Historical and Theoretical Perspectives on War and Peace in Western and Islamic Traditions*. New York: Greenwood Press, 1991.

Kleiderer, John, Paula Minaert, and Mark Mossa. *Just War, Lasting Peace: What Christian Traditions Can Teach Us*. Maryknoll, NY: Orbis, 2006.

Lammers, Stephen E. "Peace." In *The New Dictionary of Catholic Social Thought*. Edited by Judith Dwyer, 717–21. Collegeville, MN: Liturgical Press, 1994.

Lincoln, Bruce. *Holy Terrors: Thinking about Religion after September 11*. Chicago: University of Chicago Press, 2002.

Marrin, Albert, ed. *War and the Christian Conscience: From Augustine to Martin Luther King Jr.* Chicago: Henry Regnery, 1971.

Miles, Jack, and Sohail Hashmi, eds. *Islamic Political Ethics: Civil Society, Pluralism, and Conflict*. Princeton, NJ: Princeton University Press, 2002.

Mosley, Alex. "Just War Theory." *The Internet Encyclopedia of Philosophy* (2006). Available at *http://www.iep.utm.edu/j/justwar.htm*.

Niebuhr, Reinhold. "Why the Christian Church Is Not Pacifist." In *The Essential Reinhold Niebuhr*. Edited by Robert McAfee Brown, 102–119. New Haven: Yale University Press, 1986.

Orend, Brian. *The Morality of War*. Peterborough, Ontario: Broadview Press, 2006.

———. "*Jus Post Bellum*." *Journal of Social Philosophy* 31.1 (Spring 2000): 117-37.

———. "Justice after War." *Ethics and International Affairs* 61.1 (2002): 43-56.

Ramsey, Paul. *The Just War: Force and Political Responsibility*. New York: Scribner & Sons, 1968.

Smith-Christopher, Daniel, ed. *Subverting Hatred: The Challenge of Nonviolence in Religious Traditions*. Maryknoll, NY: Orbis, 2007.

Smock, David. *Religious Perspectives on War: Christian, Muslim, and Jewish Attitudes toward Force after the Gulf War*. Washington, DC: United States Institute for Peace Press, 1992.

Solomon, Norman. "Judaism and the Ethics of War." *International Review of the Red Cross* 87.858 (June 2005): 295–309.

Stassen, Glen H., ed. *Just Peacemaking: Ten Practices for Abolishing War*. Cleveland, OH: Pilgrim Press, 1998.

———. *Just Peacemaking: Transforming Initiatives for Justice and Peace*. Louisville, KY: Westminster/John Knox Press, 1992.

Walzer, Michael. *Just and Unjust Wars: A Moral Argument with Historical Illustrations*. 3rd ed. New York: Basic Books, 2000.

———. *Arguing about War*. New Haven, CT: Yale University Press, 2004.

Wink, Walter. *Engaging the Powers: Discernment and Resistance in a World of Domination*. Minneapolis, MN: Augsburg Fortress, 1992.

———. *Jesus and Nonviolence: A Third Way*. Minneapolis, MN: Augsburg Fortress, 2003.

Winright, Tobias. "Just Cause and Preemptive Strikes in the War on Terrorism: Insights from a Just-Policing Perspective." *Journal of the Society of Christian Ethics* 26.2 (2006): 157–81.

Yoder, John Howard. *The Politics of Jesus*. Grand Rapids, MI: Eerdmans, 1972, 1990.

———. *When War Is Unjust: Being Honest in Just War Thinking*. Minneapolis, MN: Augsburg Fortress, 1984/Eugene, OR: Wipf & Stock, 2001.

INDEX